REX MUNDI
Book Two

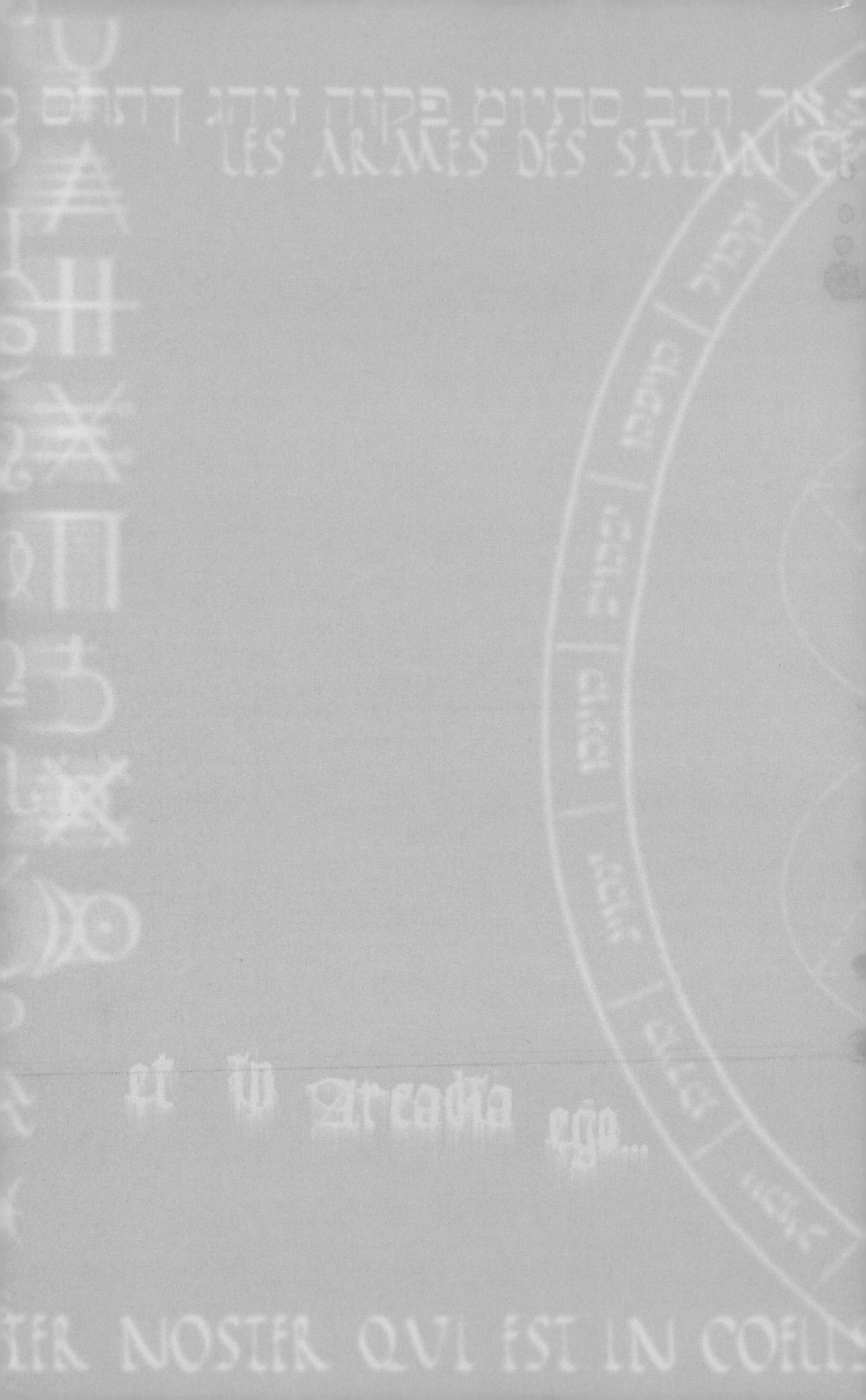
LES ARMES DES SATAN
et in Arcadia ego...
TER NOSTER QUI EST IN COELI

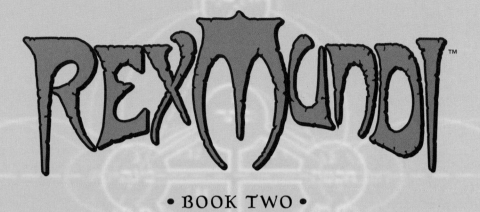

• BOOK TWO •

The River Underground

writer **ARVID NELSON**

artist **ERICJ**

color artist **JEROMY COX**

cover artist **JUAN FERREYRA**

Rex Mundi created by **ARVID NELSON** and **ERICJ**

DARK HORSE BOOKS™

publisher
MIKE RICHARDSON

editors
SCOTT ALLIE and MIKE CARRIGLITTO

assistant editor
RYAN JORGENSEN

letterer and newspaper designer
ARVID NELSON

book designer
AMY ARENDTS

art director
LIA RIBACCHI

Special thanks to Jason Rickerd.
Archival photographs: Eugène Atget.

REX MUNDI BOOK TWO: THE RIVER UNDERGROUND

This volume collects issues six through eleven of the comic-book series *Rex
Mundi*, originally published by Image Comics.

Published by
Dark Horse Books
A division of Dark Horse Comics, Inc.
10956 SE Main Street
Milwaukie, OR 97222

darkhorse.com

To find a comics shop in your area, call the Comic Shop Locator
Service toll-free at 1-888-266-4226

First edition:
ISBN-10: 1-59307-682-7
ISBN-13: 9-781-59307-682-5

10 9 8 7 6 5 4 3 2

Printed in China

INTRODUCTION *by Scott Allie*

IF YOU'RE READING THE INTRODUCTION to the second volume of *Rex Mundi*, it's fairly certain that you've read at least some of the story so far. You're familiar with Julien Saunière, and the Duke of Lorraine, and all the characters caught between them in a struggle that, as of this volume, even Julien himself doesn't fully understand. You probably have some sense of the riddles and mysteries behind it all—questions about the Holy Grail, John the Baptist, and Christ himself. And you're into it enough that you'll even read a prose introduction to a graphic novel. Hear, hear. I'm with you.

With this series, Arvid Nelson and his collaborators—in this volume, EricJ—have tapped a literary vein that readers find intoxicating. There're the obvious comparisons to *The Da Vinci Code*. That book does share notable similarities with this one—the most striking of which appeared in *Rex Mundi*'s earliest issues, published before *The Da Vinci Code* saw print, just to be perfectly clear. There are also unmistakable connections to *Holy Blood, Holy Grail*, the nonfiction book that popularized some of the historical situations central to both *Rex Mundi* and *The Da Vinci Code*.

More importantly, for me, *Rex Mundi* takes its place in a tradition springing from Umberto Eco's novel/doorstop *Foucault's Pendulum*. Arvid's never read *Foucault's Pendulum*, but I might have sworn that he had. Eco's book is not a great work of literature, nor is it a page-turning piece of pop fiction, though it has been called a thriller [apparently by someone with a more patient sense of thrills than I have]. It was an international literary sensation in the 1980s, with its mix of deconstructionist history, mysticism, conspiracy, and secrets that could bring down Western civilization, all decorated with kabalistic chapter breaks—sound familiar? Arvid never read it, although we mystically inclined types might perceive something more than mere coincidence.

I say *Foucault's Pendulum* wasn't necessarily a great work of literature because it was more intellectualism than art, more about characters sitting around talking—and talking and talking and talking—in an impersonal way, tearing down the preconceptions of European Christian culture. It was an intellectual exercise of sorts—and people loved it.

Rex Mundi sprang from the same creative font and has gripped its readers in the same way. And why? Why are some of us so eager to see our histories rewritten before our eyes, our beliefs questioned and our faith disproved?

Through world wars and economic intertwining, the twentieth century saw the Western world unified to a degree previously impossible, a singular Western culture knit together, bringing the past of Europe hand in hand with an American continent that was once recognized as The Future. We've weathered the end of a century rife with growing pains—we've seen the end of a millennium, a calendar event so significant we have nothing to compare it to—it's only our second, and we really don't remember much of the first one. We can only be sure that the world looks a lot different now. And that suggests that it *means* something different, too. We're a brand new culture, built upon pieces of the past. We've achieved a milestone, and it's human nature, now, to ask a few questions.

Rex Mundi asks those questions, and in its answers it makes the kinds of leaps that reward readers. It offers possibilities that strike bold chords. It says something in the way that the best fiction should, elevating a page–turner into something more by displaying ideas from which readers may discover whatever meanings ring truest to them.

Rex Mundi is fantasy—Arvid declares that, more clearly than some of his peers in this literary vein, by setting his story in a past which is clearly not our own. But his colorful recreation of early twentieth–century Europe shouldn't distract you from his very honest examination of what it means to be a Westerner, the way some of us are driven to conquer and some to seek, and what sorts of secrets we might find in our own past.

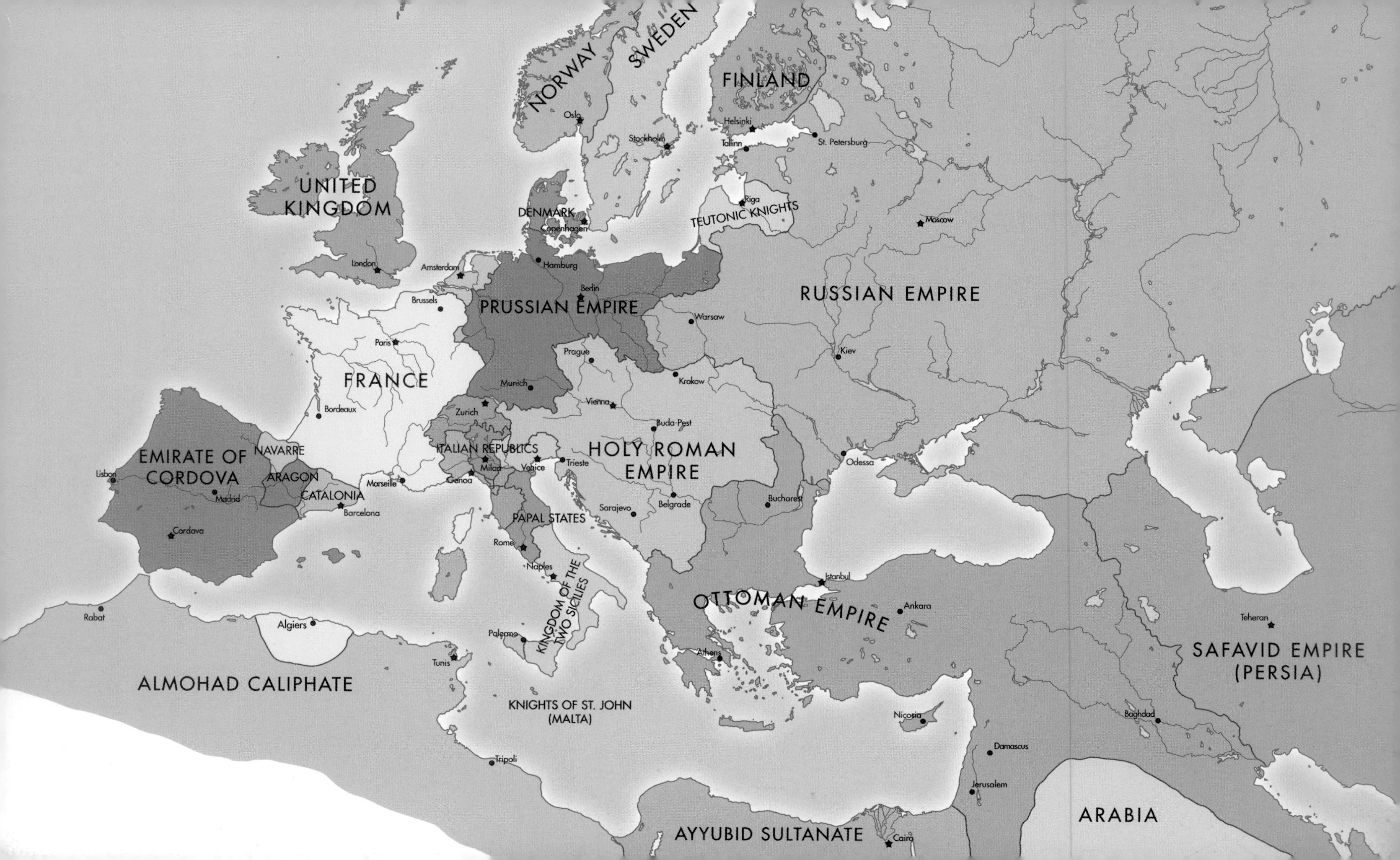
NORWAY
SWEDEN
FINLAND
Oslo
Stockholm
Helsinki
Tallinn
St. Petersburg
UNITED KINGDOM
London
DENMARK
Copenhagen
Riga
TEUTONIC KNIGHTS
Moscow
Amsterdam
Hamburg
Berlin
Brussels
PRUSSIAN EMPIRE
Warsaw
RUSSIAN EMPIRE
Paris
Prague
Kiev
FRANCE
Munich
Krakow
Bordeaux
Zurich
Vienna
Buda-Pest
EMIRATE OF CORDOVA
NAVARRE
ITALIAN REPUBLICS
HOLY ROMAN EMPIRE
Lisbon
ARAGON
Milan
Venice
Trieste
Odessa
Marseille
Genoa
Madrid
CATALONIA
Barcelona
Bucharest
Sarajevo
Belgrade
PAPAL STATES
Cordova
Rome
Naples
KINGDOM OF THE TWO SICILIES
Istanbul
OTTOMAN EMPIRE
Ankara
Rabat
Algiers
Palermo
Teheran
Tunis
Athens
SAFAVID EMPIRE (PERSIA)
ALMOHAD CALIPHATE
KNIGHTS OF ST. JOHN (MALTA)
Nicosia
Baghdad
Damascus
Tripoli
Jerusalem
ARABIA
AYYUBID SULTANATE
Cairo

REX MUNDI BOOK TWO:
The River Underground

PARIS, 1933. THE PROTESTANT REFORMATION failed. Europe is in the grip of feudalism, and sorcerers stalk the streets at night. It is the world of *Rex Mundi*.

An encrypted medieval scroll is stolen from priest Gérard Marin. The father had revealed the existence of the scroll to a prostitute, and now fears retribution from the Church. He goes to Master Physician Julien Saunière, his longtime friend, for help.

Saunière finds the prostitute murdered the next day, and a mysterious assassin, the Man in White, kills Marin soon after.

A trail of corpses leads to the powerful Duke of Lorraine, apparent mastermind of a secret society with origins in the murky history of the First Crusade. The society has infiltrated the highest ranks of government and is manipulating rising political tensions for sinister aims.

Saunière's private investigation arouses the ire of the Holy Inquisition, but the doctor persists in spite of warnings from the brutal Grand Inquisitor Moricant and his master, the cold, calculating Archbishop of Sens.

Genevieve Tournon, Saunière's old flame and fellow doctor, has been appointed personal physician to the Duke of Lorraine. She is having an affair with the powerful Duke, but she also rekindles her romance with Saunière, muddying her motives and loyalties.

Saunière follows the Man in White into a temple hidden in the sewers of Paris, where he is discovered and forced to run for his life. The doctor's street urchin friends help him escape, apparently killing the Man in White . . .

et in arcadia ego...

ER NOSTER QVI EST IN COELI

CHAPTER ONE

THE KNIGHTS OF THE TEMPLE

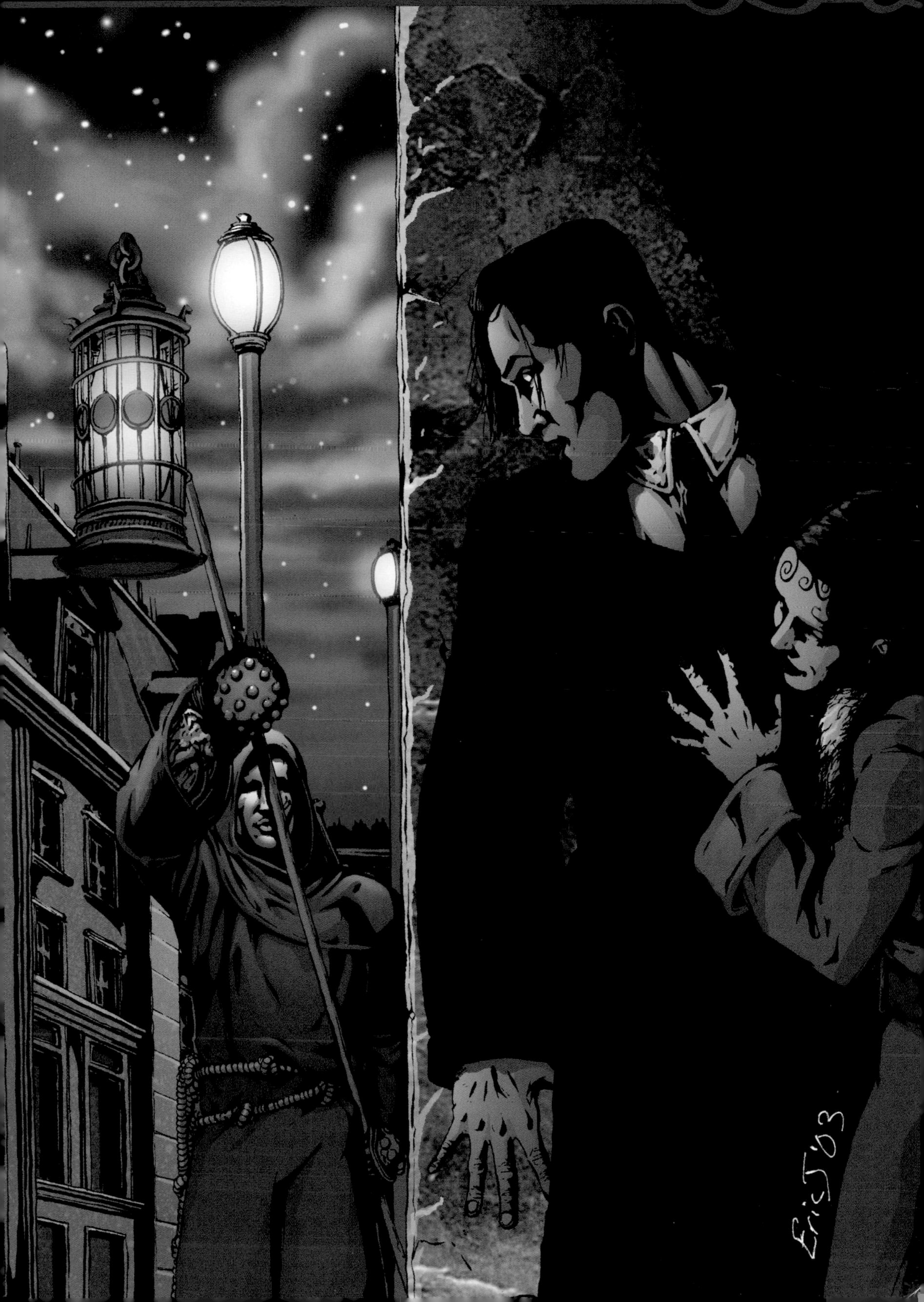

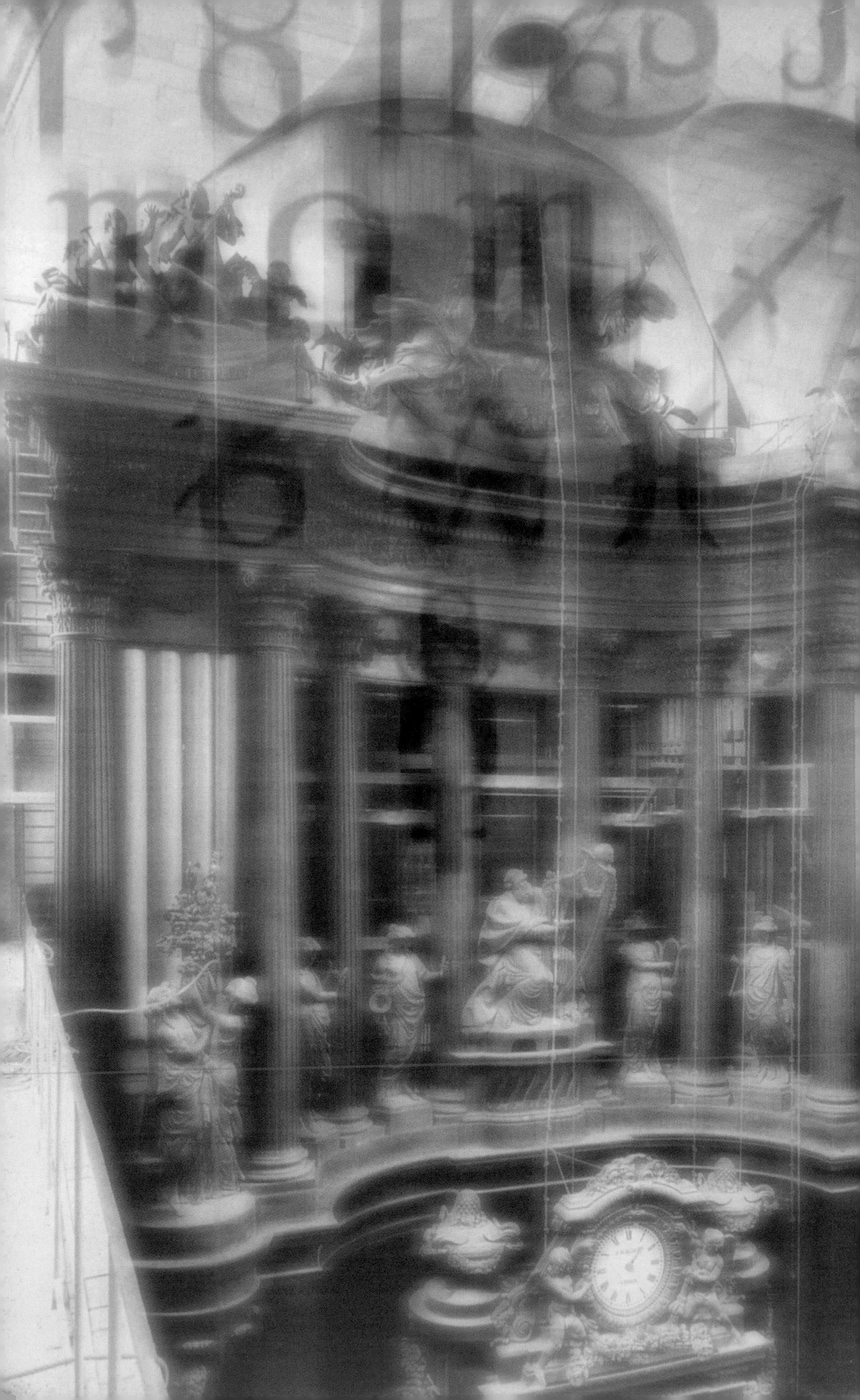

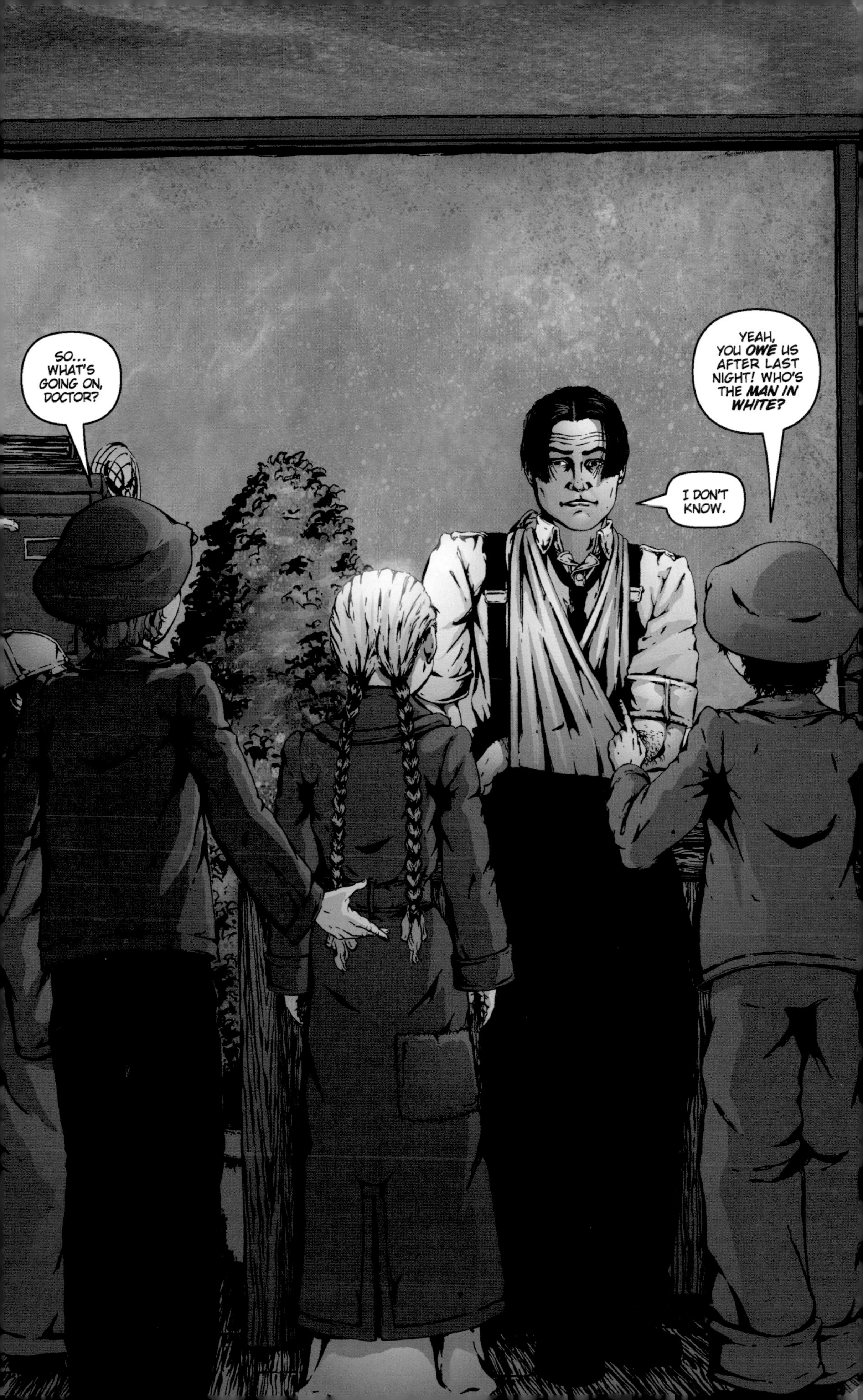
SO... WHAT'S GOING ON, DOCTOR?
YEAH, YOU OWE US AFTER LAST NIGHT! WHO'S THE MAN IN WHITE?
I DON'T KNOW.

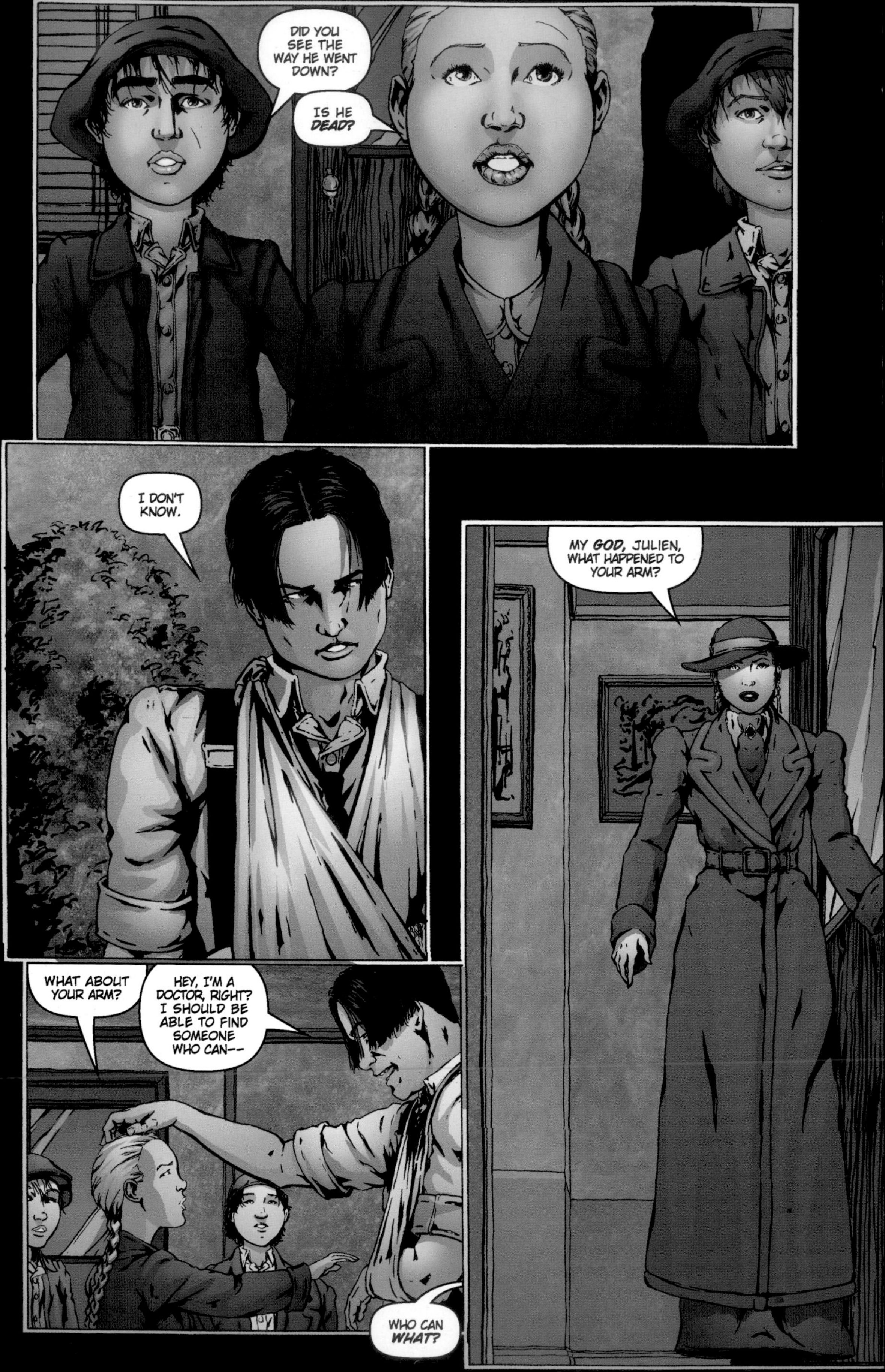
DID YOU SEE THE WAY HE WENT DOWN?
IS HE *DEAD?*
I DON'T KNOW.
MY *GOD*, JULIEN, WHAT HAPPENED TO YOUR ARM?
WHAT ABOUT YOUR ARM?
HEY, I'M A DOCTOR, RIGHT? I SHOULD BE ABLE TO FIND SOMEONE WHO CAN--
WHO CAN *WHAT?*

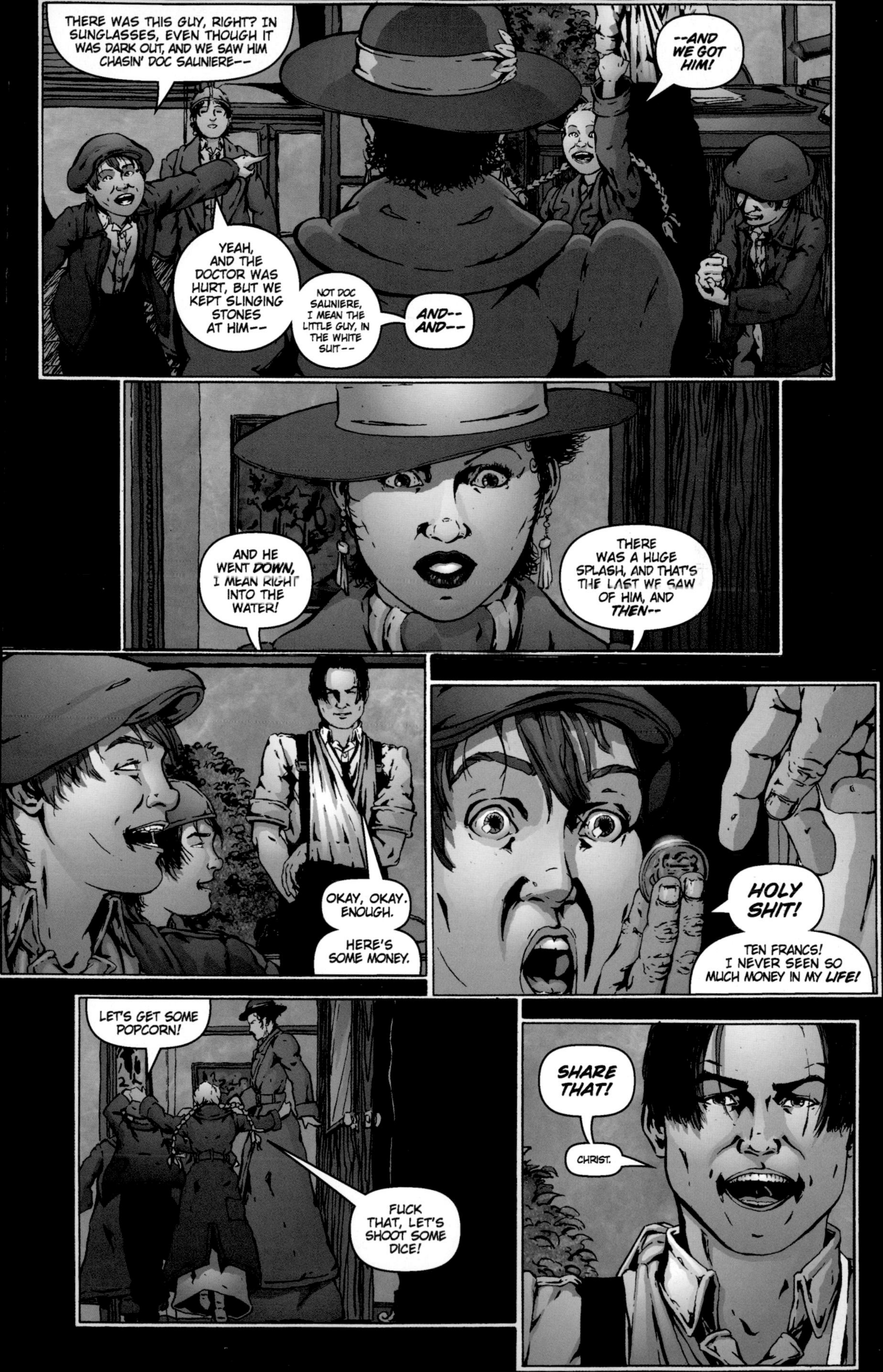
THERE WAS THIS GUY, RIGHT? IN SUNGLASSES, EVEN THOUGH IT WAS DARK OUT, AND WE SAW HIM CHASIN' DOC SAUNIERE--
--AND WE GOT HIM!
YEAH, AND THE DOCTOR WAS HURT, BUT WE KEPT SLINGING STONES AT HIM--
NOT DOC SAUNIERE, I MEAN THE LITTLE GUY, IN THE WHITE SUIT--
AND-- AND--
AND HE WENT DOWN, I MEAN RIGHT INTO THE WATER!
THERE WAS A HUGE SPLASH, AND THAT'S THE LAST WE SAW OF HIM, AND THEN--
OKAY, OKAY. ENOUGH.
HERE'S SOME MONEY.
HOLY SHIT!
TEN FRANCS! I NEVER SEEN SO MUCH MONEY IN MY LIFE!
LET'S GET SOME POPCORN!
FUCK THAT, LET'S SHOOT SOME DICE!
SHARE THAT!
CHRIST.

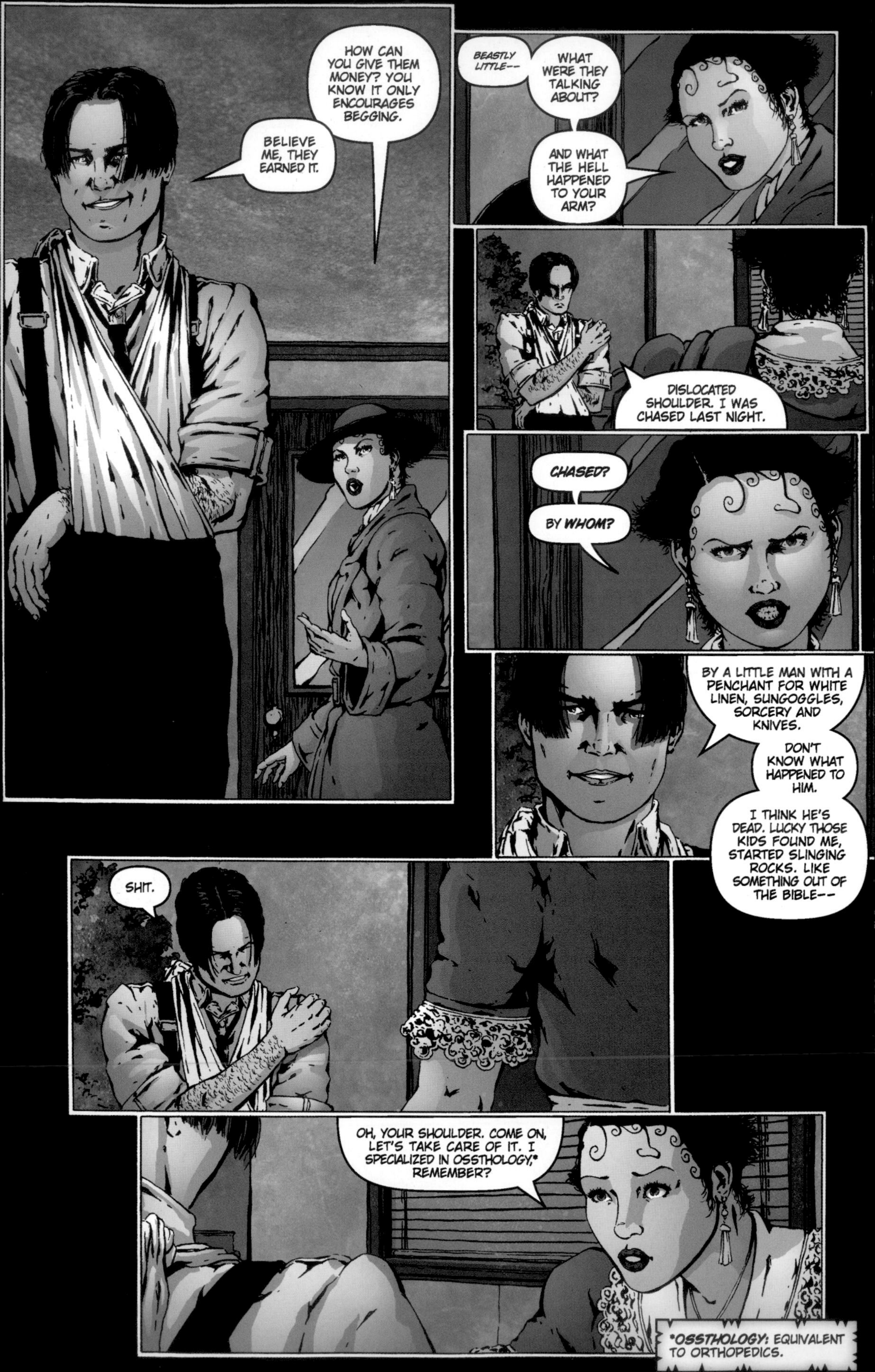
HOW CAN YOU GIVE THEM MONEY? YOU KNOW IT ONLY ENCOURAGES BEGGING.
BELIEVE ME, THEY EARNED IT.
BEASTLY LITTLE--
WHAT WERE THEY TALKING ABOUT?
AND WHAT THE HELL HAPPENED TO YOUR ARM?
DISLOCATED SHOULDER. I WAS CHASED LAST NIGHT.
CHASED?
BY WHOM?
BY A LITTLE MAN WITH A PENCHANT FOR WHITE LINEN, SUNGOGGLES, SORCERY AND KNIVES.
DON'T KNOW WHAT HAPPENED TO HIM.
I THINK HE'S DEAD. LUCKY THOSE KIDS FOUND ME, STARTED SLINGING ROCKS. LIKE SOMETHING OUT OF THE BIBLE--
SHIT.
OH, YOUR SHOULDER. COME ON, LET'S TAKE CARE OF IT. I SPECIALIZED IN OSSTHOLOGY,* REMEMBER?
*OSSTHOLOGY: EQUIVALENT TO ORTHOPEDICS.

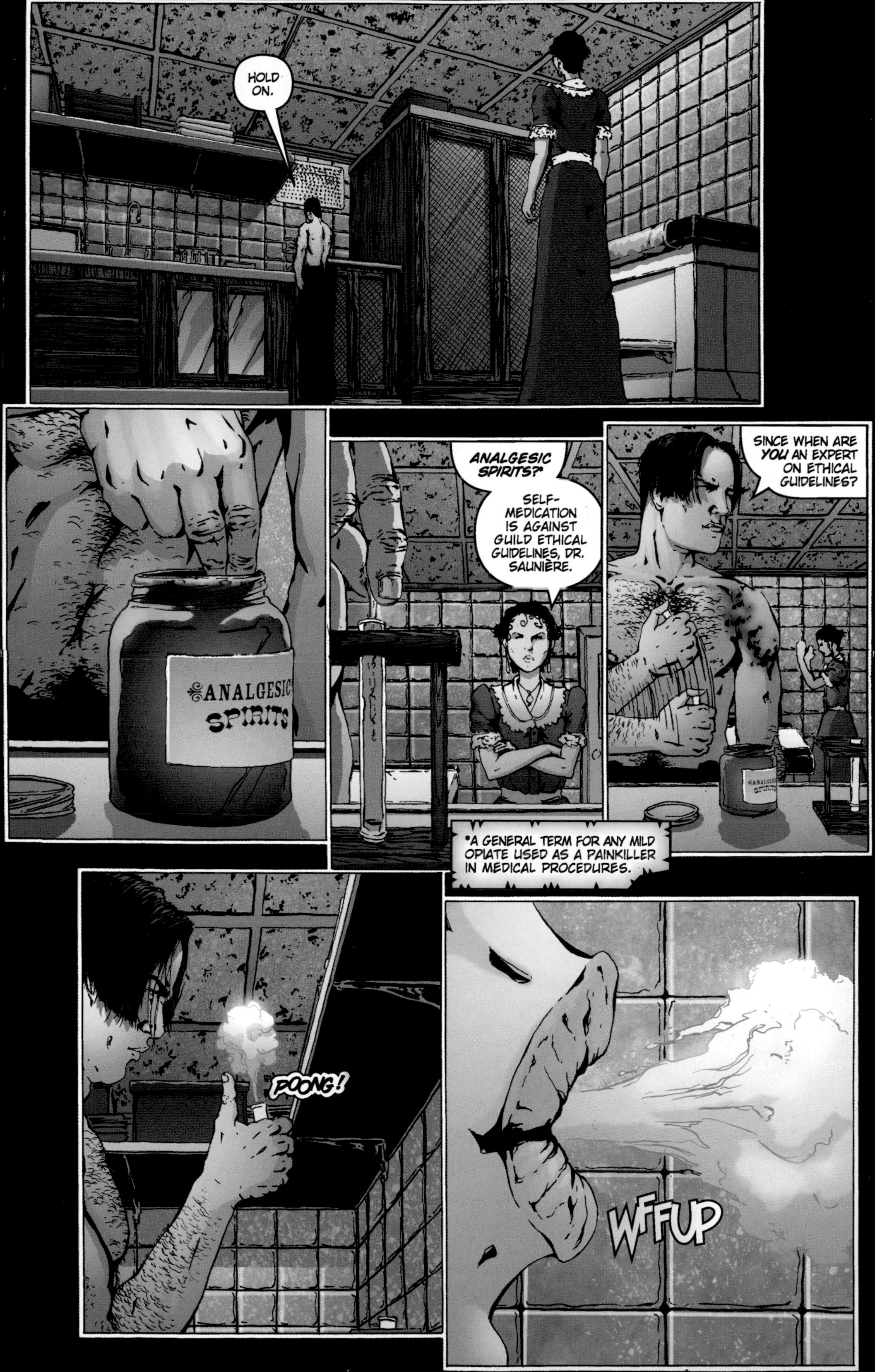
HOLD ON.
ANALGESIC SPIRITS
ANALGESIC SPIRITS?*
SELF-MEDICATION IS AGAINST GUILD ETHICAL GUIDELINES, DR. SAUNIÈRE.
SINCE WHEN ARE YOU AN EXPERT ON ETHICAL GUIDELINES?
ANALGESIC SPIRITS
*A GENERAL TERM FOR ANY MILD OPIATE USED AS A PAINKILLER IN MEDICAL PROCEDURES.
POONG!
WFFUP

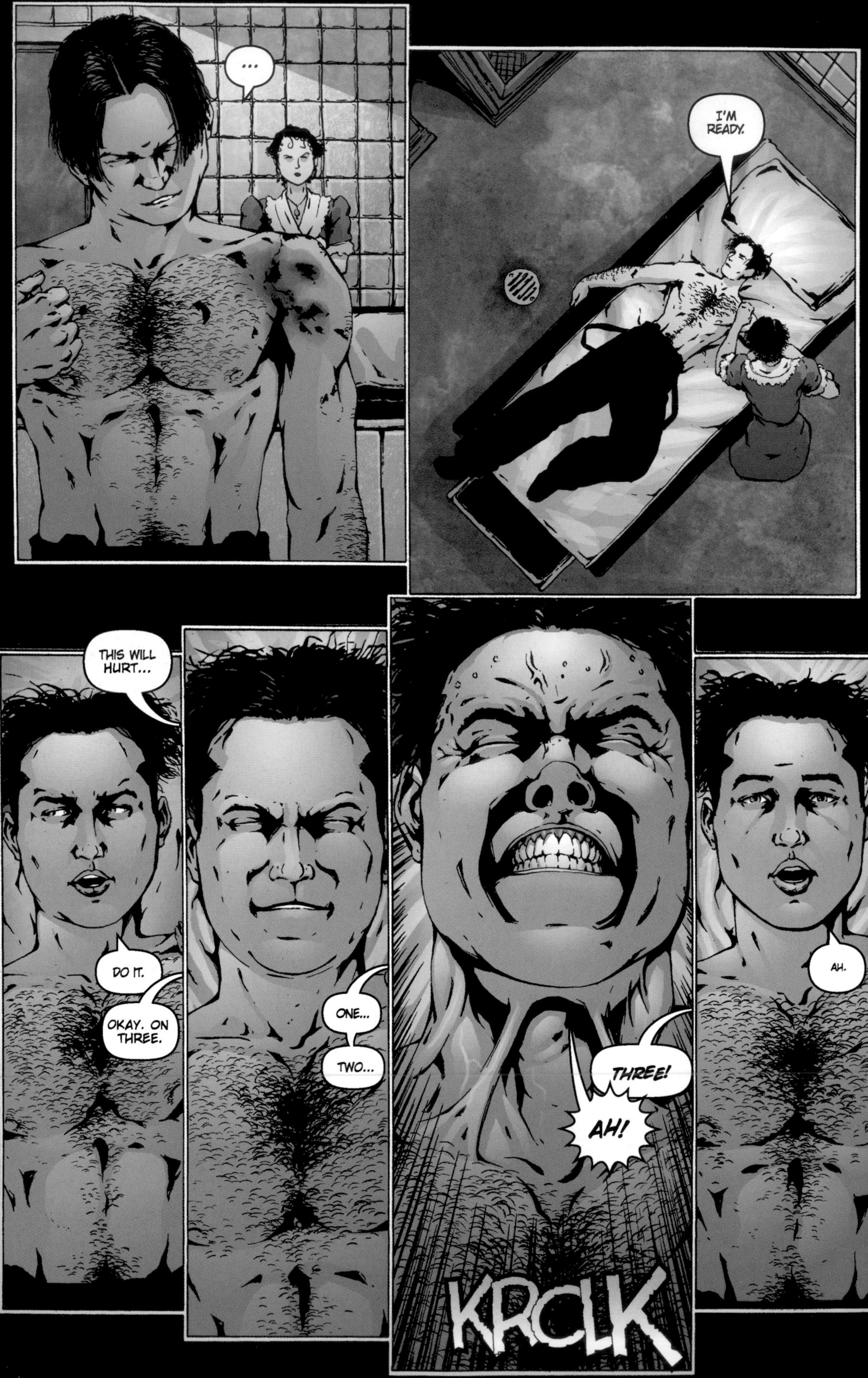
...
I'M READY.
THIS WILL HURT...
DO IT.
OKAY. ON THREE.
ONE...
TWO...
THREE!
AH!
KRCLK
AH.

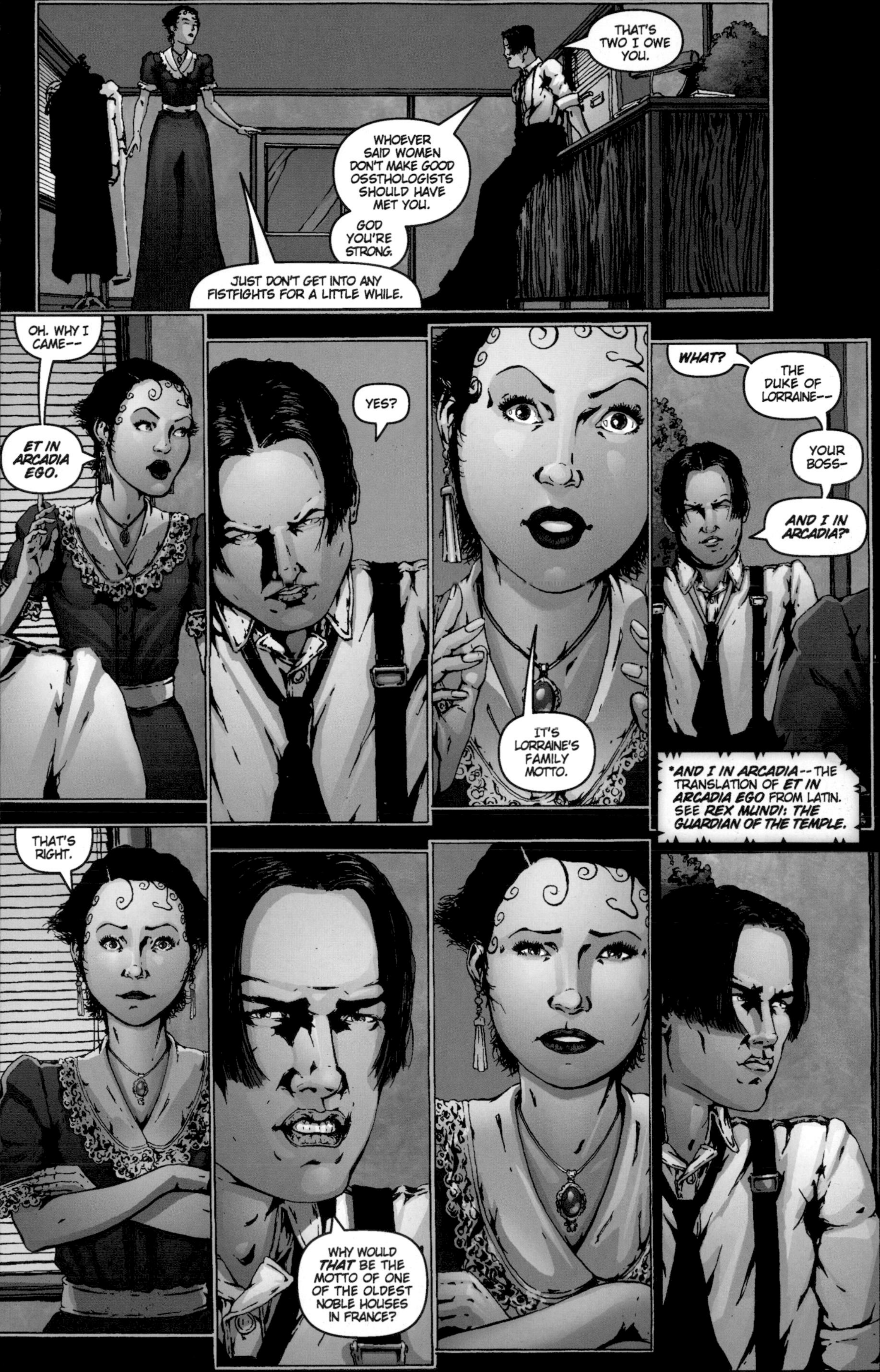
THAT'S TWO I OWE YOU.
WHOEVER SAID WOMEN DON'T MAKE GOOD OSSTHOLOGISTS SHOULD HAVE MET YOU.
GOD YOU'RE STRONG.
JUST DON'T GET INTO ANY FISTFIGHTS FOR A LITTLE WHILE.
OH. WHY I CAME--
ET IN ARCADIA EGO.
YES?
IT'S LORRAINE'S FAMILY MOTTO.
WHAT?
THE DUKE OF LORRAINE--
YOUR BOSS-
AND I IN ARCADIA?*
*AND I IN ARCADIA--THE TRANSLATION OF ET IN ARCADIA EGO FROM LATIN. SEE REX MUNDI: THE GUARDIAN OF THE TEMPLE.
THAT'S RIGHT.
WHY WOULD THAT BE THE MOTTO OF ONE OF THE OLDEST NOBLE HOUSES IN FRANCE?

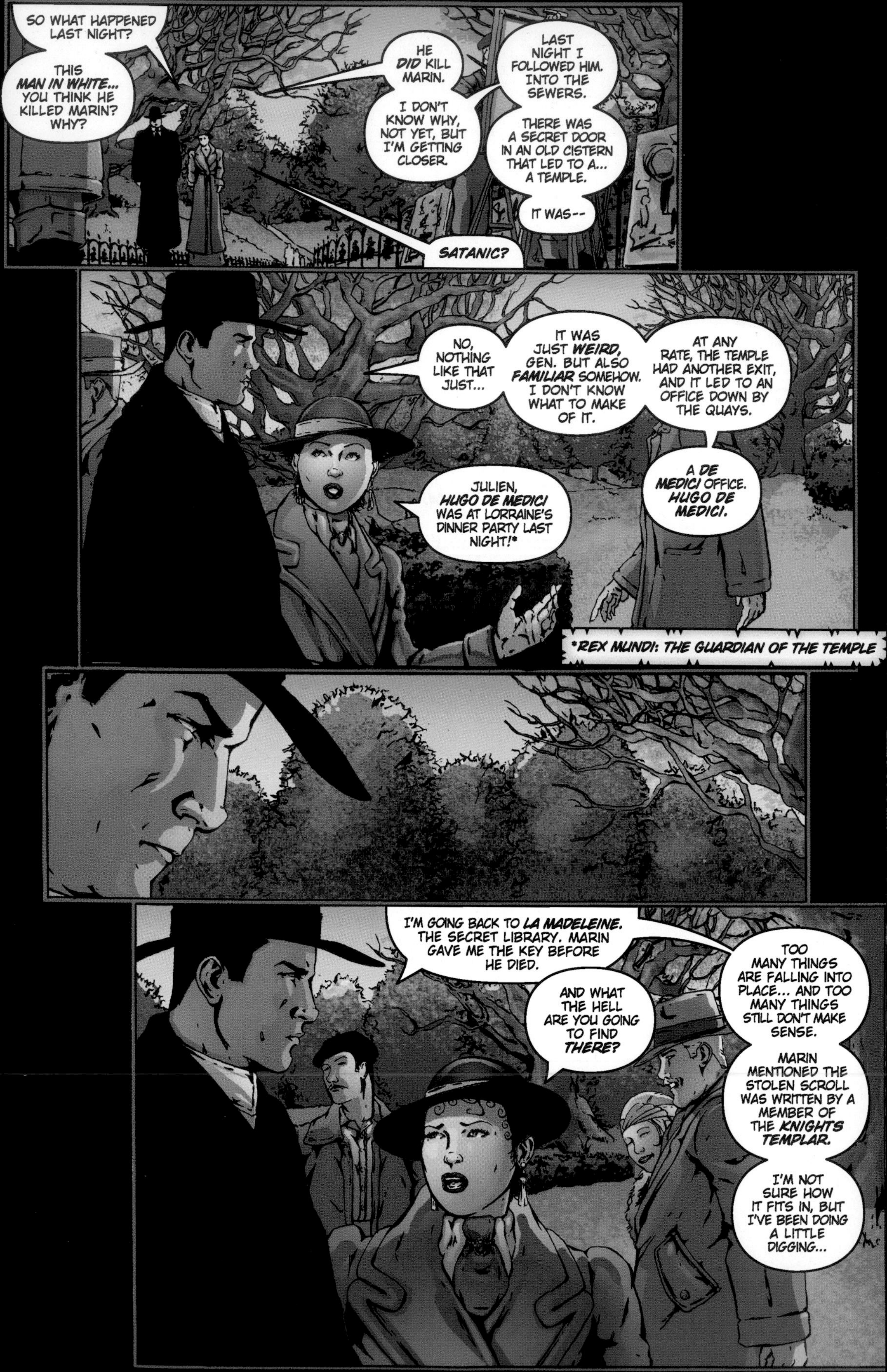
SO WHAT HAPPENED LAST NIGHT?
THIS MAN IN WHITE... YOU THINK HE KILLED MARIN? WHY?
HE DID KILL MARIN.
I DON'T KNOW WHY, NOT YET, BUT I'M GETTING CLOSER.
LAST NIGHT I FOLLOWED HIM. INTO THE SEWERS.
THERE WAS A SECRET DOOR IN AN OLD CISTERN THAT LED TO A... A TEMPLE.
IT WAS--
SATANIC?
NO, NOTHING LIKE THAT JUST...
IT WAS JUST WEIRD, GEN. BUT ALSO FAMILIAR SOMEHOW. I DON'T KNOW WHAT TO MAKE OF IT.
AT ANY RATE, THE TEMPLE HAD ANOTHER EXIT, AND IT LED TO AN OFFICE DOWN BY THE QUAYS.
A DE MEDICI OFFICE. HUGO DE MEDICI.
JULIEN, HUGO DE MEDICI WAS AT LORRAINE'S DINNER PARTY LAST NIGHT!*
*REX MUNDI: THE GUARDIAN OF THE TEMPLE
I'M GOING BACK TO LA MADELEINE. THE SECRET LIBRARY. MARIN GAVE ME THE KEY BEFORE HE DIED.
AND WHAT THE HELL ARE YOU GOING TO FIND THERE?
TOO MANY THINGS ARE FALLING INTO PLACE... AND TOO MANY THINGS STILL DON'T MAKE SENSE.
MARIN MENTIONED THE STOLEN SCROLL WAS WRITTEN BY A MEMBER OF THE KNIGHTS TEMPLAR.
I'M NOT SURE HOW IT FITS IN, BUT I'VE BEEN DOING A LITTLE DIGGING...

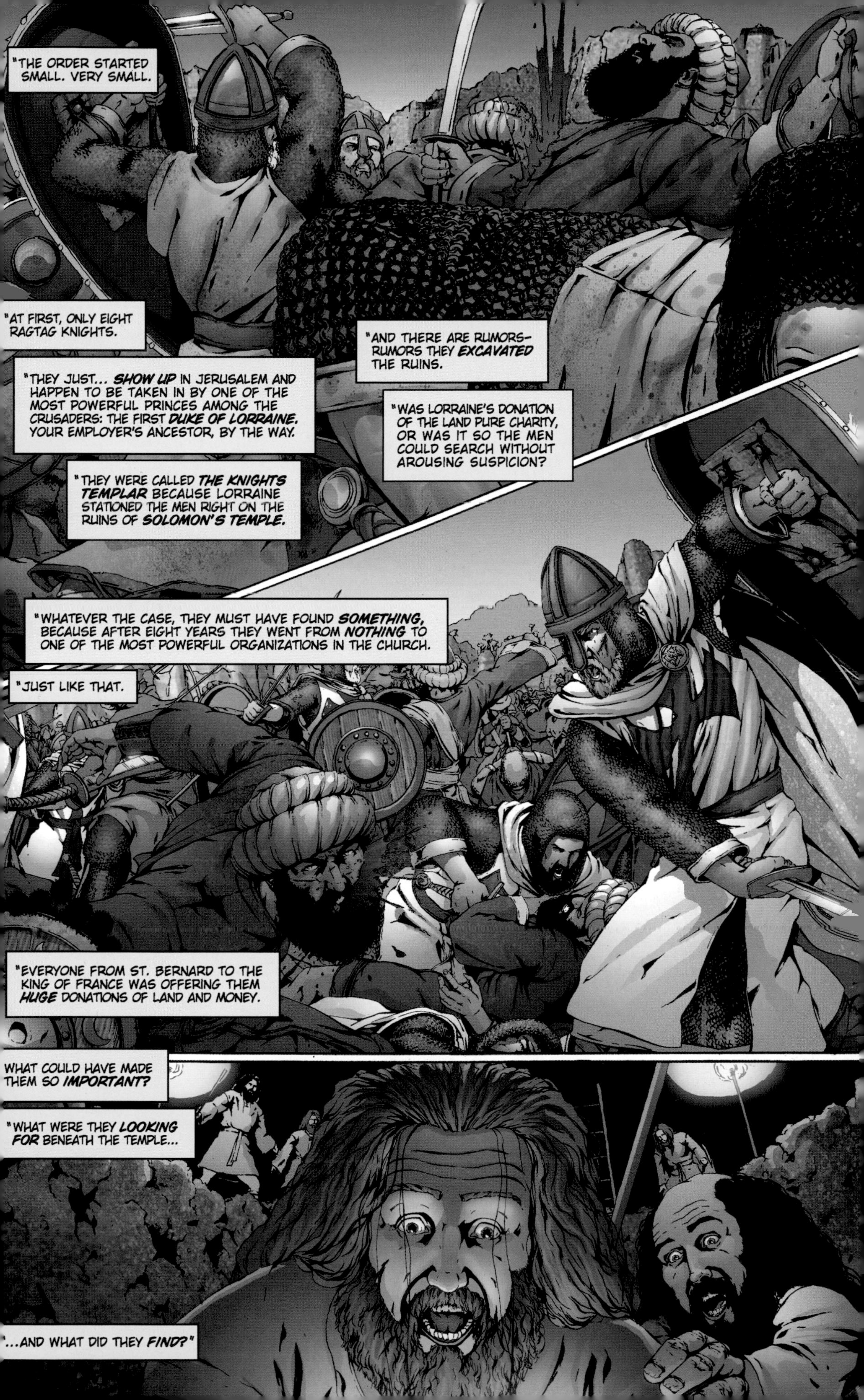
"THE ORDER STARTED SMALL. VERY SMALL.
"AT FIRST, ONLY EIGHT RAGTAG KNIGHTS.
"THEY JUST... SHOW UP IN JERUSALEM AND HAPPEN TO BE TAKEN IN BY ONE OF THE MOST POWERFUL PRINCES AMONG THE CRUSADERS: THE FIRST DUKE OF LORRAINE. YOUR EMPLOYER'S ANCESTOR, BY THE WAY.
"THEY WERE CALLED THE KNIGHTS TEMPLAR BECAUSE LORRAINE STATIONED THE MEN RIGHT ON THE RUINS OF SOLOMON'S TEMPLE.
"AND THERE ARE RUMORS-RUMORS THEY EXCAVATED THE RUINS.
"WAS LORRAINE'S DONATION OF THE LAND PURE CHARITY, OR WAS IT SO THE MEN COULD SEARCH WITHOUT AROUSING SUSPICION?
"WHATEVER THE CASE, THEY MUST HAVE FOUND SOMETHING, BECAUSE AFTER EIGHT YEARS THEY WENT FROM NOTHING TO ONE OF THE MOST POWERFUL ORGANIZATIONS IN THE CHURCH.
"JUST LIKE THAT.
"EVERYONE FROM ST. BERNARD TO THE KING OF FRANCE WAS OFFERING THEM HUGE DONATIONS OF LAND AND MONEY.
WHAT COULD HAVE MADE THEM SO IMPORTANT?
"WHAT WERE THEY LOOKING FOR BENEATH THE TEMPLE...
...AND WHAT DID THEY FIND?"

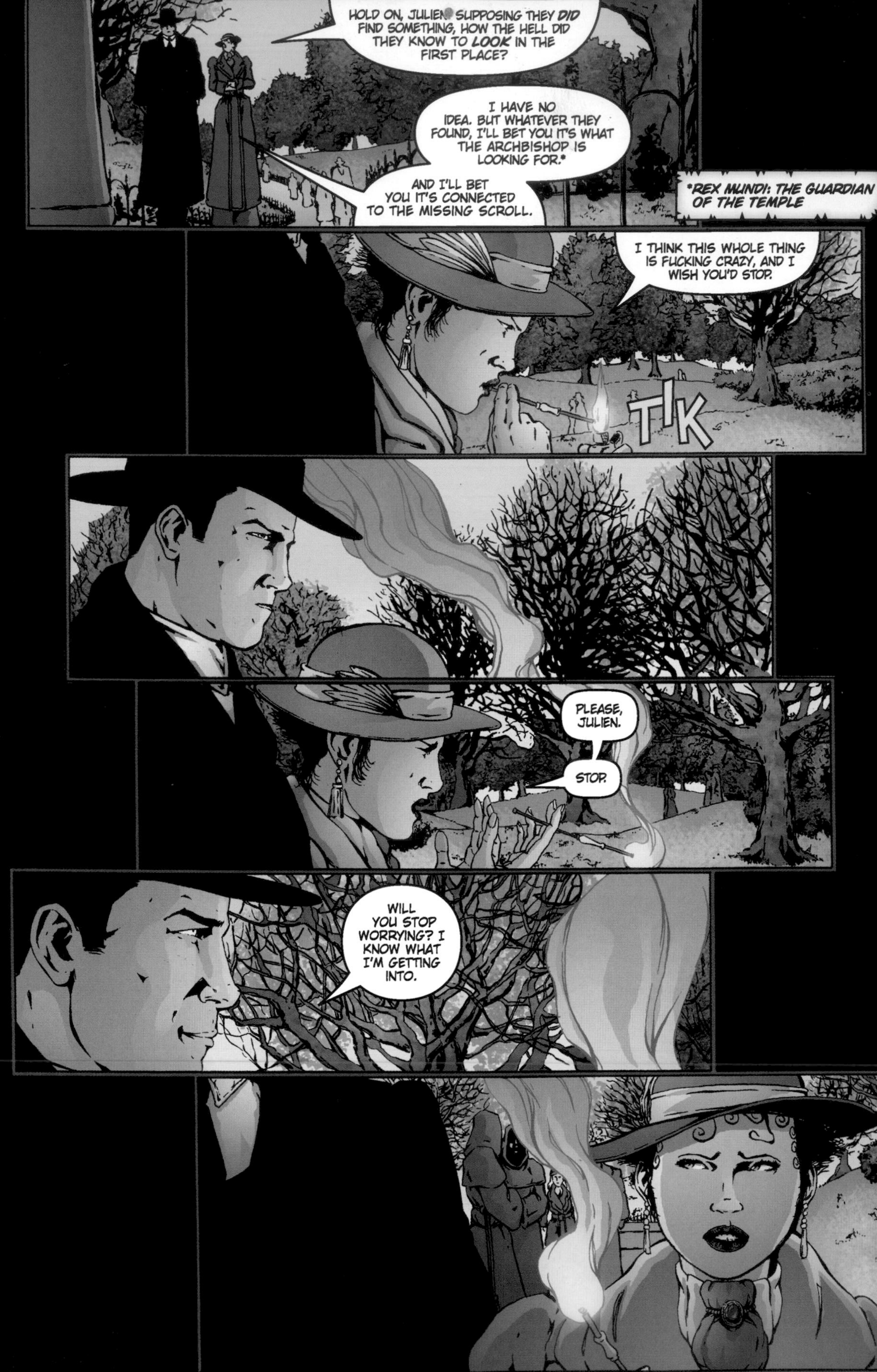

HOLD ON, JULIEN. SUPPOSING THEY DID FIND SOMETHING, HOW THE HELL DID THEY KNOW TO LOOK IN THE FIRST PLACE?
I HAVE NO IDEA. BUT WHATEVER THEY FOUND, I'LL BET YOU IT'S WHAT THE ARCHBISHOP IS LOOKING FOR.*
AND I'LL BET YOU IT'S CONNECTED TO THE MISSING SCROLL.
*REX MUNDI: THE GUARDIAN OF THE TEMPLE
I THINK THIS WHOLE THING IS FUCKING CRAZY, AND I WISH YOU'D STOP.
TIK
PLEASE, JULIEN.
STOP.
WILL YOU STOP WORRYING? I KNOW WHAT I'M GETTING INTO.

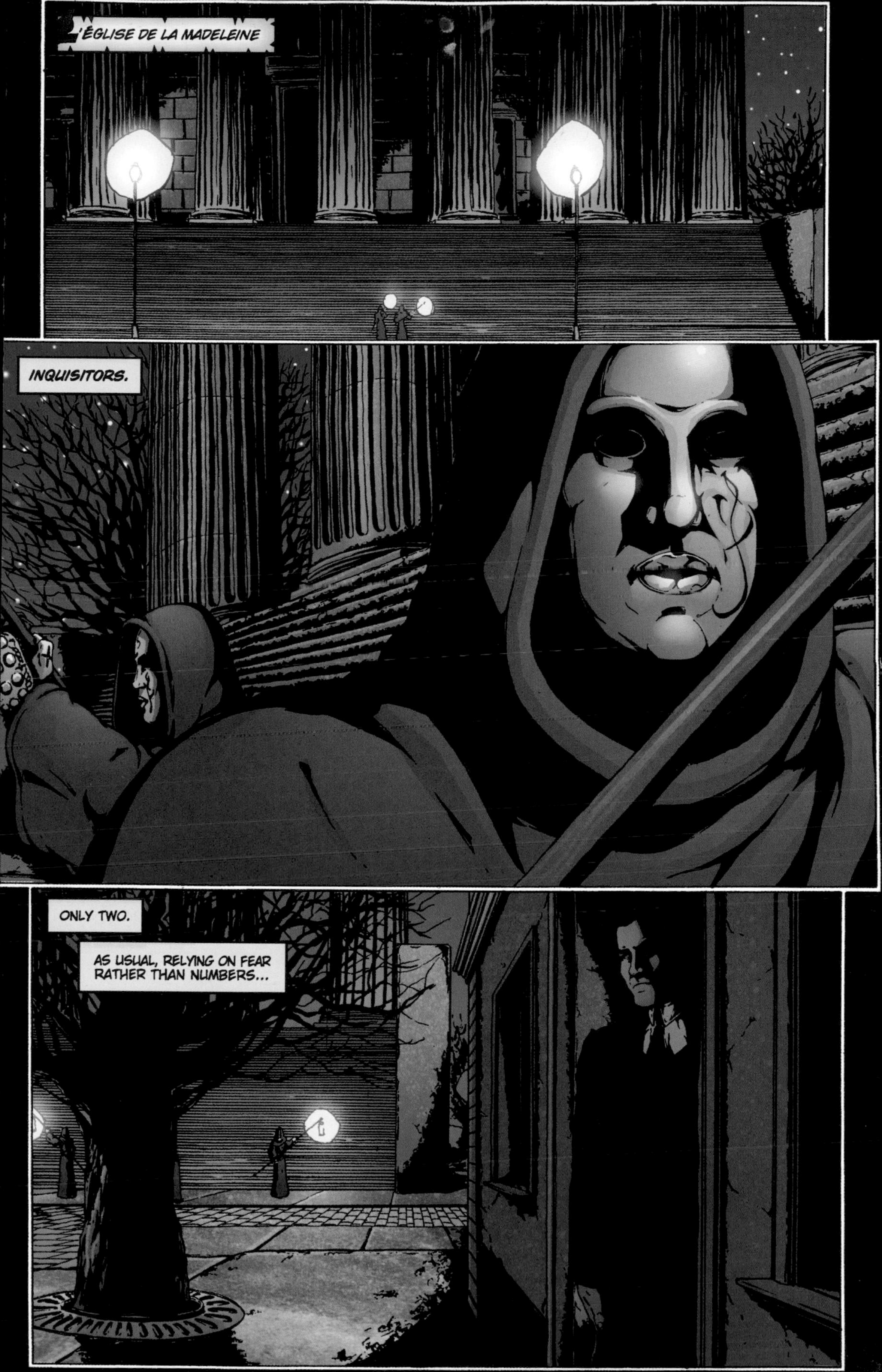

L'ÉGLISE DE LA MADELEINE
INQUISITORS.
ONLY TWO.
AS USUAL, RELYING ON FEAR RATHER THAN NUMBERS...

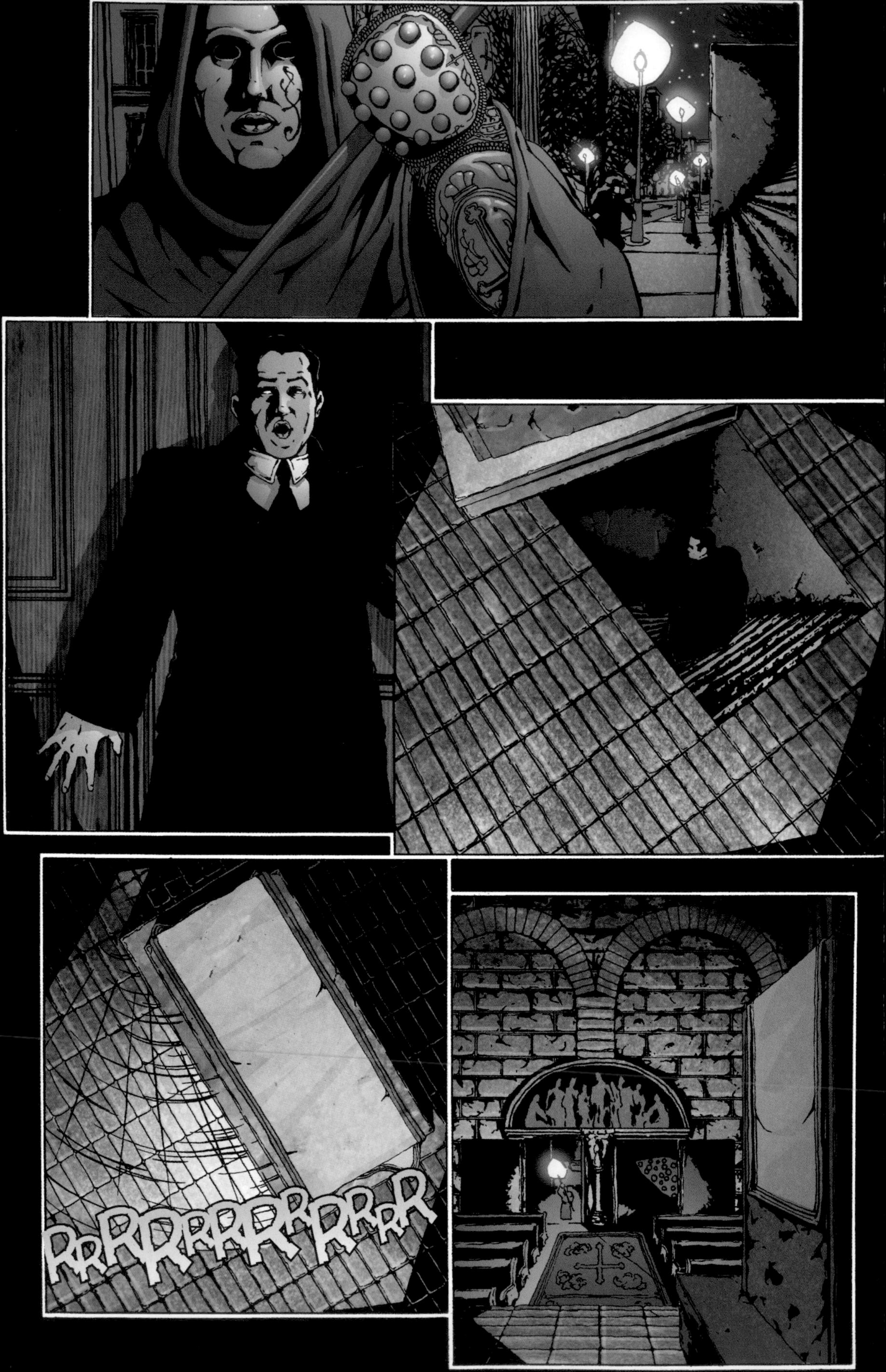
RRRRRRRRRRRRRRR

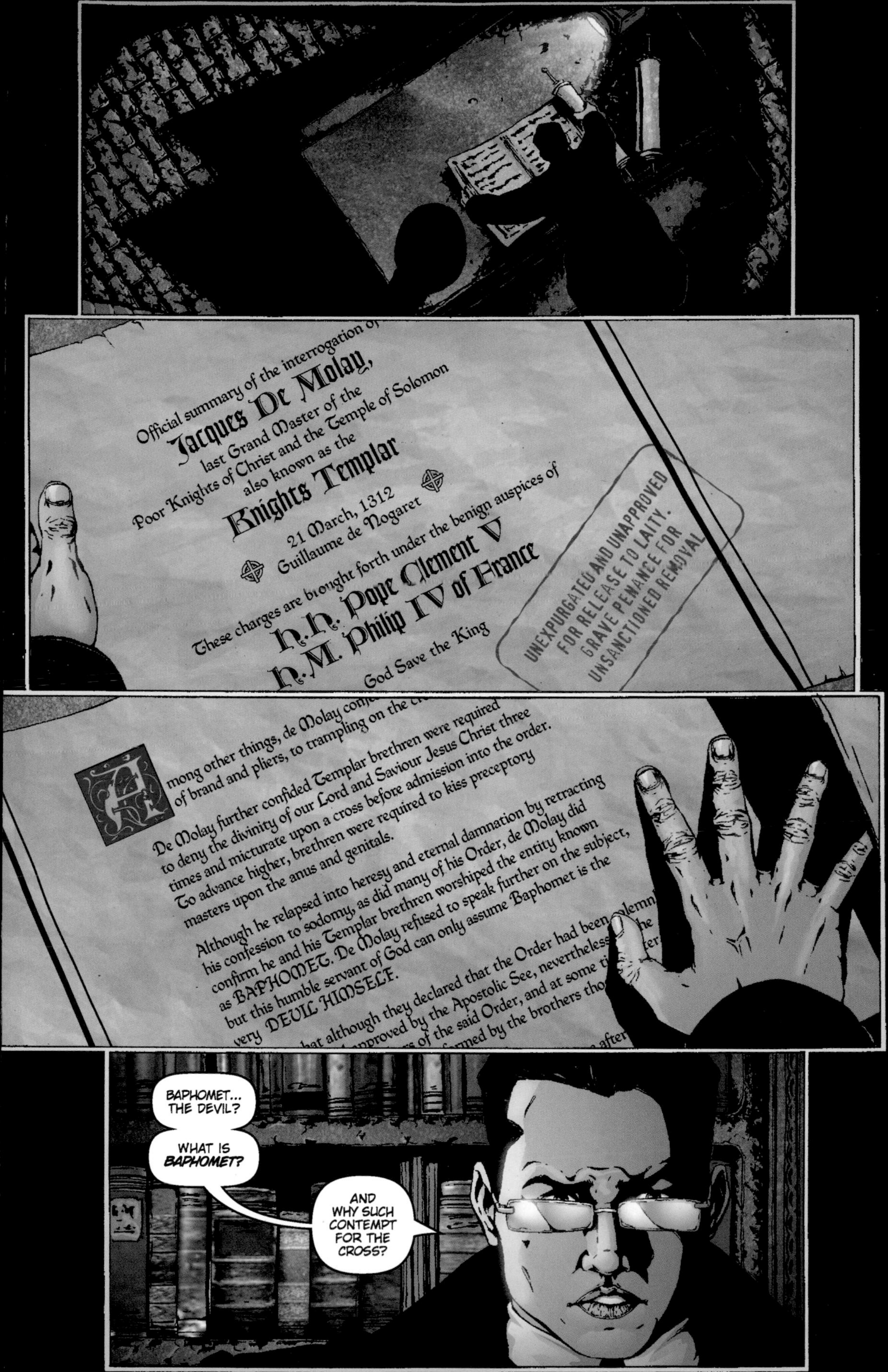
Official summary of the interrogation of
Jacques De Molay,
last Grand Master of the
Poor Knights of Christ and the Temple of Solomon
also known as the
Knights Templar
21 March, 1312
Guillaume de Nogaret
These charges are brought forth under the benign auspices of
H.H. Pope Clement V
H.M. Philip IV of France
God Save the King
UNEXPURGATED AND UNAPPROVED FOR RELEASE TO LAITY. GRAVE PENANCE FOR UNSANCTIONED REMOVAL
Among other things, de Molay
of brand and pliers, to trampling on the
De Molay further confided Templar brethren were required to deny the divinity of our Lord and Saviour Jesus Christ three times and micturate upon a cross before admission into the order. To advance higher, brethren were required to kiss preceptory masters upon the anus and genitals.
Although he relapsed into heresy and eternal damnation by retracting his confession to sodomy, as did many of his Order, de Molay did confirm he and his Templar brethren worshiped the entity known as BAPHOMET. De Molay refused to speak further on the subject, but this humble servant of God can only assume Baphomet is the very DEVIL HIMSELF.
BAPHOMET... THE DEVIL?
WHAT IS *BAPHOMET?*
AND WHY SUCH CONTEMPT FOR THE CROSS?

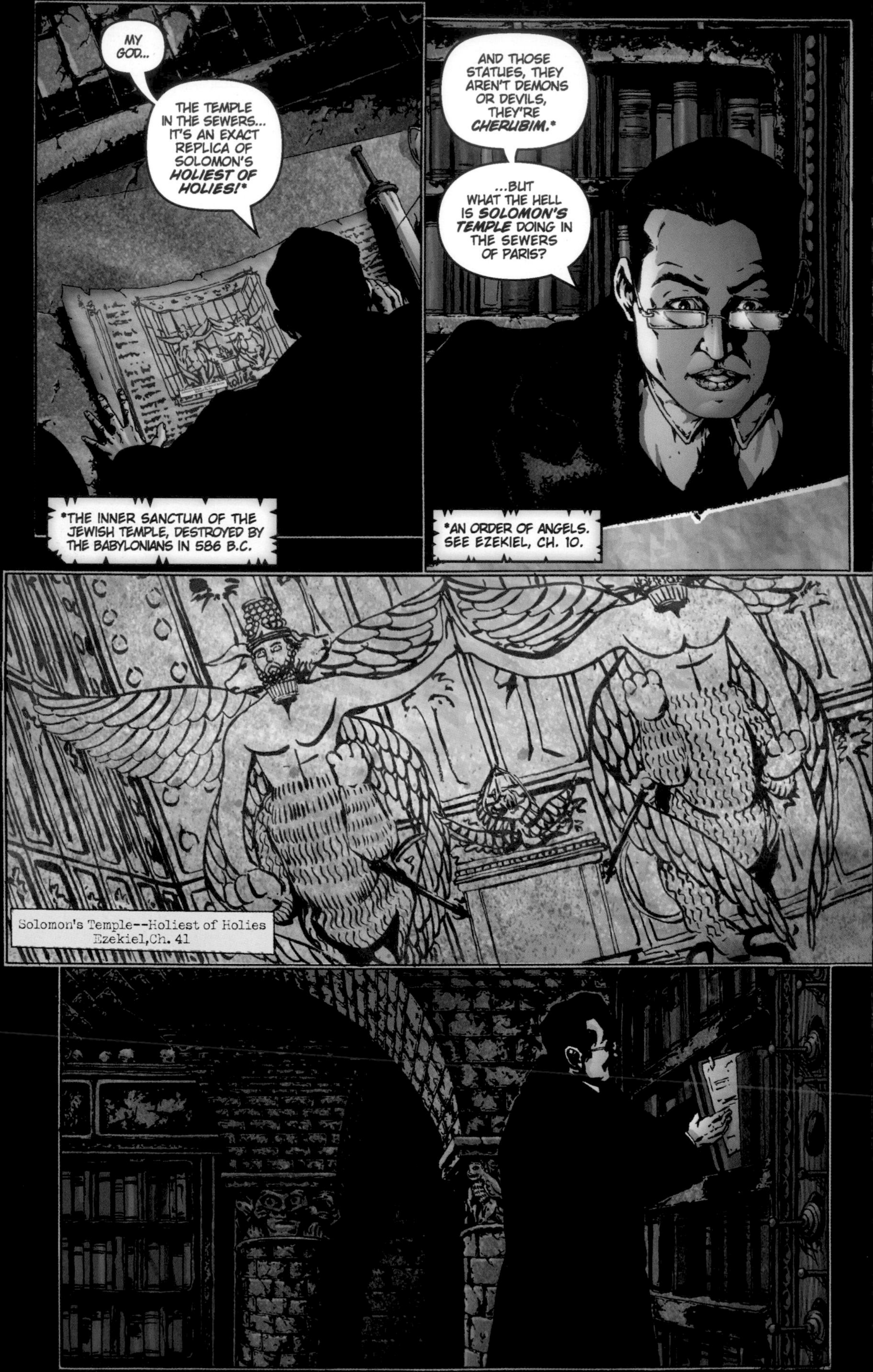
MY GOD...
THE TEMPLE IN THE SEWERS... IT'S AN EXACT REPLICA OF SOLOMON'S HOLIEST OF HOLIES!*
*THE INNER SANCTUM OF THE JEWISH TEMPLE, DESTROYED BY THE BABYLONIANS IN 586 B.C.
AND THOSE STATUES, THEY AREN'T DEMONS OR DEVILS, THEY'RE CHERUBIM.*
...BUT WHAT THE HELL IS SOLOMON'S TEMPLE DOING IN THE SEWERS OF PARIS?
*AN ORDER OF ANGELS. SEE EZEKIEL, CH. 10.
Solomon's Temple--Holiest of Holies
Ezekiel,Ch. 41

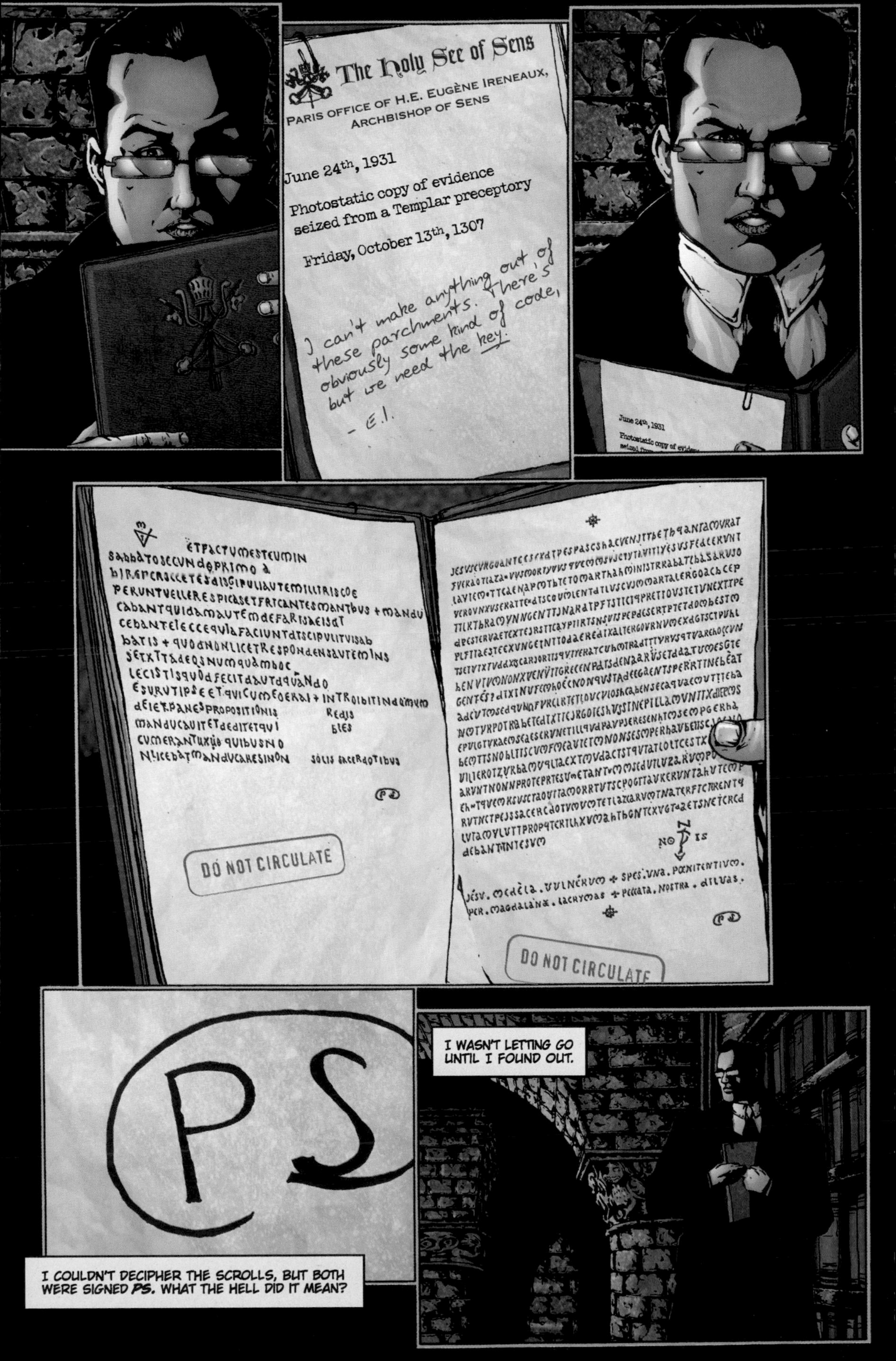

The Holy See of Sens

PARIS OFFICE OF H.E. EUGÈNE IRENEAUX,
ARCHBISHOP OF SENS

June 24th, 1931

Photostatic copy of evidence
seized from a Templar preceptory

Friday, October 13th, 1307

I can't make anything out of
these parchments. There's
obviously some kind of code,
but we need the key.

— E.I.

DO NOT CIRCULATE

DO NOT CIRCULATE

I WASN'T LETTING GO
UNTIL I FOUND OUT.

I COULDN'T DECIPHER THE SCROLLS, BUT BOTH
WERE SIGNED PS. WHAT THE HELL DID IT MEAN?

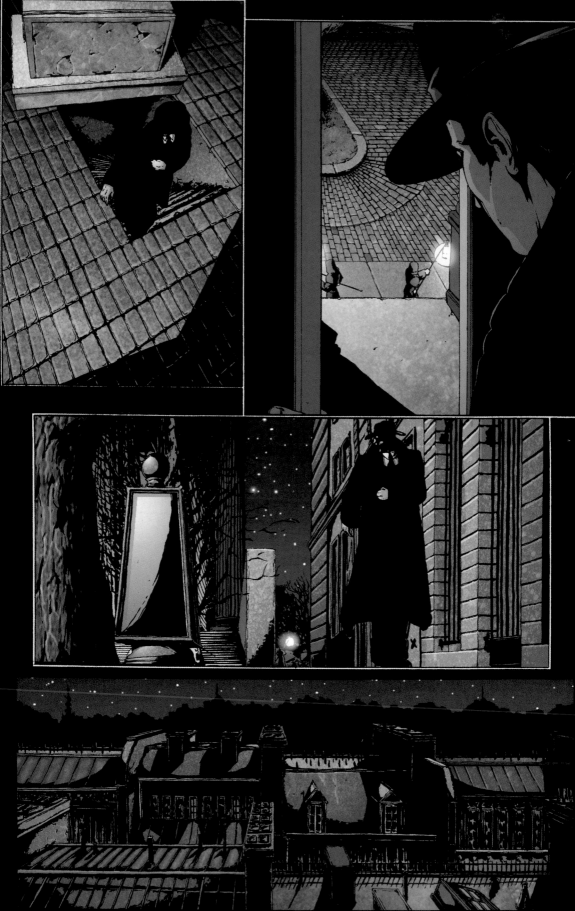

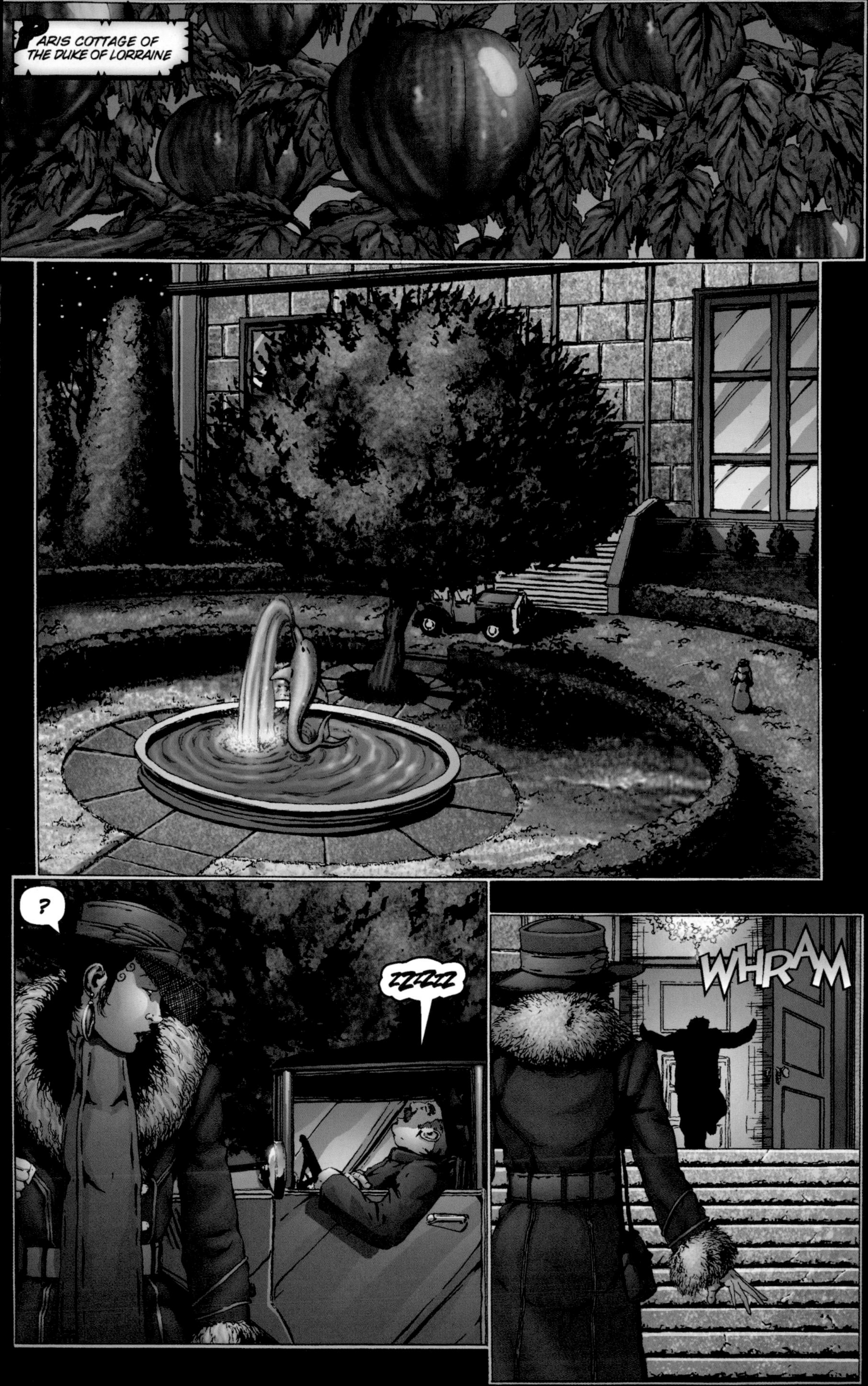

PARIS COTTAGE OF THE DUKE OF LORRAINE
?
ZZZZZZ
WHRAM

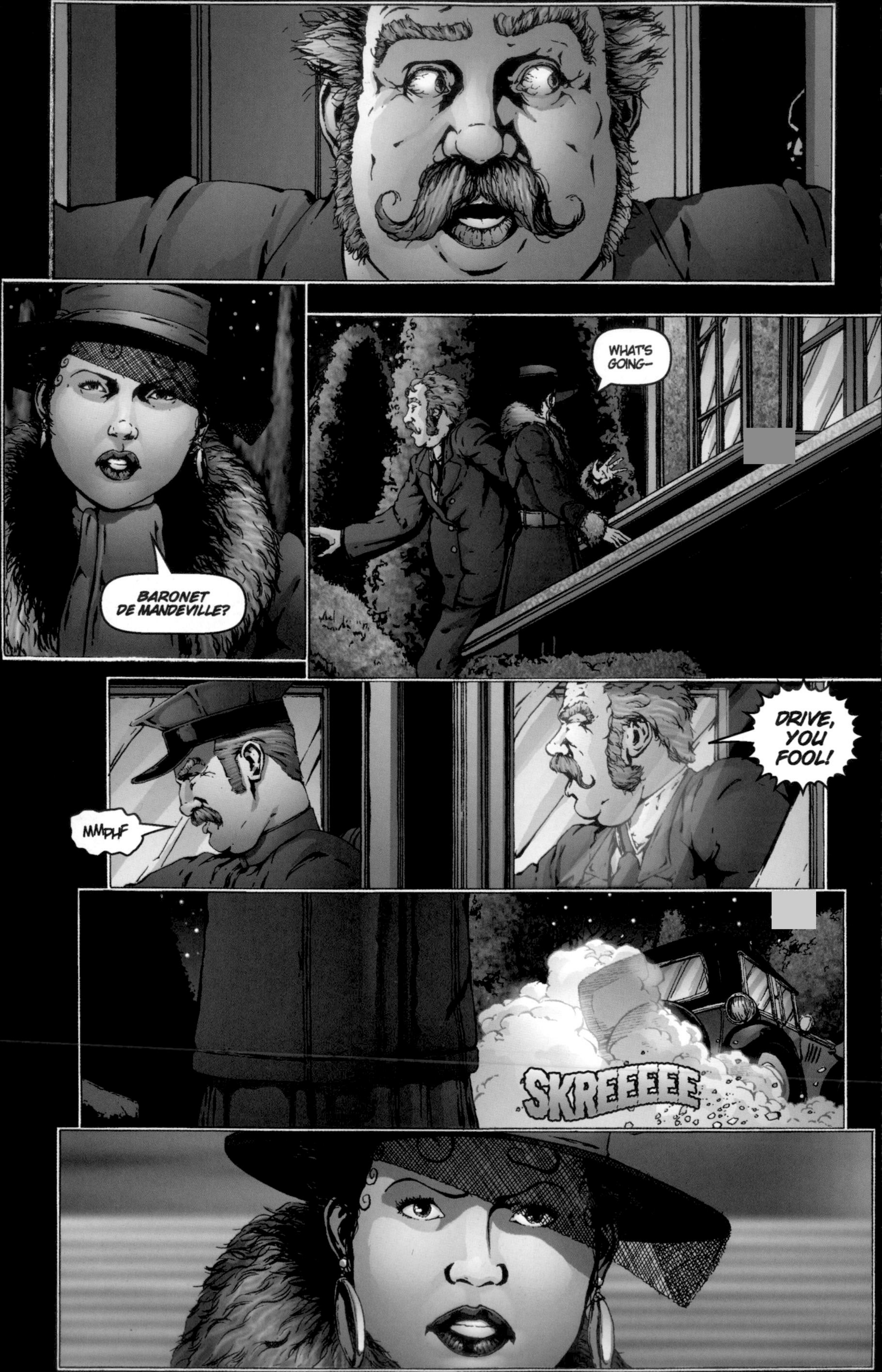
BARONET DE MANDEVILLE?
WHAT'S GOING–
MMPHF
DRIVE, YOU FOOL!
SKREEEEE

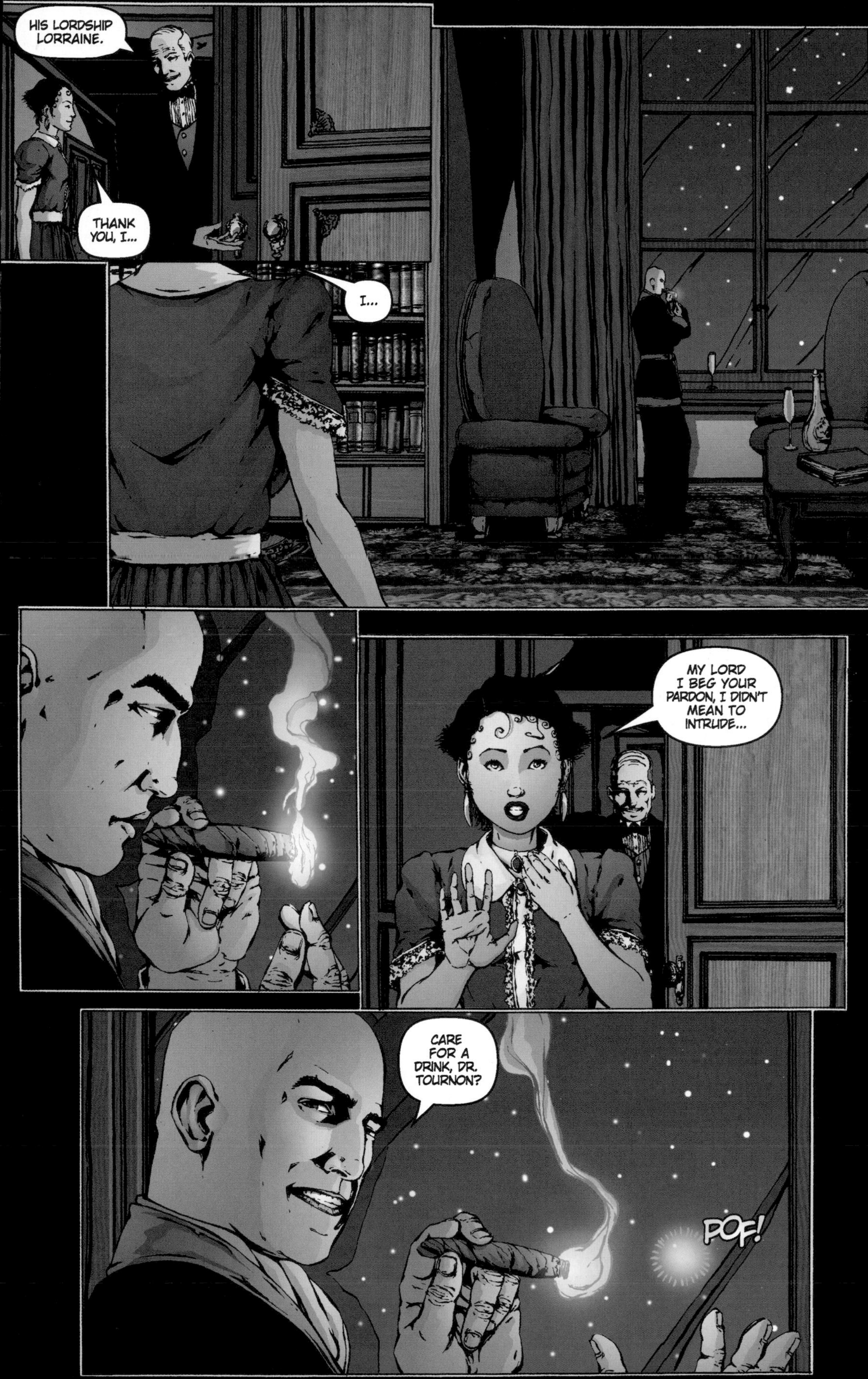
HIS LORDSHIP LORRAINE.
THANK YOU, I...
I...
MY LORD I BEG YOUR PARDON, I DIDN'T MEAN TO INTRUDE...
CARE FOR A DRINK, DR. TOURNON?
POF!

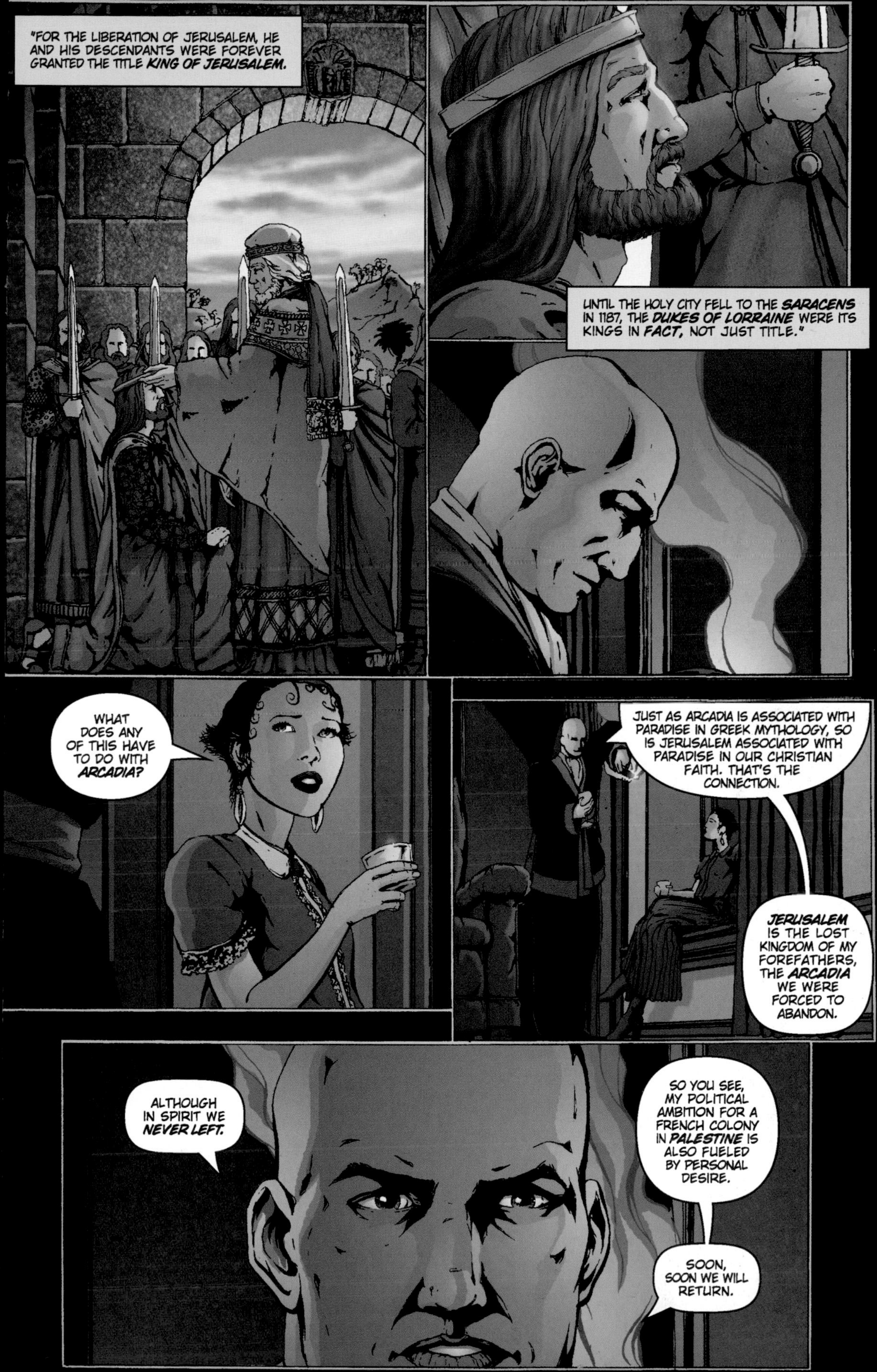
"FOR THE LIBERATION OF JERUSALEM, HE AND HIS DESCENDANTS WERE FOREVER GRANTED THE TITLE *KING OF JERUSALEM.*
UNTIL THE HOLY CITY FELL TO THE *SARACENS* IN 1187, THE *DUKES OF LORRAINE* WERE ITS KINGS IN *FACT,* NOT JUST TITLE."
WHAT DOES ANY OF THIS HAVE TO DO WITH *ARCADIA?*
JUST AS ARCADIA IS ASSOCIATED WITH PARADISE IN GREEK MYTHOLOGY, SO IS JERUSALEM ASSOCIATED WITH PARADISE IN OUR CHRISTIAN FAITH. THAT'S THE CONNECTION.
JERUSALEM IS THE LOST KINGDOM OF MY FOREFATHERS, THE *ARCADIA* WE WERE FORCED TO ABANDON.
ALTHOUGH IN SPIRIT WE *NEVER LEFT.*
SO YOU SEE, MY POLITICAL AMBITION FOR A FRENCH COLONY IN *PALESTINE* IS ALSO FUELED BY PERSONAL DESIRE.
SOON, SOON WE WILL RETURN.

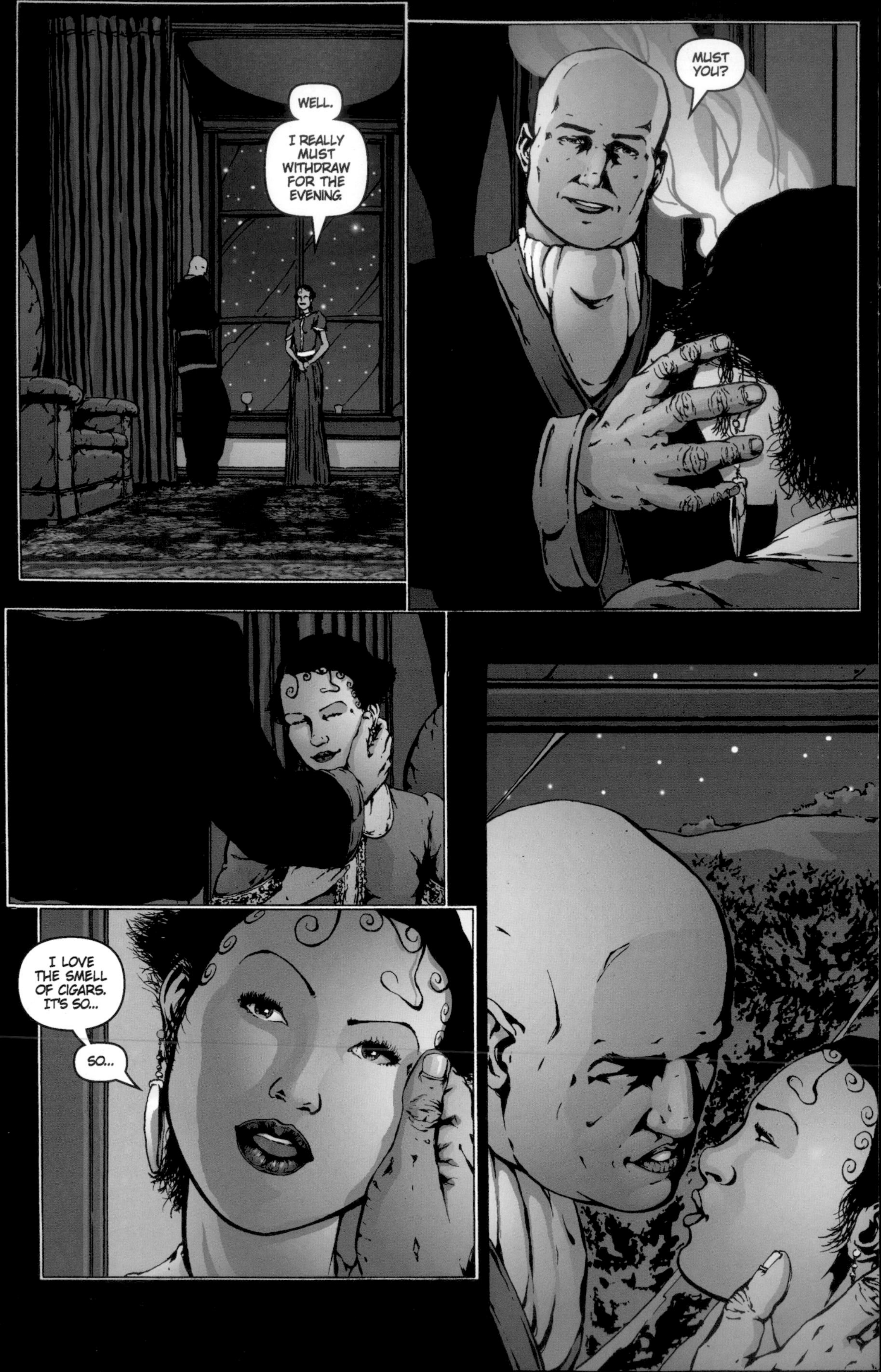
WELL.
I REALLY MUST WITHDRAW FOR THE EVENING.
MUST YOU?
I LOVE THE SMELL OF CIGARS. IT'S SO...
SO...

Le Journal de la Liberté

Paris's leading anglophone newspaper • vol. 205, no. 101 • Oct. 24, MCMXXXIII

Editors in Chief: M. Tait Bergstrom, M. Matthew Pasteris. **Story Editor:** M. Arvid Nelson. **Art Editors:** M. EricJ, M. Jeromy Cox. **Photography Editor:** M. Alexander Waldman. **Layout Supervisor:** M. William Kartalopoulos. **Editors Emeritus:** M. Clark A. Smith, M. Howard P. Lovecraft, M. Robert E. Howard. Redacted by the Holy Parisian Inquisition under the direction of His Excellency Archbishop Emile-Jean Ireneaux. Le Journal de Liberté is printed under the benign auspices of his most puissant majesty KING LOUIS XXII of FRANCE. GOD SAVE THE KING.

Papal Seal

of Approval

KING'S SUPPORTERS BLAST LORRAINE'S PROPOSED COLONIZATION OF THE HOLY LAND

ough Talk in the Hall of the Robe

"I know I speak for an overhelming majority of my colgues when I say that I have never en a more rash, a more ill-conived or a more misguided piece legislation in my tenure in the all of the Robe," Baronet Aristide Mandeville, speaker of the Hall the Robe, said yesterday.

He spoke before the members the Robe regarding legislation oposed by the Hall of the Sword enable French colonization of e Holy Land.

DeMandeville received loud eers and applause during his eech.

Members of the Robe made very clear the colonial designs the Holy Land proposed by e Duke of Lorraine last week ould be rejected if it came a vote in the Hall of the obe. "Without the support of e Robe, the scheme proposed the Sword is a dead letter," Mandeville said.

The members of the Robe erwhelmingly proclaimed their pport for King Louis XXII's licy of "unstringing the bow," e term political analysts have ven to the King's foreign policy ategy aimed at easing tensions Europe and abroad.

"Christendom can ill afford idespread conflict. We do not vocate a policy of peace because ance is weak, but because France strong," deMandeville said.

"All the monarchies of rope would be in grave peril

should war break out. Now is a time when, for the good of the common man as well as the highest lord, Christian kings should band together to fight the twin hydras of political libertarianism and radical nationalism."

These sentiments are hardly unexpected, since the Robe is entirely made up of Louis XXII's closest political allies.

Charles Martel, the king's mayor of the court, expressed his satisfaction with the proclamations made the other day in the Hall of the Robe.

"The King and the Robe are in complete concurrence on this matter," he said.

The Robe's sentiments were received coolly by members of the Hall of the Sword.

"It is unfortunate we are unable to reach consensus on this issue," Baron Robert Teniers, a spokesman for the Duke of Lorraine, said. "But the members of the Hall of the Sword believe a policy of aggressive colonialism centered on the conquest of the Holy Land is the best course of action for France, given the avowedly aggressive stance of our neighbors."

"Also consider the enormous petrochemical reserves that lie beneath the sands of the Near East,"

continued on page A3

THREE DUTCH MERCHANT VESSELS GUTTED IN CARIBBEAN WATERS

The "Bermuda Triangle" has claimed three more ships.

The gutted hulks of three merchant ships were observed floating adrift about ninety miles East of Eleuthera Island in the Bahamas. All the vessels were Dutch in origin, and all were laden with cotton, sugar and tobacco from the Confederate States of America.

A British naval ship, the *HMS Dauntless*, was alerted to the hulks' presence by plumes of smoke on the horizon.

Immediate suspicion fell on pirates, who are a persistent menace in the region.

"It's quite unsettling to come upon a ship that's been ravaged by pirates," said First Mate Nicholas Englund of the *Dauntless*. "It's like encountering a ghost ship. The most unnerving aspect of this incident was the fact that we didn't find any bodies. Not a one."

Piracy has, of course, evolved since the days of flintlocks and canvas sails.

"Today's pirates use smaller, wood- or metal-hulled vessels with outboard motors. They can subdue a much larger ship with small, high-powered rifles. They're fast and ruthless," Englund said.

In an unusual joint statement,

continued on page E5

Bizarre Nighttime Chase Disturbs Pedestrians; Scraggly Street Urchins Observed Participating in Fracas

Late-night revelers and pedestrians were disturbed last evening in the Fifteenth Arrondissement by an unusual foot chase. By the time Inquisition and Gendarmerie officers arrived at the scene, the parties involved had disappeared.

"We have no more information about this incident than you," Inquisitor Sanival, who was questioning witnesses last night after the incident, said.

Eyewitnesses described the bizarre scene.

"The guy being chased was actually a lot bigger than the guy being chased. Don't know what the problem was, but they were both running hard," Matthieu

Carette, who operates a crepe stand in the area, said.

Further reports indicated the pursued man wore a black suit.

"Like a mortician, he was kind of creepy," an eyewitness who spoke on the condition of anonymity said.

But by all accounts, the pursuer was the more peculiar of the pair.

"He was a little guy, looked like he was maybe in his fifties," said Carette. "He was wearing all white. Even his hat and his tie. He was a little bit pudgy, but he sure did run fast."

Several eyewitnesses said the man wore sungoggles, in spite of the darkness.

"The glasses were mirrored, I

couldn't see his eyes," said Martha Huguet, who was returning home from the theater when she observed the chase. "There was something about him, something not quite right, if you know what I mean. The kind of person you might avoid on the street."

Perhaps the strangest part of last night's incident was the fact that a band of young street waifs was seen entering into the chase, "close on the heels of the man in white," Huguet said.

"Imagine it. First you see someone in black whip by. Then someone in white. Then a group of noisy children dressed in rags, brandishing slings and screaming

continued on page B11

⇒ INSIDE ⇐

THE KEY TO FRANCE: A REPORT ON THE HALL OF THE ROBI

Tensions between the Hall of the Robe and the Hall of the Sword have been boiling over in the past few days, due in large part to a controversial plan for the colonization of the Holy Land submitted by the Duke of Lorraine, Speaker for the Hall of the Sword.

But political conflict in the Assemblée Nationale is nothing new, and neither is the expected outcome of this latest round of strife. Although the endeavor proposed by Lord Lorraine has broad-based support in the Sword, most analysts believe it will never be realized.

This is because the members of the Hall of the Robe have unanimously denounced the measure and made it very clear they do not support its passage into law. As is often the case, the Robe's position perfectly reflects the wishes of the King.

"The Hall of the Robe is the key to France," an official for King Louis XXII who spoke on the condition of anonymity said. "And the key is firmly in the King's hand."

But what makes the Hall of the Robe so pivotal, why does it have so much sway in the affairs of France, and why does His Majesty Louis XXII "hold the key"?

One needs only to understand the origins and workings of our constitutional monarchy to appreciate the Robe's importance.

The Origins of France's Constitutional Monarchy

The foundation of our current government was laid in 1799, when royalist French troops rallied and forced the defeat of the so-called "Republicans," bringing and end to over a decade of brutal mob rule and barbaric disregard for the sanctity of France's ancient and noble institutions.

Indeed, the Monarchy nearly perished—the Dauphin Louis XVII's near capture by a murderous Jacobin mob and his harrowing flight to Luxembourg left a deep scar on the house of Bourbon and the institution of the Monarchy itself.

Therefore in 1801 the Crown, having solely ruled France for over a millennia, finally acquiesced to the demands of the landed aristocracy. A constitutional monarchy was formed, limiting the power of the King with a bicameral diet known as the "National Assembly."

But in many ways the King retained the upper hand.

The Sword and the Robe

The Hall of the Sword derives its name from the ancient oath of martial fealty medieval lords swore to a King. It is exclusively composed of members of ancient noble houses who can trace their lineage back to the time of the First Crusade – almost eight hundred and fifty years ago!

This means the Hall of the Sword is vastly smaller than the Hall of the Robe, and therefore its power is far more concentrated.

In theory, anyway.

"The reality is that the noble families represented in the Sword often have conflicting viewpoints and are usually at odds with one another due to long-standing feuds and rivalries," Georges Fresnay, a professor of political theology at the Sorbonne, said. "This makes it very difficult for the Sword to coordinate any kind of political strategy."

Fresnay admits the Sword has coalesced as a unified political body over the last few years due to the leadership of the Duke of Lorraine.

"Lorraine's rallying of the Sword is nothing short of a miracle," Fresnay said. "He has taken a very willful group of people and convinced them to work for their collective interests. It's simply unprecedented."

Versailles, court of Louis XXII. Also the nominal center of power for the Hall of the Robe and therefore France itself. Photo: Eugène Atget, staff photographe

But all this is for naught when the Hall of the Robe is taken into consideration.

Members of the Robe are hand-selected by the King. The term "Robe" therefore refers to the robes of a merchant or a state official.

"The King selects Robe members based on loyalty to the Crown and common political interest. And no one can interfere with the selection process. It's the King's exclusive right," Fresnay said.

Thus, while the Robe is much larger than the Sword, with over 300 members at any given time, it is politically much more cohesive—and fiercely loyal to the Crown.

"The King deliberately cultivates relationships with members of his entourage who demonstrate exemplary loyalty and service for placement into the Hall of the Robe," Fresnay said. "There's no secret about that."

The Crown, the Sword and the Robe each have one vote on proposed legislation. The King casts a vote alone. For either

> ## "The Hall of the Robe is the key to France. And the key is firmly in the King's hand."

house to endorse a propos a two-thirds majority vote required. Two out of three of th Crown, Robe and Sword mu endorse a measure for it to l signed into law.

Since the first session of th Assemblée Nationale in 180 the Robe has never once vote against the King.

Thus the Sword finds itse out-maneuvere time and tim again by th King throug the agency of t Robe. There no indication th this latest rou of voting—o Lorraine's colon policy—will be any different.

"The Robe is nothing mo than the King's puppet, and o so-called constitutional mo archy exists only on paper," member of the Hall of the Swo who spoke on the condition anonymity said.

Members of the Robe de this characterization. Says Ro member Jean-Michel Modot:

"We simply want what's be for France, and, as loyal subjec we believe in our King."

France's three legislative bodies, in which is invested the vast majority of the powers of government:

The crest of the House of Bourbon, the reigning kings of France. Because the King reserves the sole power to admit members into the Hall of the Robe, he is assured a virtual monopoly in French politics.

The Hall of the Robe is composed of the King's most loyal supporters. A noble title is also a requirement for entry, but because King Louis XXII has the right to confer titles, this is mere formality.

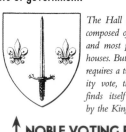

The Hall of the Sword composed of France's olde and most prestigious nol houses. But since legislati requires a two-thirds majoity vote, the Sword oft finds itself outmaneuver by the King and the Rob

↑ ROYAL VOTING BLOC | **↑ NOBLE VOTING BLOCK**

CHAPTER TWO
FATHER OF WISDOM

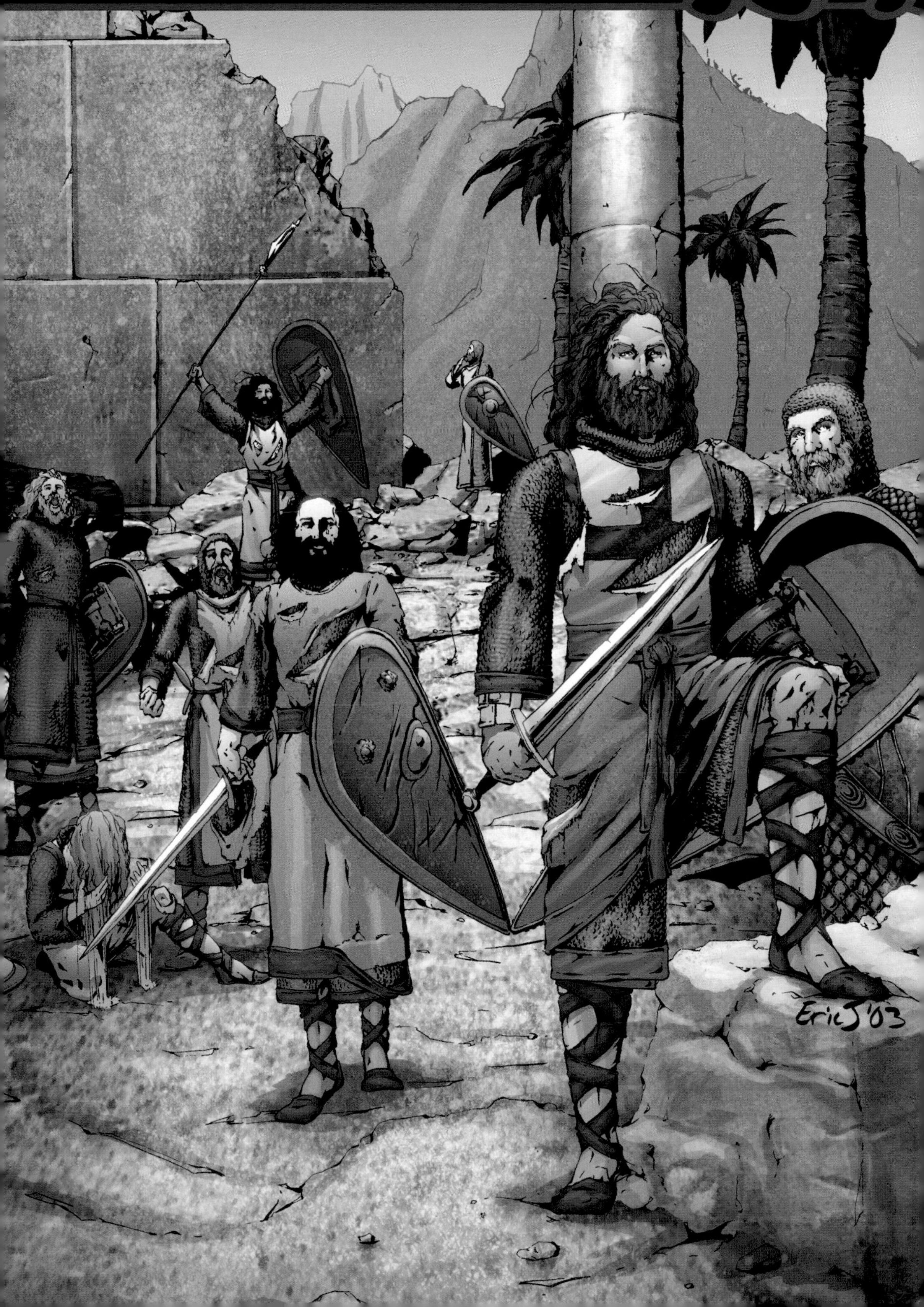
EricJ'03

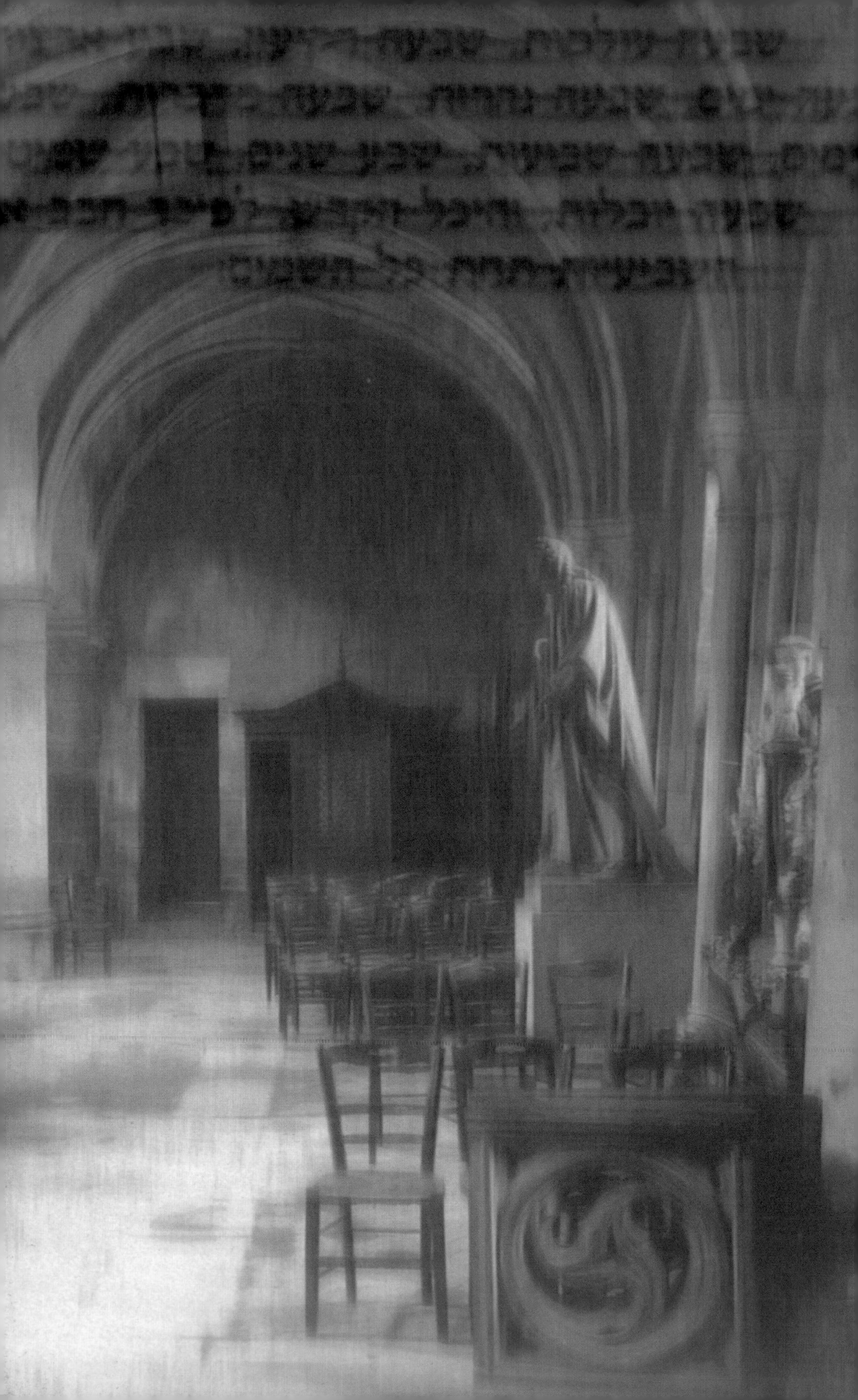
שבעה עולמות, שבעה רקיעים,
שבעה נהרות, שבעה מדברות,
שבעה שבועות, שבע שנים, שבע שמיטות,
שבעה יובלות, והיכל הקדש. לפיכך חבב
שביעיות תחת כל השמים

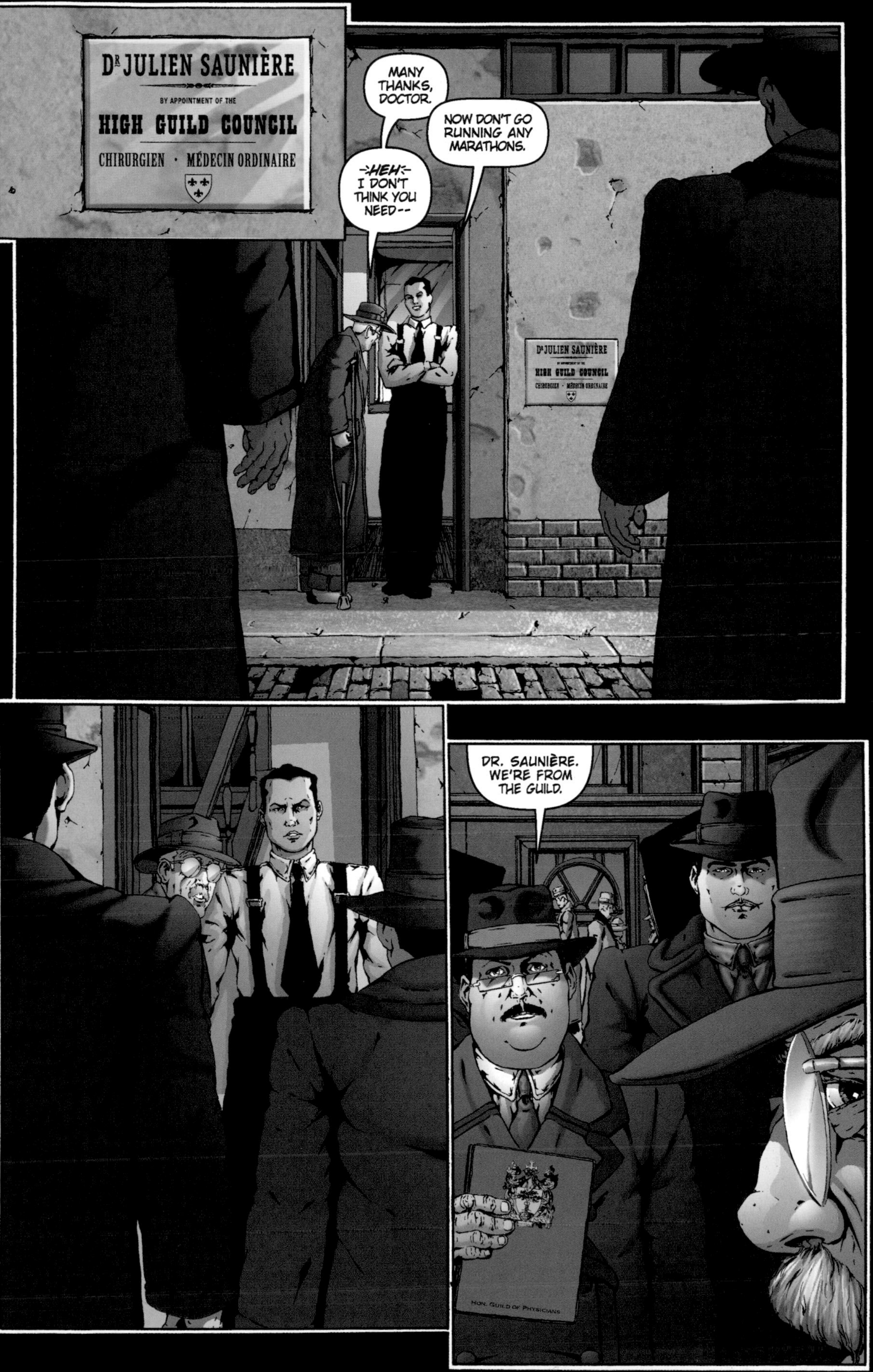
DR JULIEN SAUNIÈRE
BY APPOINTMENT OF THE
HIGH GUILD COUNCIL
CHIRURGIEN · MÉDECIN ORDINAIRE
MANY THANKS, DOCTOR.
NOW DON'T GO RUNNING ANY MARATHONS.
-HEH- I DON'T THINK YOU NEED--
DR JULIEN SAUNIÈRE
HIGH GUILD COUNCIL
CHIRURGIEN · MÉDECIN ORDINAIRE
DR. SAUNIÈRE. WE'RE FROM THE GUILD.
HON. GUILD OF PHYSICIANS

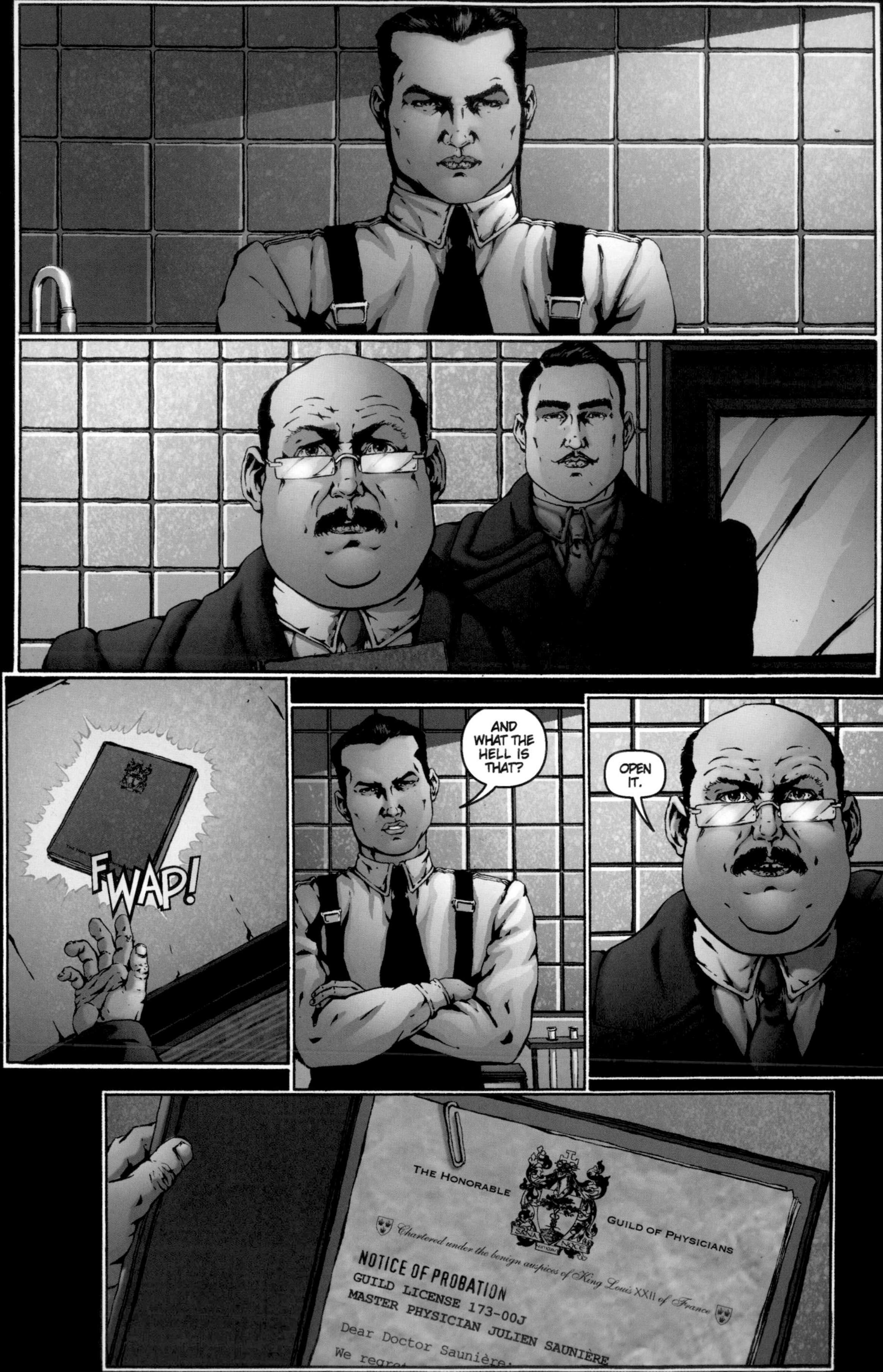
FWAP!
AND WHAT THE HELL IS THAT?
OPEN IT.
THE HONORABLE
GUILD OF PHYSICIANS
Chartered under the benign auspices of King Louis XXII of France
NOTICE OF PROBATION
GUILD LICENSE 173-00J
MASTER PHYSICIAN JULIEN SAUNIÈRE
Dear Doctor Saunière:

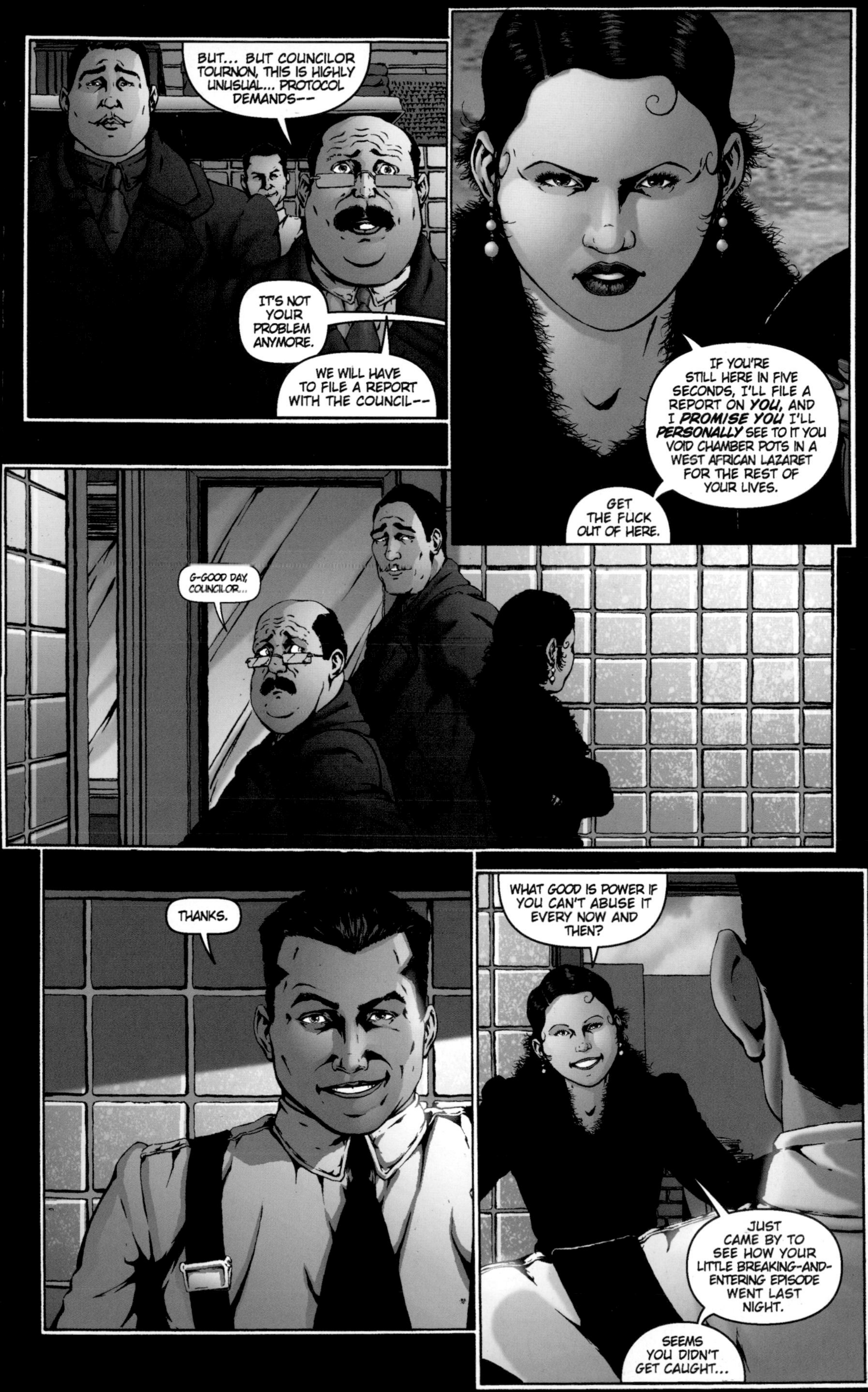
BUT... BUT COUNCILOR TOURNON, THIS IS HIGHLY UNUSUAL... PROTOCOL DEMANDS--
IT'S NOT YOUR PROBLEM ANYMORE.
WE WILL HAVE TO FILE A REPORT WITH THE COUNCIL--
IF YOU'RE STILL HERE IN FIVE SECONDS, I'LL FILE A REPORT ON *YOU,* AND I ***PROMISE YOU*** I'LL ***PERSONALLY*** SEE TO IT YOU VOID CHAMBER POTS IN A WEST AFRICAN LAZARET FOR THE REST OF YOUR LIVES.
GET THE FUCK OUT OF HERE.
G-GOOD DAY, COUNCILOR...
THANKS.
WHAT GOOD IS POWER IF YOU CAN'T ABUSE IT EVERY NOW AND THEN?
JUST CAME BY TO SEE HOW YOUR LITTLE BREAKING-AND-ENTERING EPISODE WENT LAST NIGHT.
SEEMS YOU DIDN'T GET CAUGHT...

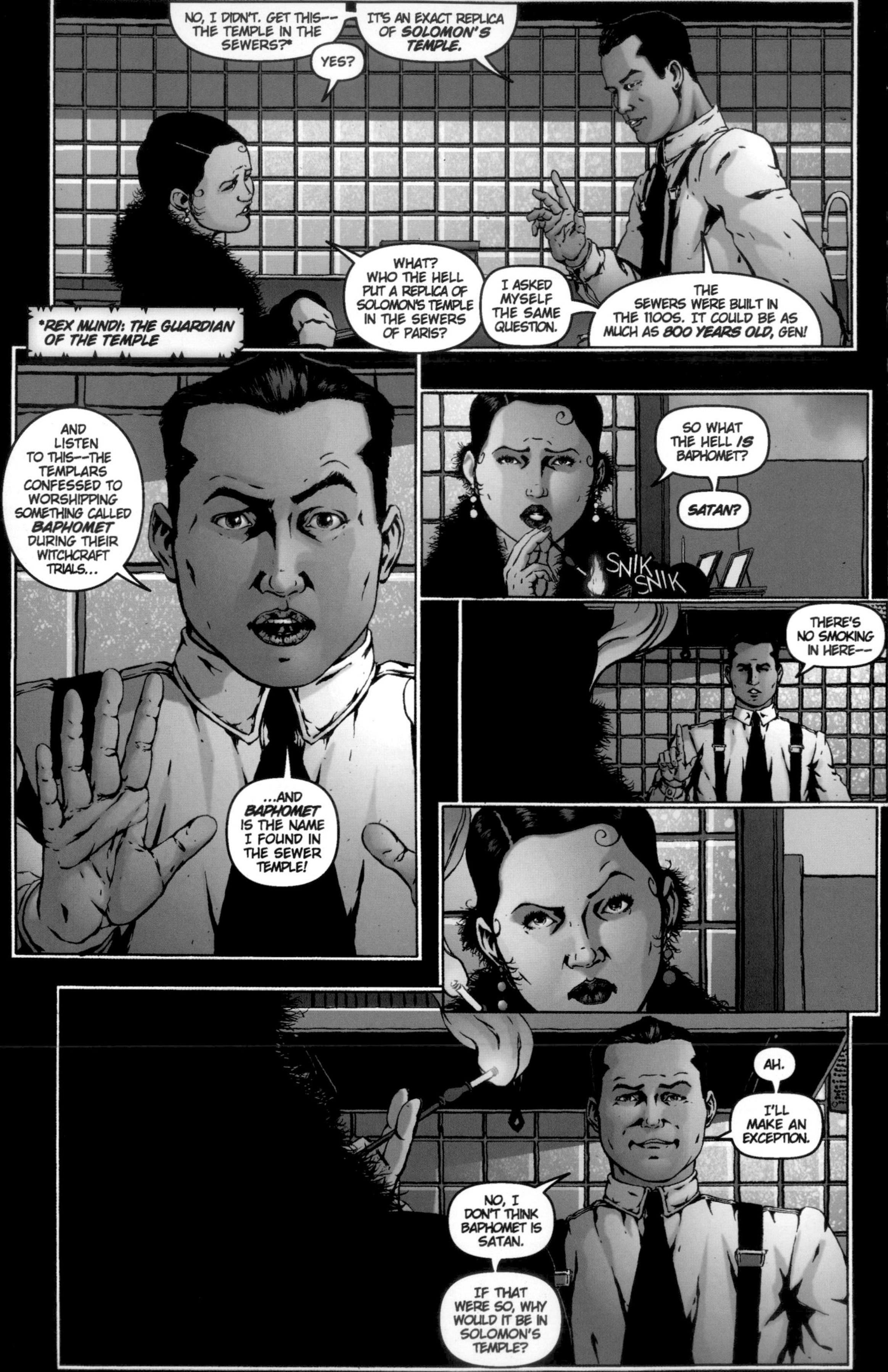
NO, I DIDN'T. GET THIS-- THE TEMPLE IN THE SEWERS?*
YES?
IT'S AN EXACT REPLICA OF SOLOMON'S TEMPLE.
WHAT? WHO THE HELL PUT A REPLICA OF SOLOMON'S TEMPLE IN THE SEWERS OF PARIS?
I ASKED MYSELF THE SAME QUESTION.
THE SEWERS WERE BUILT IN THE 1100S. IT COULD BE AS MUCH AS 800 YEARS OLD, GEN!
*REX MUNDI: THE GUARDIAN OF THE TEMPLE
AND LISTEN TO THIS--THE TEMPLARS CONFESSED TO WORSHIPPING SOMETHING CALLED BAPHOMET DURING THEIR WITCHCRAFT TRIALS...
...AND BAPHOMET IS THE NAME I FOUND IN THE SEWER TEMPLE!
SO WHAT THE HELL IS BAPHOMET?
SATAN?
SNIK SNIK
THERE'S NO SMOKING IN HERE--
AH.
I'LL MAKE AN EXCEPTION.
NO, I DON'T THINK BAPHOMET IS SATAN.
IF THAT WERE SO, WHY WOULD IT BE IN SOLOMON'S TEMPLE?

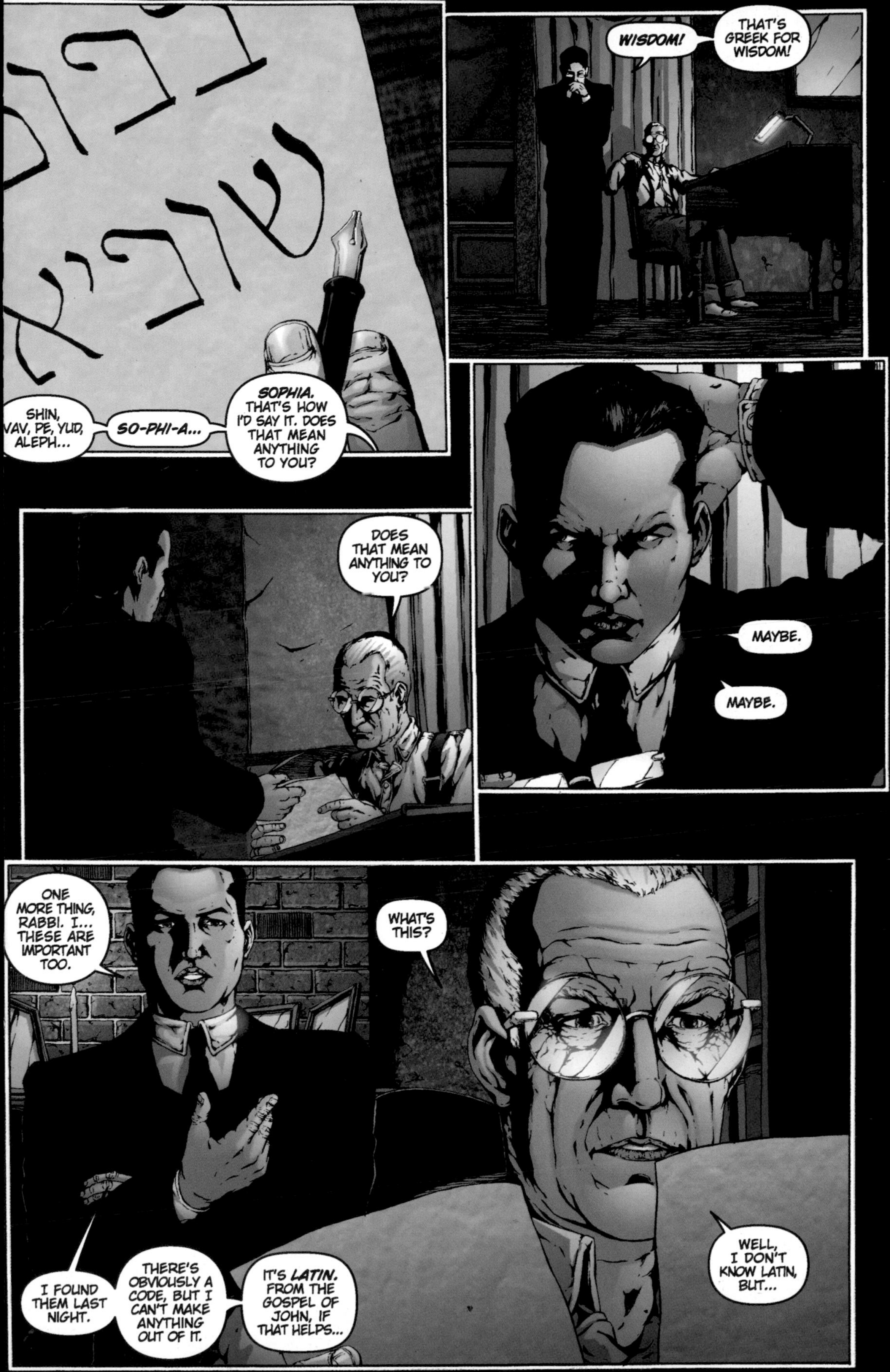

SHIN, VAV, PE, YUD, ALEPH...
SO-PHI-A...
SOPHIA. THAT'S HOW I'D SAY IT. DOES THAT MEAN ANYTHING TO YOU?
WISDOM!
THAT'S GREEK FOR WISDOM!
DOES THAT MEAN ANYTHING TO YOU?
MAYBE.
MAYBE.
ONE MORE THING, RABBI. I... THESE ARE IMPORTANT TOO.
WHAT'S THIS?
I FOUND THEM LAST NIGHT.
THERE'S OBVIOUSLY A CODE, BUT I CAN'T MAKE ANYTHING OUT OF IT.
IT'S *LATIN.* FROM THE GOSPEL OF JOHN, IF THAT HELPS...
WELL, I DON'T KNOW LATIN, BUT...

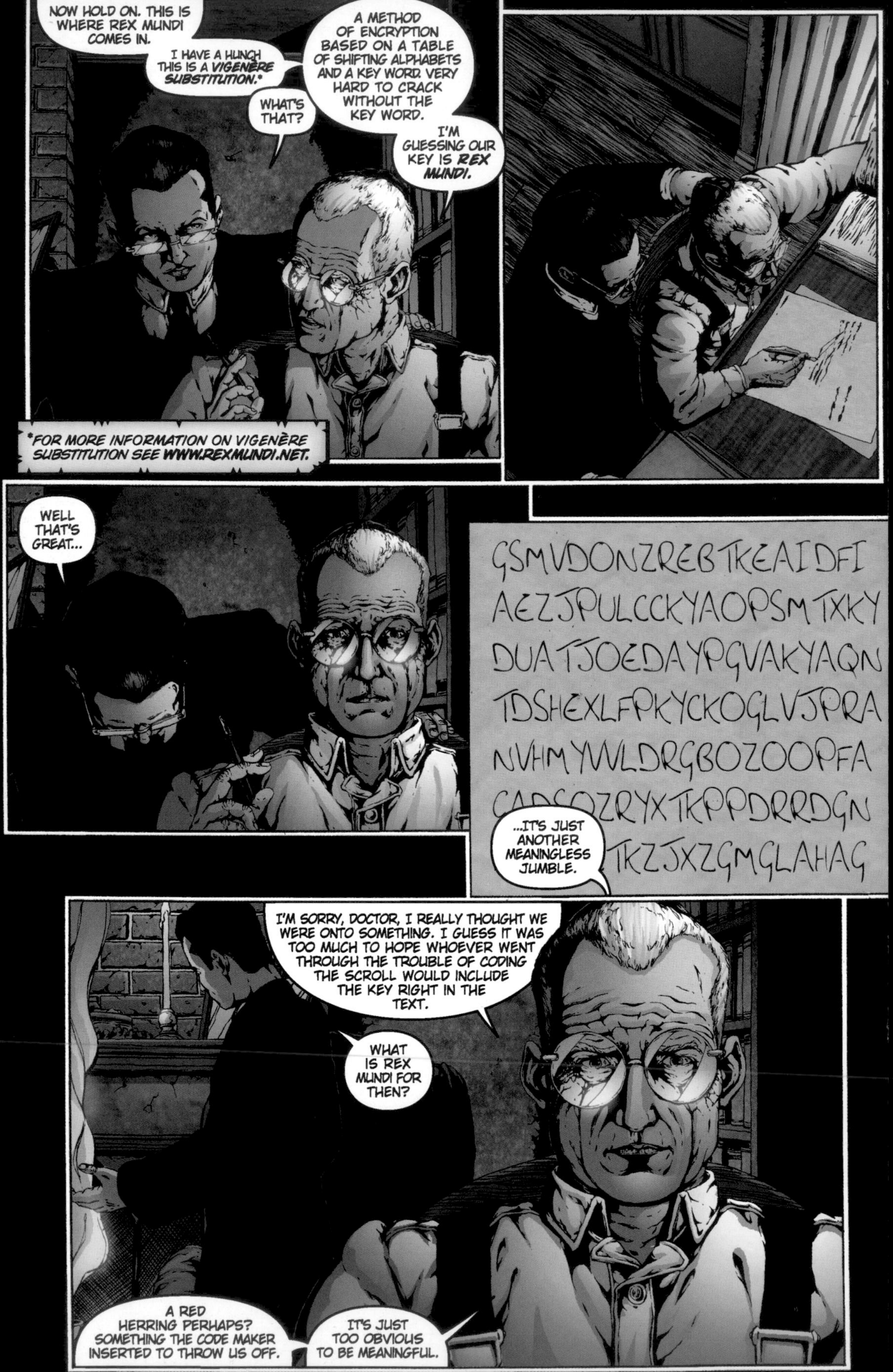
NOW HOLD ON. THIS IS WHERE REX MUNDI COMES IN.
I HAVE A HUNCH THIS IS A *VIGENÈRE SUBSTITUTION.**
WHAT'S THAT?
A METHOD OF ENCRYPTION BASED ON A TABLE OF SHIFTING ALPHABETS AND A KEY WORD. VERY HARD TO CRACK WITHOUT THE KEY WORD.
I'M GUESSING OUR KEY IS ***REX MUNDI.***
*FOR MORE INFORMATION ON VIGENÈRE SUBSTITUTION SEE **WWW.REXMUNDI.NET.***
WELL THAT'S GREAT...
GSMVDONZREBTKEAIDFI
AEZJPULCCKYAOPSMTXKY
DUATJOEDAYPGVAKYAQN
TDSHEXLFPKYCKOGLVJPRA
NVHMYWLDRGBOZOOPFA
CADSOZRYXTKPPDRRDGN
TKZJXZGMGLAHAG
...IT'S JUST ANOTHER MEANINGLESS JUMBLE.
I'M SORRY, DOCTOR, I REALLY THOUGHT WE WERE ONTO SOMETHING. I GUESS IT WAS TOO MUCH TO HOPE WHOEVER WENT THROUGH THE TROUBLE OF CODING THE SCROLL WOULD INCLUDE THE KEY RIGHT IN THE TEXT.
WHAT IS REX MUNDI FOR THEN?
A RED HERRING PERHAPS? SOMETHING THE CODE MAKER INSERTED TO THROW US OFF.
IT'S JUST TOO OBVIOUS TO BE MEANINGFUL.

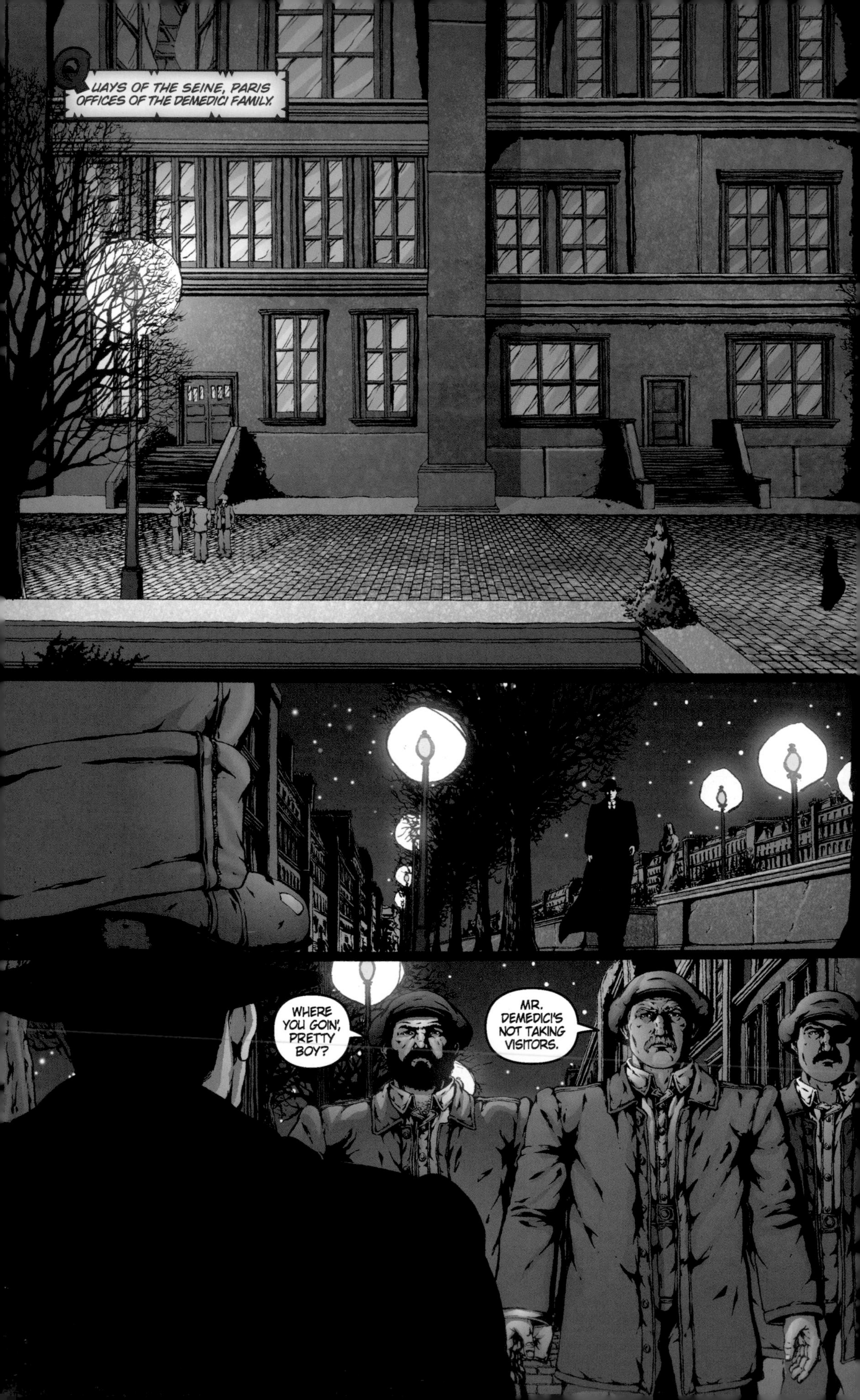
QUAYS OF THE SEINE, PARIS
OFFICES OF THE DEMEDICI FAMILY.
WHERE YOU GOIN', PRETTY BOY?
MR. DEMEDICI'S NOT TAKING VISITORS.

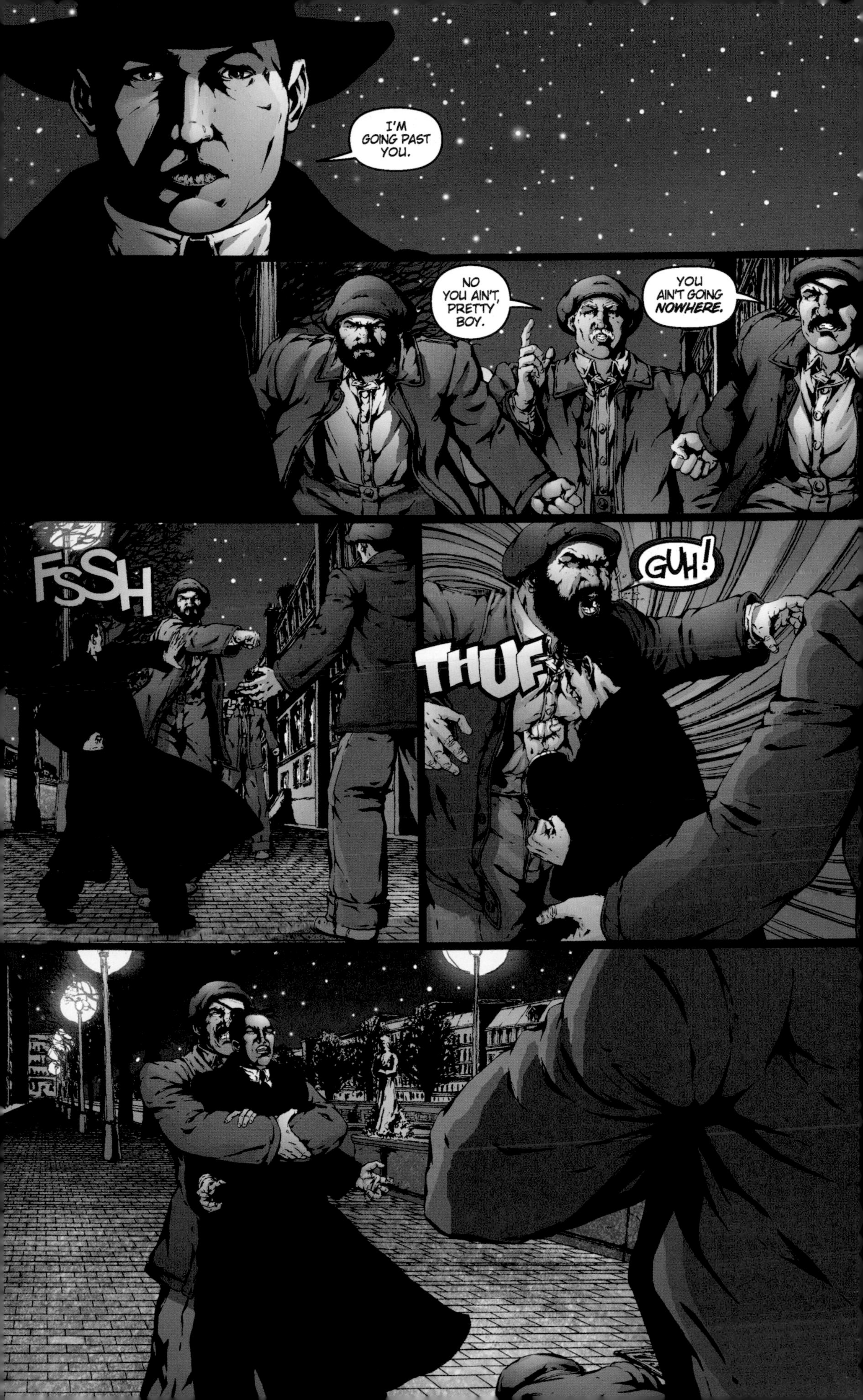
I'M GOING PAST YOU.
NO YOU AIN'T, PRETTY BOY.
YOU AIN'T GOING *NOWHERE.*
FSSH
GUH!
THUF

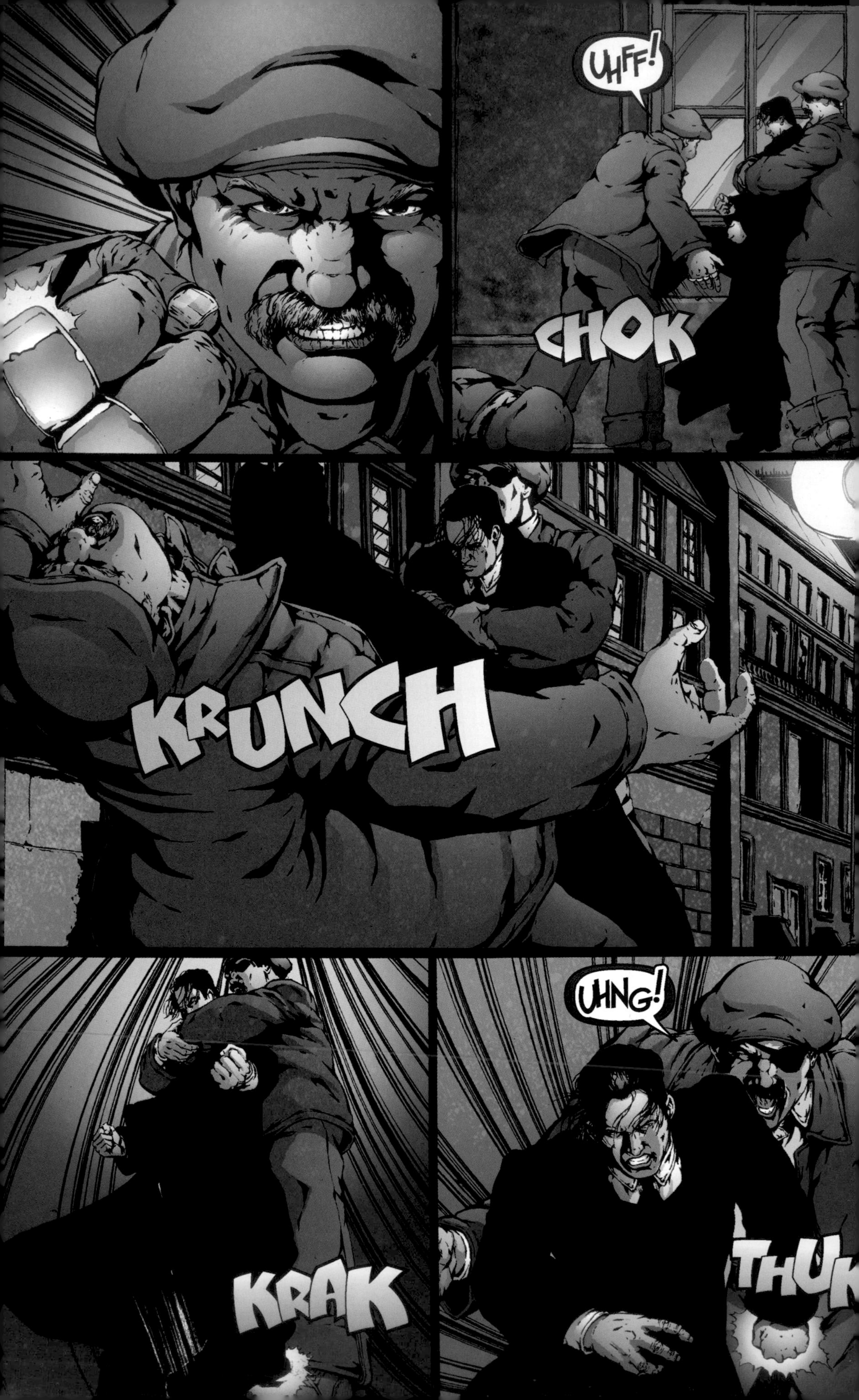
UHFF!
CHOK
KRUNCH
KRAK
UHNG!
THUK

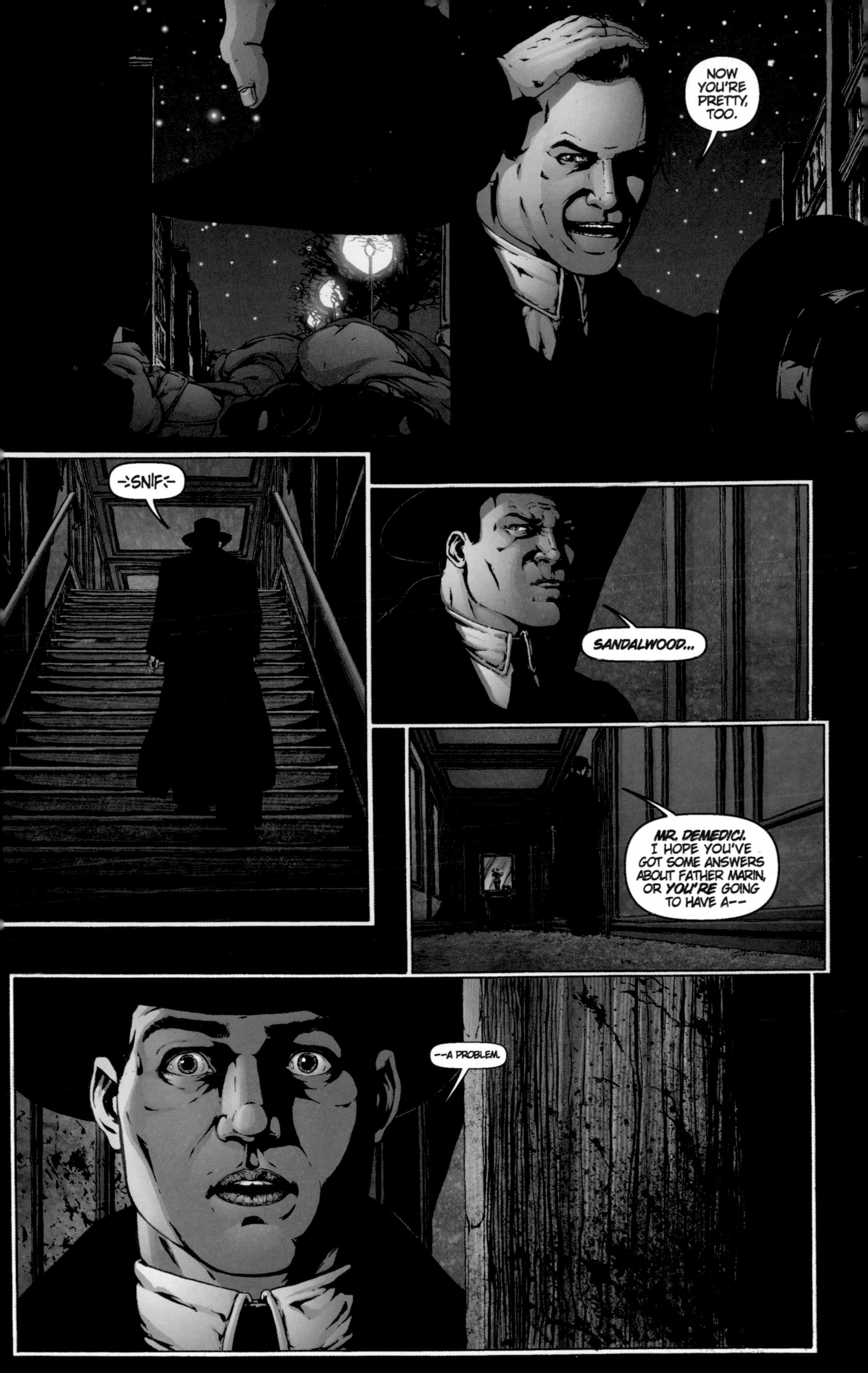
NOW YOU'RE PRETTY, TOO.
-SNIF-
SANDALWOOD...
MR. DEMEDICI. I HOPE YOU'VE GOT SOME ANSWERS ABOUT FATHER MARIN, OR YOU'RE GOING TO HAVE A--
--A PROBLEM.

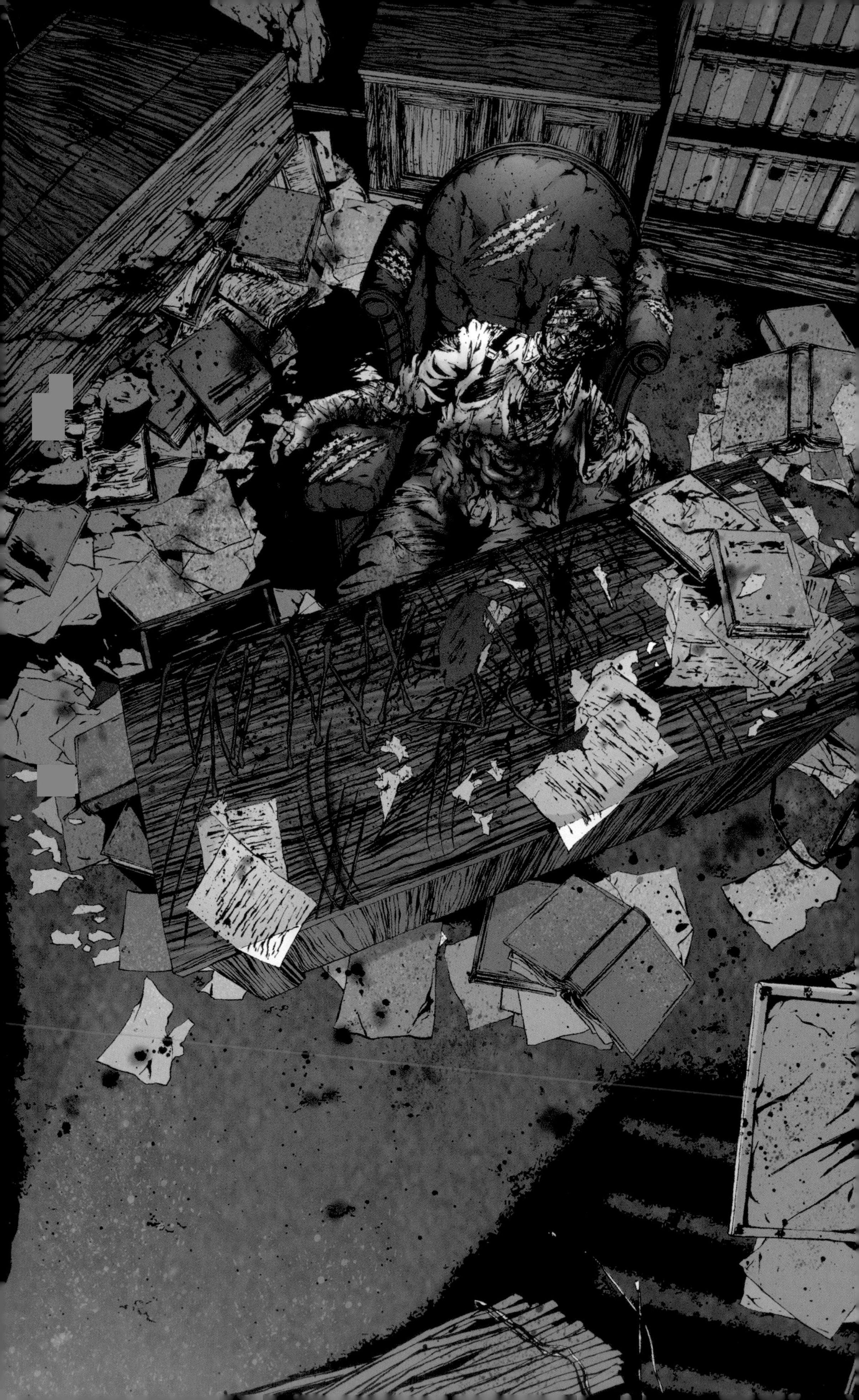

Le Journal de la Liberté

Paris's leading anglophone newspaper • vol. 205, no. 102 • Oct. 25, MCMXXXIII

Editors in Chief: M. Tait Bergstrom, M. Matthew Pasteris. **Story Editor:** M. Arvid Nelson. **Art Editors:** M. EricJ, M. Jeromy Cox. **Photography Editor:** M. Alexander Waldman. **Layout Supervisor:** M. William Kartalopoulos. **Editors Emeritus:** M. Clark A. Smith, M. Howard P. Lovecraft, M. Robert E. Howard. Redacted by the Holy Parisian Inquisition under the direction of His Excellency Archbishop Emile-Jean Ireneaux. Le Journal de Liberté is printed under the benign auspices of his most puissant majesty KING LOUIS XXII of FRANCE. GOD SAVE THE KING.

Papal Seal   of Approval

HOLY FATHER CALLS ECUMENICAL COUNCIL

first in nearly 400 years; topics to be discussed include Holy Church's relation to the state

t. Peter's Basilica, where Pope John XIV has convened the first cumenical Council since Trent concluded in 1563.

Vatican Hill, Rome – Citing ising spiritual and religious ten-on among the nations of Christ," pe John XIV has declared the onvention of an Ecumenical ouncil to settle theological dis-tes and formalize Church rul-gs on matters of faith.

It is the first since the Council Trent, which began in 1545 and ok place in discontinuous ses-ons until 1563. Trent formalized e anathematization of Martin uther and officially declared the –called "Protestant" movement a eresy subject to the persecution the Holy Inquisition.

"The Holy Father believes e nations of Europe are once gain in a very precarious spiritual osition," Papal Nuncio Honore uéant said.

The Council will convene at e Vatican over a period span-ng anywhere from a month to a few years.

"It all depends on how much debate there is," Guéant said.

It is expected to cover top-ics ranging from the surge of nationalism amongst the peoples of Europe to the nature of salva-tion.

"Nationalism poses a great danger to the human soul because it places the State before God," Guéant said. "It is a form of idolatry, make no mistake."

"There is also a strong senti-ment amongst the ecclesiastical community that despite Trent, the doctrine of salvation has not been explained with enough force," Guéant said. "A soul can only attain the Kingdom of Heaven through the Church."

Although this has been a part of Christian teaching for a very long time, Guéant said linger-ing Lutheran sentiments were still leading people astray.

"We need to show people that the power of the Church is absolute. Faith in Christ is faith in the Church, and vice-versa. this is what Christ meant when he said 'I am the Alpha and the Omega'."

Equally important, he said, was the sanctity of the institution of kingship.

"Christian Kings receive a mandate to rule from God and swear loyalty to the Church. This is a vital component of the Christian social order, and there is much evidence for it in scripture," Guéant said.

According to Guéant, it is even possible that this sentiment may become canonized.

"This is one of the areas about which there is debate, so it is difficult to say. The most important thing, to my mind, is the recognition of the fact that Kings receive their mandate to rule from God through the Church and the Church alone."

Guéant said the Holy Father was not convening the council out of fear the world was aban-doning God.

"The Pope is the vicar of Christ," he said. "As long as peo-ple need Christ, they will need the Church."

⚜

BRITISH TROOPS OPEN FIRE ON ANGRY CROWD IN SHANGHAI

Shanghai, Cathay – British Royal Marines opened fire on a crowd in Shanghai yesterday when, according to colonial offi-cials, a demonstration against English rule turned "ugly."

A Chinese casualty report was not available, per British policy. No British troops were harmed.

"It was a demonstration of dockworkers. They're always a rowdy crowd," said Viceroy Jonathan Mowbry, in charge of British concession in Shanghai. "This time it simply boiled over. The louts made a break for the British consulate, and our troops had no choice."

The demonstration began over what Shanghai natives consider the British viceroyalty's inabil-ity–or unwillingness–to put an end to opium smuggling.

"Opium is destroying our country. The British turn a blind eye to the rampant smuggling," a chinaman who spoke on the con-dition of anonymity said.

"Rubbish," Mowbry said. "If the Chinese would open up their ports we wouldn't have this smug-gling problem, which far exceeds anyone's ability to control."

Asked whether he feared a revisitation of the Opium Riots of 1928, Mowbry was dismissive.

"We showed the superiority of British military technology dur-ing the riots. I daresay the rabble-rousers aren't anxious to go at it continued on page A9

Plus sanctimonious editorials by eds. A. Nelson and EricJ

Prussians Re-Affirm Support for Habsburg Presence in Serbia; Tzar Expresses "Displeasure"

Belgrade, Serbia – Prussian Chancellor Karl von Haugwitz issued a statement yesterday reaf-firming Prussian support for Emperor Rudolph's continued presence in the troubled Balkan province in a move that will strengthen Austrian claims to the land – and further strain Russo-Prussian relations.

"The German people rec-ognize the right of Emperor Rudolph to bring peace and prosperity to the troubled Serbian nation," von Haugwitz wrote in the statement, "and we recognize the legitimacy of their continued presence in that country."

Russian officials expressed the Tzar's misgivings about the Prussian statement.

"Russia has long-standing eco-nomic and cultural ties to Serbia. We dispute the claim that the Austrians have a 'sole right' to occupy Serbia, especially against the will of the Serbian people," Yevgeny Morischenko, Russian ambassador to France, said.

However, in the same state-ment, von Haugwitz declared Prussian support for the freedom of the northern Italian republics from Austrian influence.

"It is the Kaiser's belief that the Italian people are in a position to determine their own political destiny," von Haugwitz wrote.

"In political terms, the Prussians are trying to have it both ways," French Foreign Ministry official Artaud Farrand said. "They see a threat in the Russians, so they want to court the Habsburgs. But they also see a threat in France and England, so they want to court the Italians. They are walk-ing a precarious line, because they are caught between two powers. It is the classic problem of continued on page A2

LE JOURNAL SPECIAL: A NATION DIVIDED

FORMER UNITED STATES OF AMERICA

"NEBRASKA CORRIDOR"

CITY-STATE of NEW YORK

- ▢ FEDERAL REPUBLIC OF AMERICA
- ▢ CONFEDERATE STATES OF AMERICA
- ▢ DISPUTED TERRITORIES

The lands of the former continental United States of America. The failed United States Constitution is regarded as "incontrovertible proof of the impossibility of popular government." The Federal Republic of America (FRA) and the Confederate States of America (CSA) are drained by chronic border skirmishes and a vast, lawless western frontier.

"No one dared as highly or failed as catastrophically, as the founding fathers of the United States of America." So says Winston Churchill, first lord of the British admiralty. His sentiment perfectly sums up the prevailing wisdom regarding the ill-fated "American experiment."

The United States of America was coming into eminence as a regional power when it was torn asunder by a brutal four-year civil war from 1861–1864. It never recovered.

"There is a tragic quality to the American experiment," Sir Emile Desrossiers of the Royal Academy of Historians, said. "Tragic because it began with such noble goals and such high aspirations. But there was always a tension in the country between North and South. It proved too much for a government based on popular elections to bear."

In this *Le Journal* special, we examine the history of American Civil War.

A Brief History of the War

The political conflict that ripped the United States apart began with a difference of opinion about the right of states versus the power of the federal government. Southern people generally believed state government authority superceded that of the national or "federal" government, while northern people generally believed the opposite.

This debate became explosive because it factored into the question of the legitimacy of slavery.

War inevitably erupted.

The English crown was instrumental in the success of the Confederacy over the Union. Still smarting over the loss of its American colonies, England supplied the Confederacy with the supplies it needed to protract the war into a brutal stalemate.

"England had to swallow a lot of bile to aid the Confederacy," Desrossiers said. "At the time, revenge was more important than moral qualms about slavery."

Union resolve wavered in the face of the horrors of Southern general Nathan Bedford-Forrest's campaign of wholesale destruction in Pennsylvania, the so-called "scorched earth policy," and the failure of Northern general Ulysses Grant to take the key Southern town of Vicksburg. Abraham Lincoln lost the presidential election of 1864. On taking office, President George McClellan sued for peace, and the Confederate States of America was born.

To this day an uneasy equilibrium exists between North and the South. Petty, economically draining border wars occur almost every year. Economists generally agree the CSA's dependence on slave labor, facilitated by Dutch and Italian merchant princes, means the Southern economy will always be stunted, while chronic political instability weakens the North.

Neither the CSA or the FRA have the wherewithal to take place in international or even regional politics; they are barely able to muster the resources to squabble with each other.

The West—Still Wild

The collapse of the Union created a very large problem, in the form of the western territories of the former United States. Confederacy policy dictated new territories could decide their own fate, but the federal North saw itself as the sole inheritor of the lands. The debate flared into violence on more than one occasion. Most of the former territories are now a part of the FRA, but the South was able to consolidate its hold on the lands north and west of Texas (see map above).

A large swath of the western lands remain disputed. Called the "Nebraska Corridor," it is a wide-open, lawless domain. The law of the gun prevails, and powerful cattle ranchers have all the sway of feudal lords. The cattle barons serve a dual purpose, according to Desrossiers.

"They provide beef for the cities of the North and the South, and they are a sort of proxy law-enforcement agency given the vacuum of government control."

"It's not a place for the faint of heart," says James McCreedy, a Wyoming rancher. "It is a constant battle against bandits and cattle thieves. But there are G-d-fearing men out here too."

Desrossiers believes it is not that simple.

"The distinction between a cattle baron and a well-organized gang of bandits is exceedingly hazy," he said. "In the final summa-

tion, no one suffers more than t native population, the Indians."

The City-State of New York

One must specify "state" "country" when one refers New York. The war against t South was never popular in t Union's greatest city; draft ri broke out more than once, a the city had close economic t to the slaveholding South.

When a city legislatu declared secession from t Union in 1864, a combination corruption at the highest lev of the McClellan administrati and war-weariness led to t FRA's unexpected recogniti of the independence of the Cit State of New York.

The arrangement is profital for both the North and t South; New York City acts as kind of economic brok between the two nations.

"Not since the demise ancient Athens has there been system of government like th of New York City," New Yo mayor Fiorello LaGuardia said. think democracy can only rea succeed on a municipal level. believe New York City boasts t purest form of democracy th world has ever seen."

The Persistence of Slavery

To many, the most troubli aspect of the CSA is the persi tence of slavery within its borde

Southerners defend the inst tution vigorously.

"This is our way of life. N one has a right to come in ar tell someone to change his w of life just because he doesn't li it," Arthur McClune, a Georg peanut farmer, said. "My for fathers fought and died for th principle."

"Slavery is, as Dr. Livingsto said, the sore of the world Desrossiers said. "There's no ge ting around the revulsion mo people feel for the institution. has made the CSA an interna tional pariah."

The CSA has certainly ne made any concessions to th international community, b their status might be changing fast. In the past few years, oil h been discovered in the fields Texas and Oklahoma.

"Oil is the future. It wi become the life-blood of natio within our lifetime." David-Lou Plantard, the Duke of Lorrain said. "It's hard to argue with th sort of power."

CHAPTER THREE
THE RING AND THE KEY

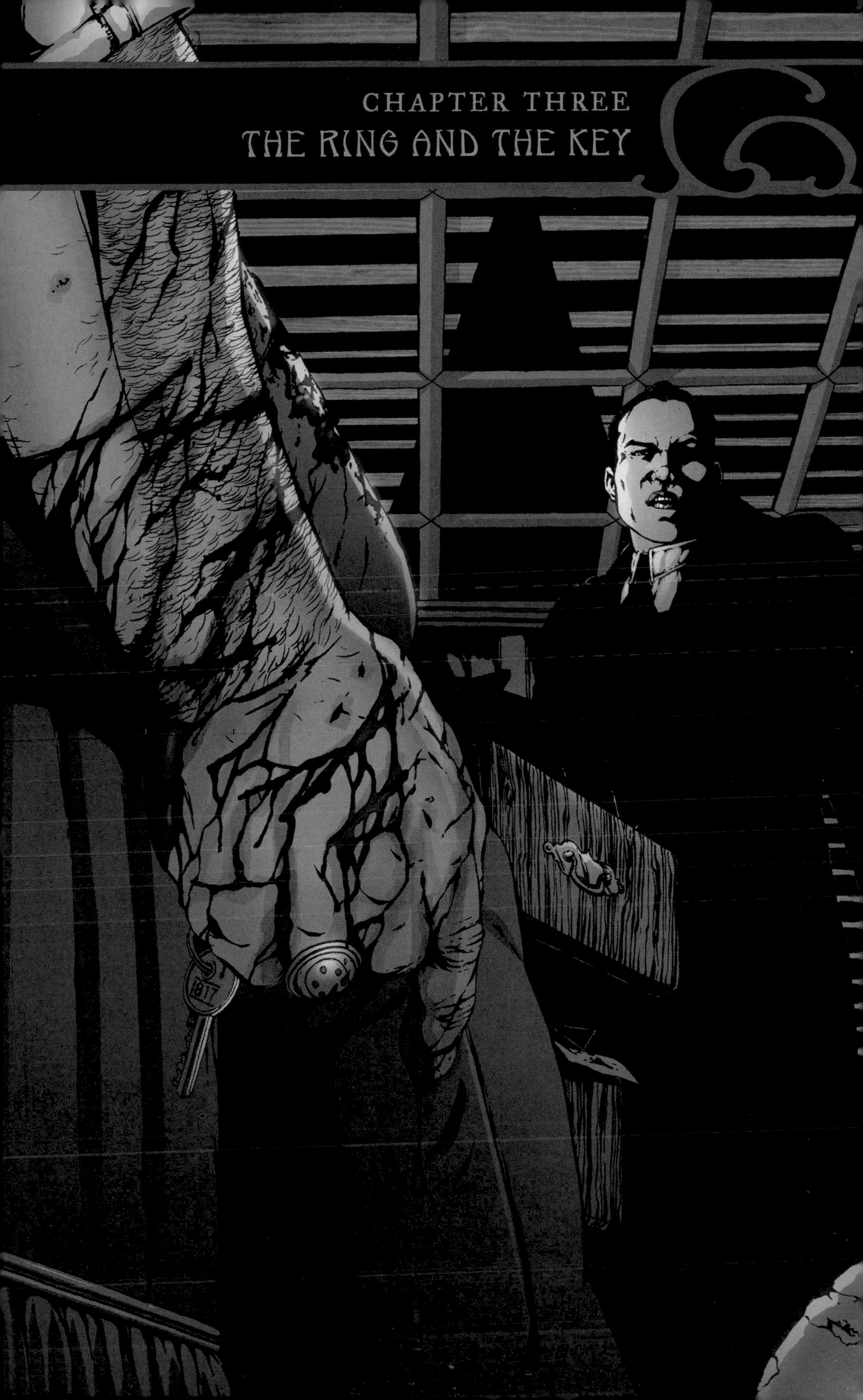

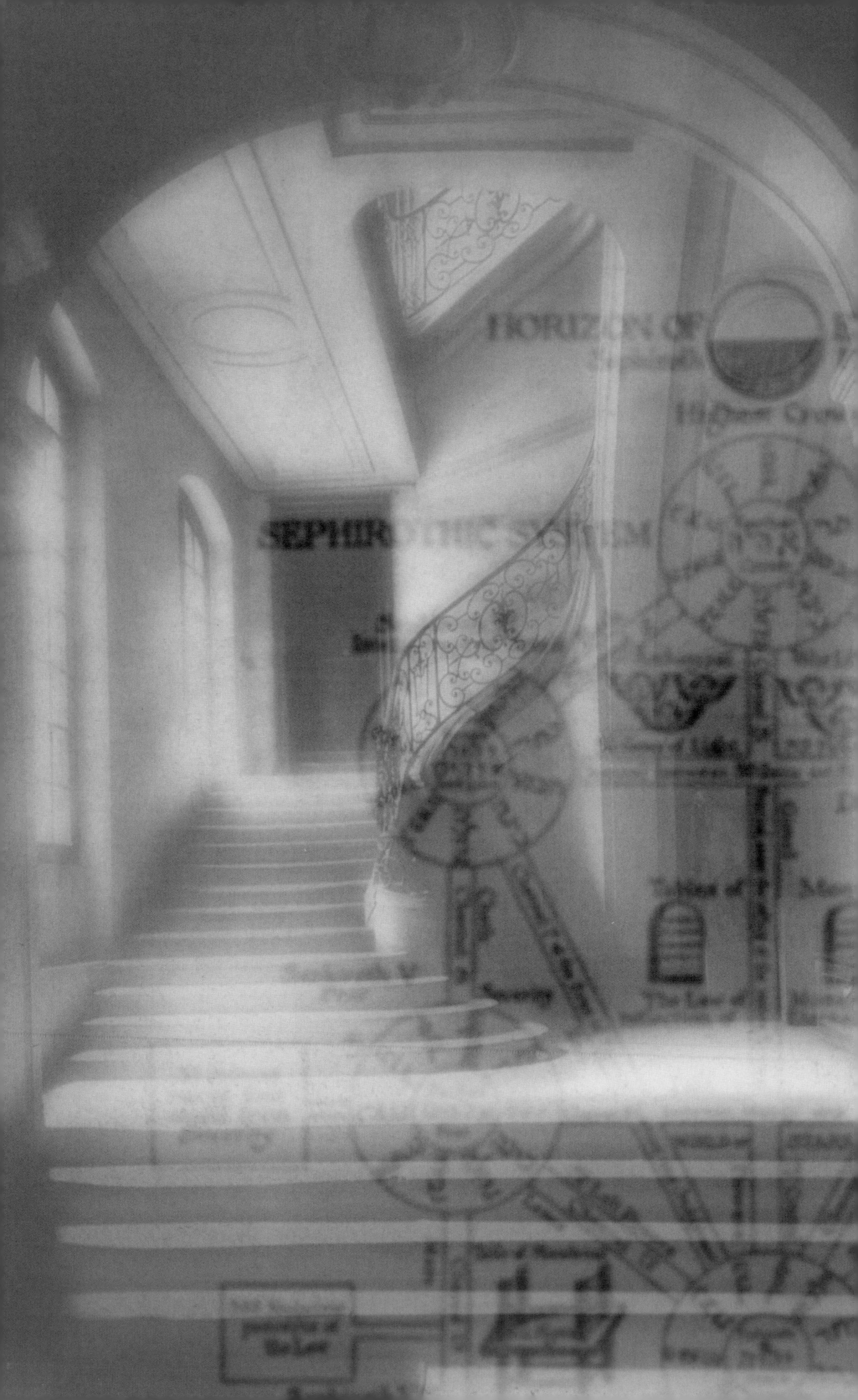

HE BLOOD WAS *FRESH.* IT HADN'T EVEN STARTED TO OXIDIZE.

STILL DRIPPING, IN FACT. DEMEDICI HAD BEEN KILLED RECENTLY.

VERY RECENTLY.

SMELL OF SANDALWOOD AND SULFUR IN THE AIR... JUST LIKE IN THE CRYPT BELOW *LA MADELEINE...*

UNLIKE THE SLAIN PROSTITUTE, THE ABRASIONS ON DEMEDICI'S BODY WERE *RANDOM.*

NO *PATTERNS* TO THE WOUNDS--NO *DIAGRAMS.*

THE GASHES SEEMED TO BE ORGANIZED INTO DEEP, JAGGED SERRATIONS, AS IF A CLAW OR SET OF KNIVES HAD RIPPED INTO THE FLESH.

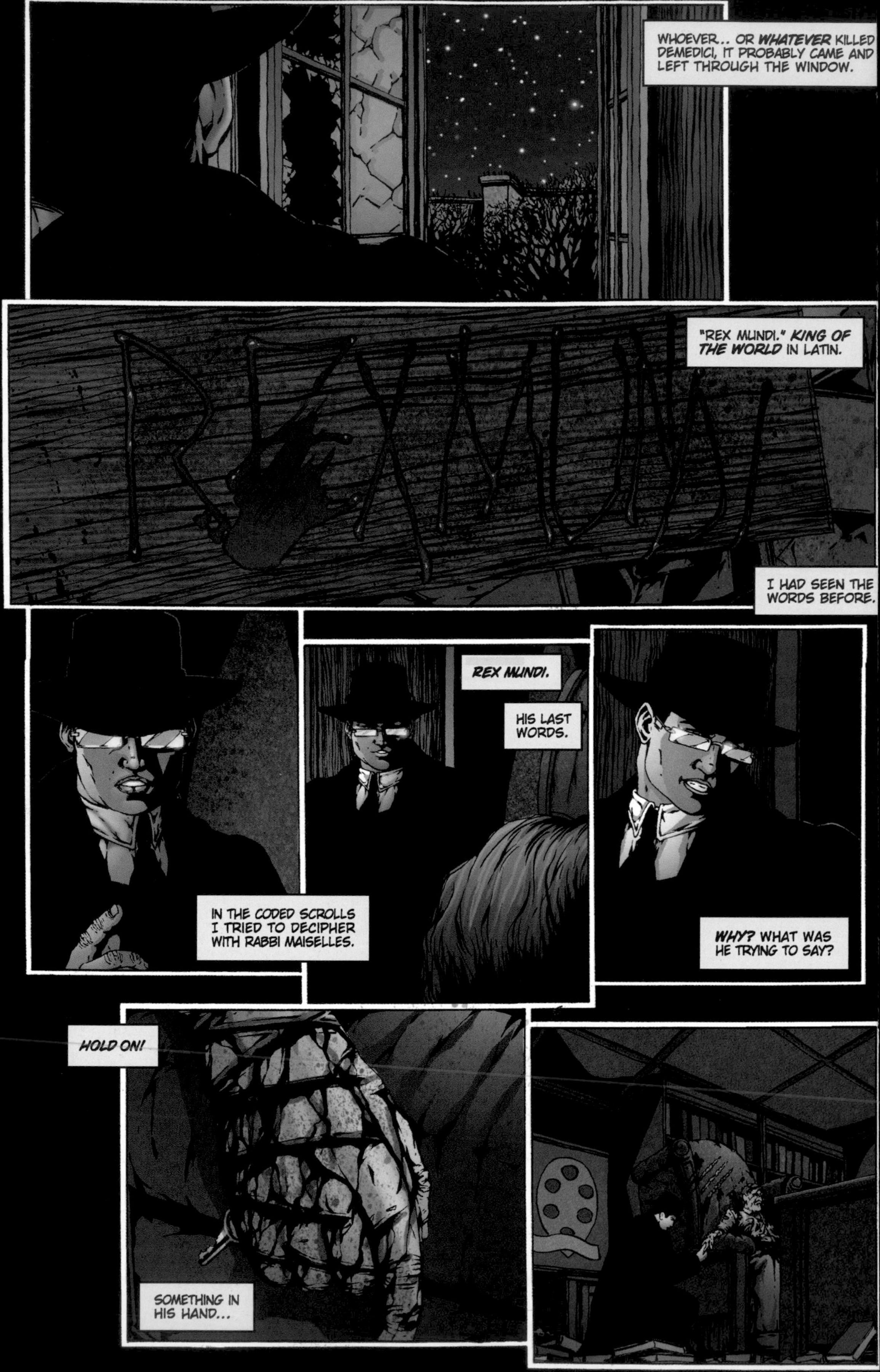
WHOEVER... OR WHATEVER KILLED DEMEDICI, IT PROBABLY CAME AND LEFT THROUGH THE WINDOW.
"REX MUNDI." KING OF THE WORLD IN LATIN.
I HAD SEEN THE WORDS BEFORE.
IN THE CODED SCROLLS I TRIED TO DECIPHER WITH RABBI MAISELLES.
REX MUNDI.
HIS LAST WORDS.
WHY? WHAT WAS HE TRYING TO SAY?
HOLD ON!
SOMETHING IN HIS HAND...

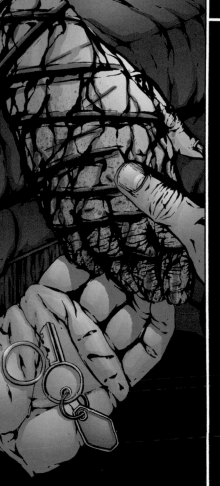

IT LOOKED LIKE A KEY TO A SAFE DEPOSIT BOX.

WHERE?

AND THE RING.

JUST A PLAIN BAND OF GOLD.

WHY DID HE PUT IT IN HIS PALM WITH THE KEY BEFORE HE DIED? WHAT WAS HE TRYING TO COMMUNICATE?

HUGE STACKS OF BILLS.

THOUSANDS OF FRANCS.

UNTOUCHED.

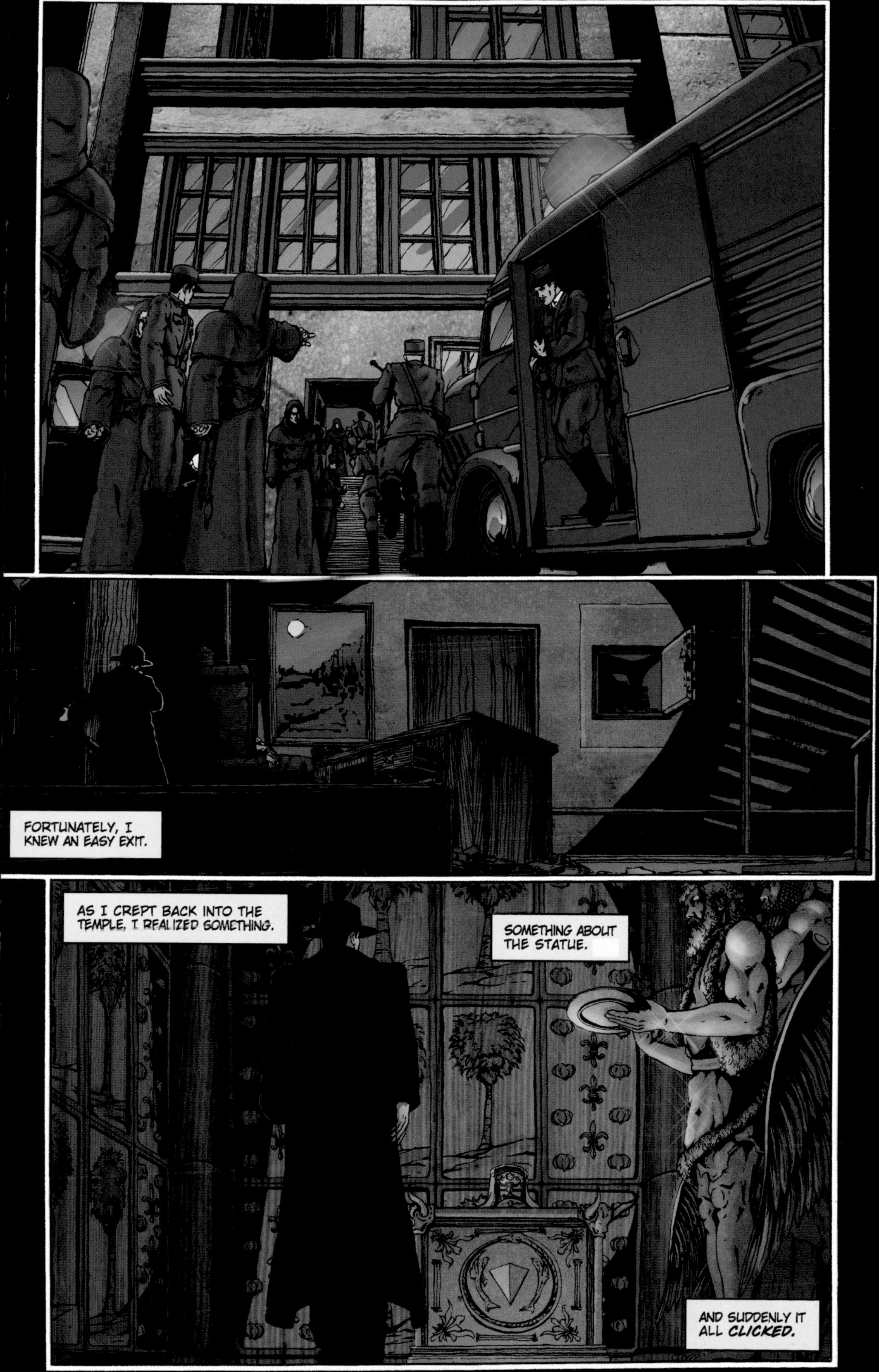
FORTUNATELY, I KNEW AN EASY EXIT.
AS I CREPT BACK INTO THE TEMPLE, I REALIZED SOMETHING.
SOMETHING ABOUT THE STATUE.
AND SUDDENLY IT ALL *CLICKED.*

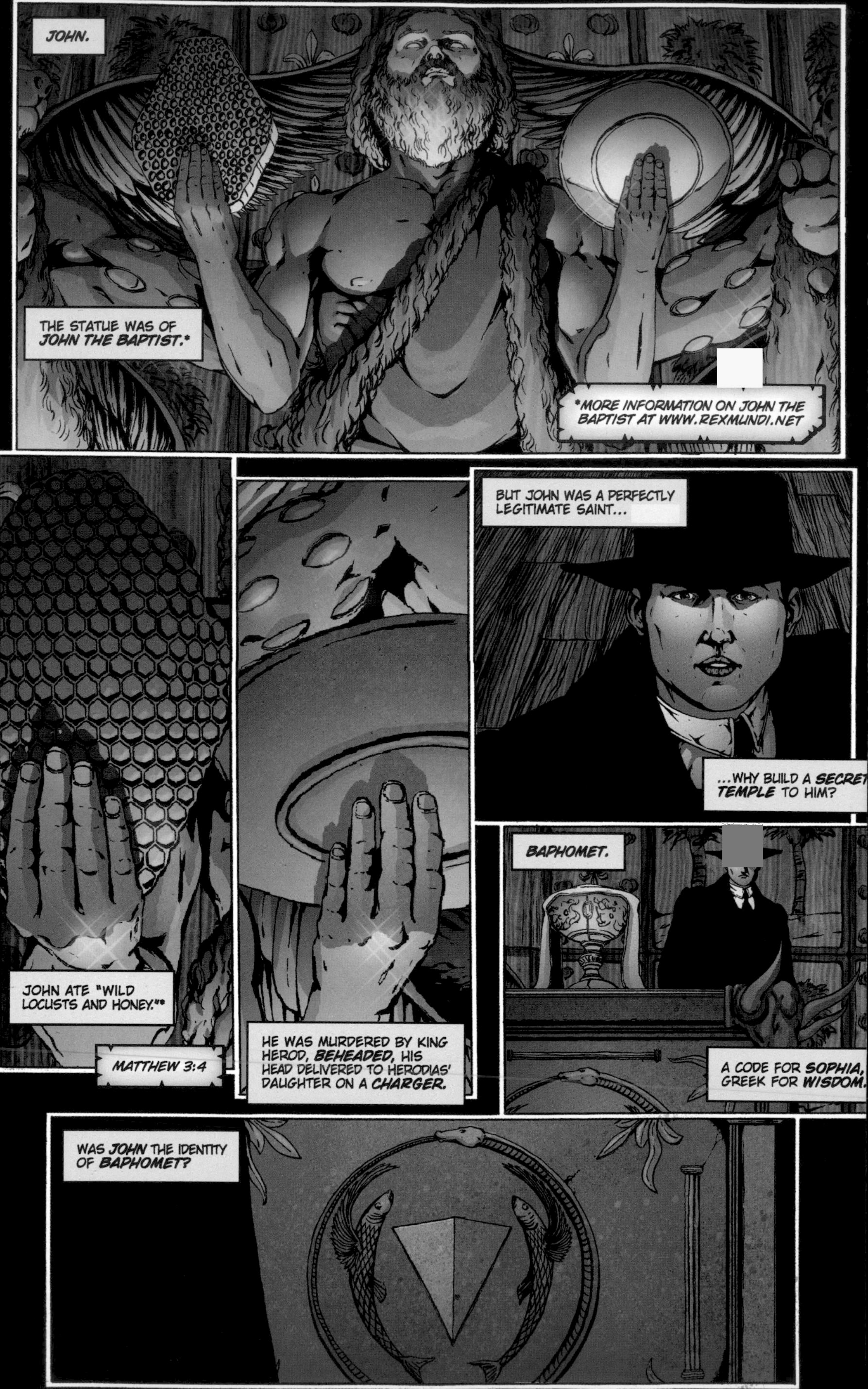
JOHN.
THE STATUE WAS OF JOHN THE BAPTIST.*
*MORE INFORMATION ON JOHN THE BAPTIST AT WWW.REXMUNDI.NET
JOHN ATE "WILD LOCUSTS AND HONEY."*
MATTHEW 3:4
HE WAS MURDERED BY KING HEROD, BEHEADED, HIS HEAD DELIVERED TO HERODIAS' DAUGHTER ON A CHARGER.
BUT JOHN WAS A PERFECTLY LEGITIMATE SAINT...
...WHY BUILD A SECRET TEMPLE TO HIM?
BAPHOMET.
A CODE FOR SOPHIA, GREEK FOR WISDOM.
WAS JOHN THE IDENTITY OF BAPHOMET?

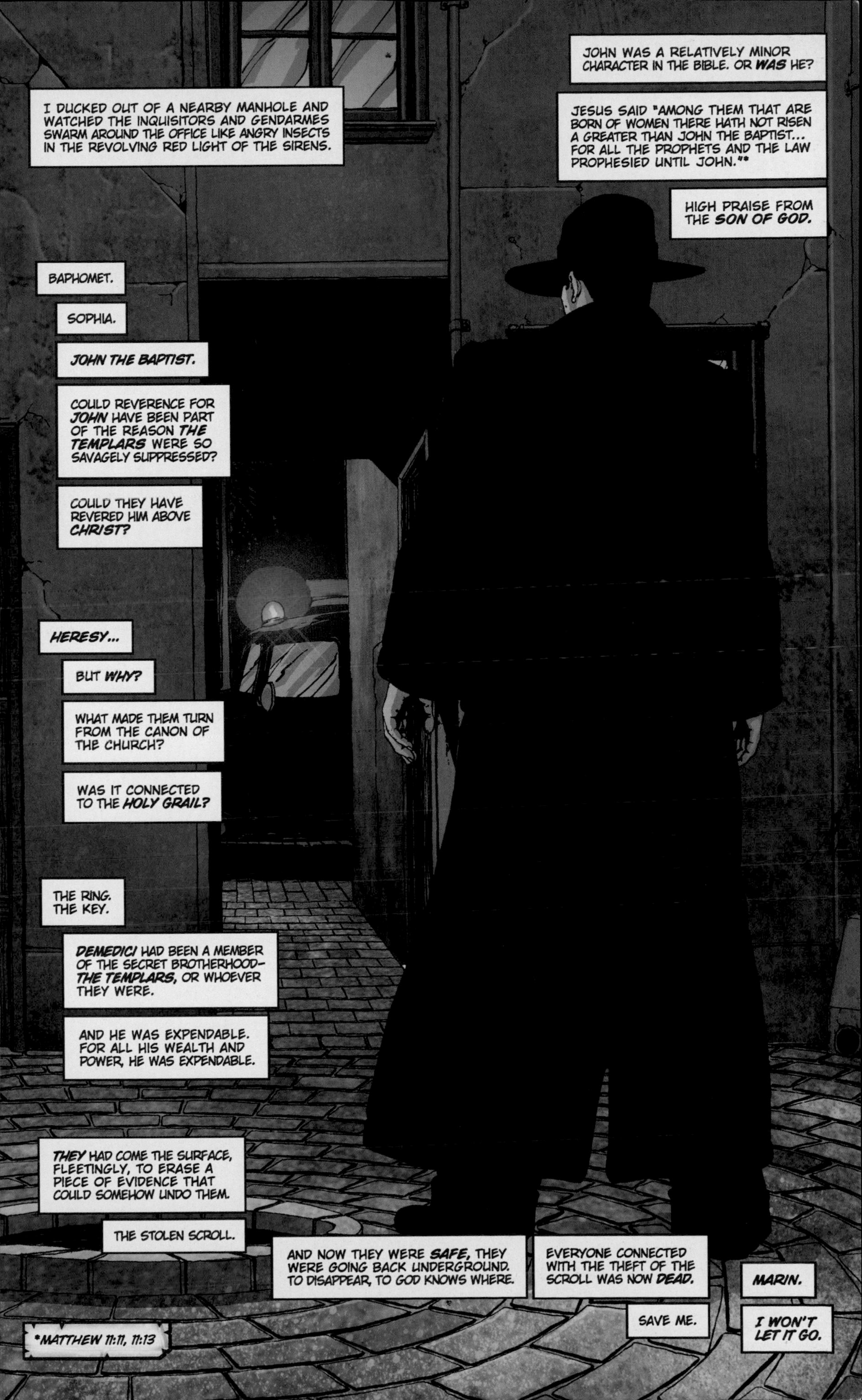
I DUCKED OUT OF A NEARBY MANHOLE AND WATCHED THE INQUISITORS AND GENDARMES SWARM AROUND THE OFFICE LIKE ANGRY INSECTS IN THE REVOLVING RED LIGHT OF THE SIRENS.
JOHN WAS A RELATIVELY MINOR CHARACTER IN THE BIBLE. OR WAS HE?
JESUS SAID "AMONG THEM THAT ARE BORN OF WOMEN THERE HATH NOT RISEN A GREATER THAN JOHN THE BAPTIST... FOR ALL THE PROPHETS AND THE LAW PROPHESIED UNTIL JOHN."*
HIGH PRAISE FROM THE SON OF GOD.
BAPHOMET.
SOPHIA.
JOHN THE BAPTIST.
COULD REVERENCE FOR JOHN HAVE BEEN PART OF THE REASON THE TEMPLARS WERE SO SAVAGELY SUPPRESSED?
COULD THEY HAVE REVERED HIM ABOVE CHRIST?
HERESY...
BUT WHY?
WHAT MADE THEM TURN FROM THE CANON OF THE CHURCH?
WAS IT CONNECTED TO THE HOLY GRAIL?
THE RING. THE KEY.
DEMEDICI HAD BEEN A MEMBER OF THE SECRET BROTHERHOOD— THE TEMPLARS, OR WHOEVER THEY WERE.
AND HE WAS EXPENDABLE. FOR ALL HIS WEALTH AND POWER, HE WAS EXPENDABLE.
THEY HAD COME THE SURFACE, FLEETINGLY, TO ERASE A PIECE OF EVIDENCE THAT COULD SOMEHOW UNDO THEM.
THE STOLEN SCROLL.
AND NOW THEY WERE SAFE, THEY WERE GOING BACK UNDERGROUND. TO DISAPPEAR, TO GOD KNOWS WHERE.
EVERYONE CONNECTED WITH THE THEFT OF THE SCROLL WAS NOW DEAD.
SAVE ME.
MARIN.
I WON'T LET IT GO.
*MATTHEW 11:11, 11:13

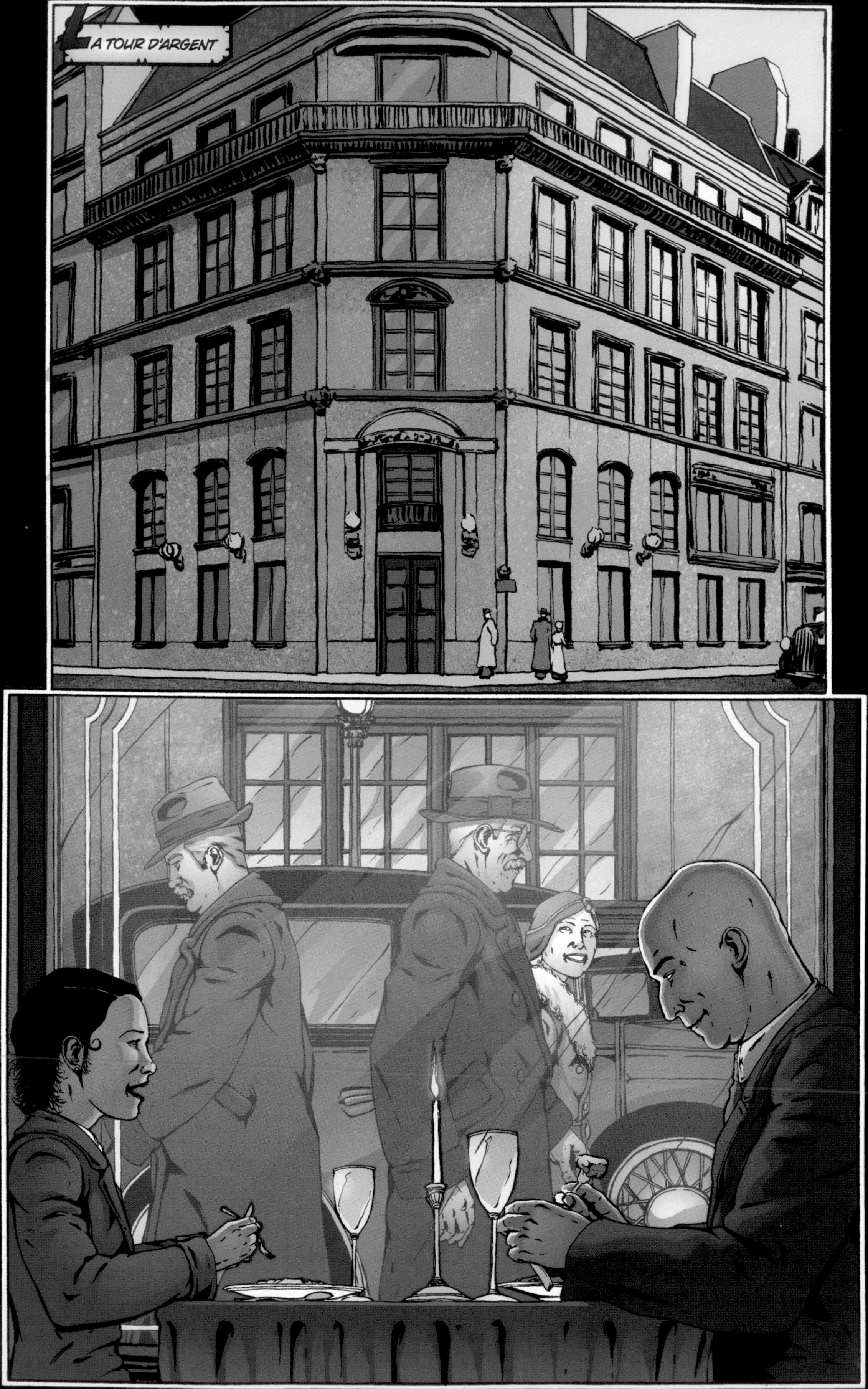
LA TOUR D'ARGENT

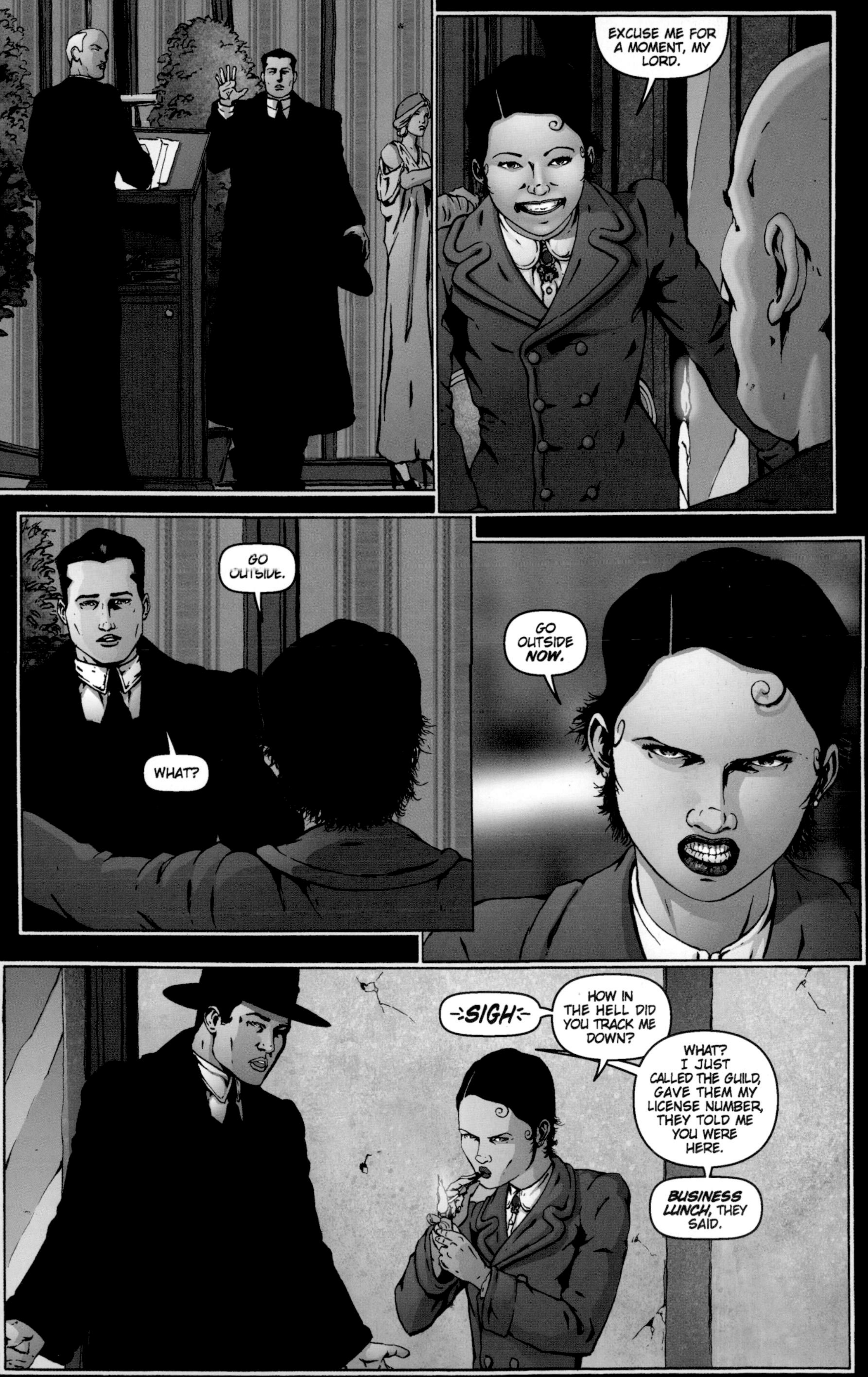
EXCUSE ME FOR A MOMENT, MY LORD.
GO OUTSIDE.
WHAT?
GO OUTSIDE *NOW.*
-SIGH-
HOW IN THE HELL DID YOU TRACK ME DOWN?
WHAT? I JUST CALLED THE GUILD, GAVE THEM MY LICENSE NUMBER, THEY TOLD ME YOU WERE HERE.
BUSINESS LUNCH, THEY SAID.

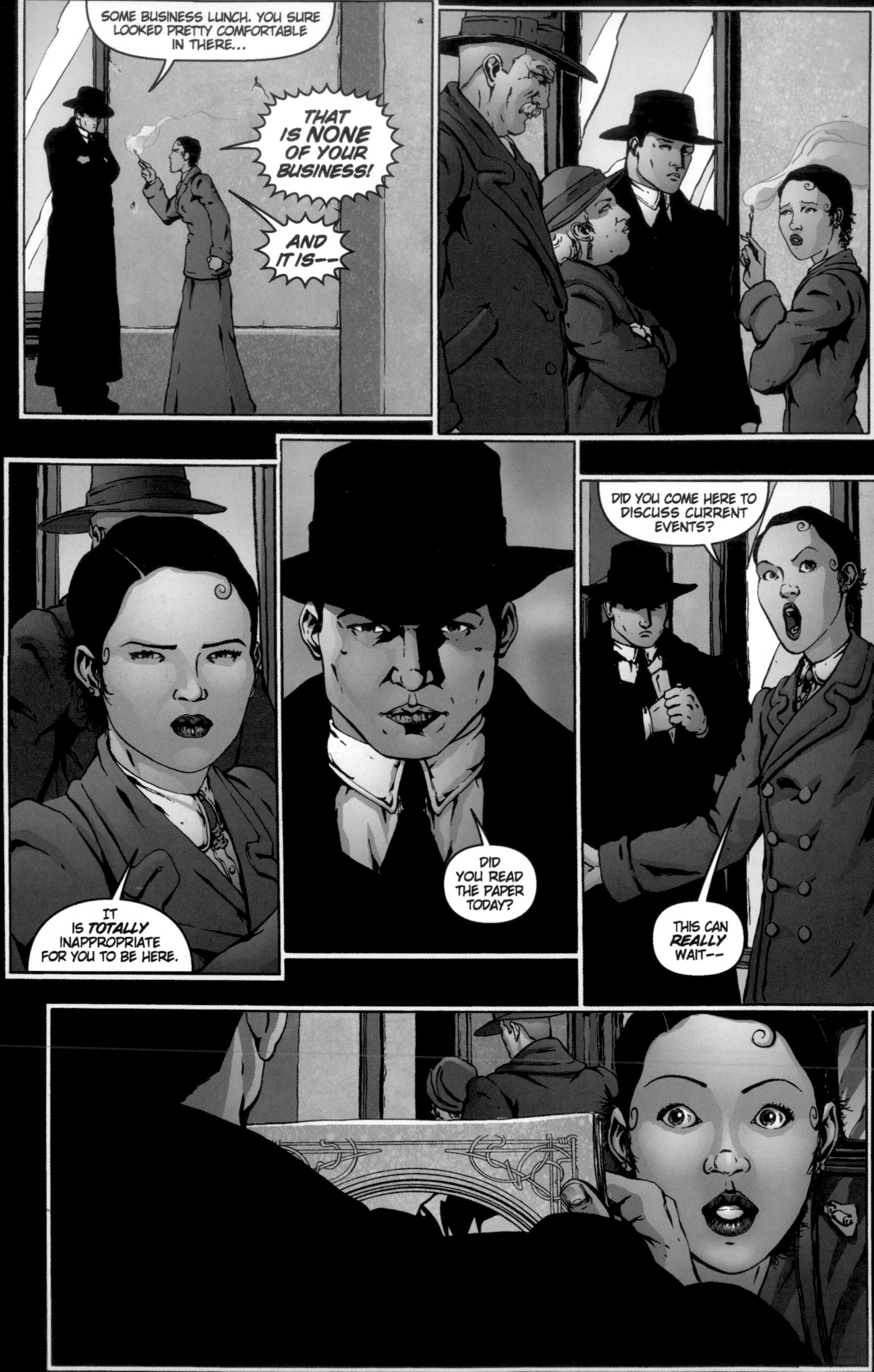
SOME BUSINESS LUNCH. YOU SURE LOOKED PRETTY COMFORTABLE IN THERE...
THAT IS NONE OF YOUR BUSINESS!
AND IT IS--
IT IS TOTALLY INAPPROPRIATE FOR YOU TO BE HERE.
DID YOU READ THE PAPER TODAY?
DID YOU COME HERE TO DISCUSS CURRENT EVENTS?
THIS CAN REALLY WAIT--

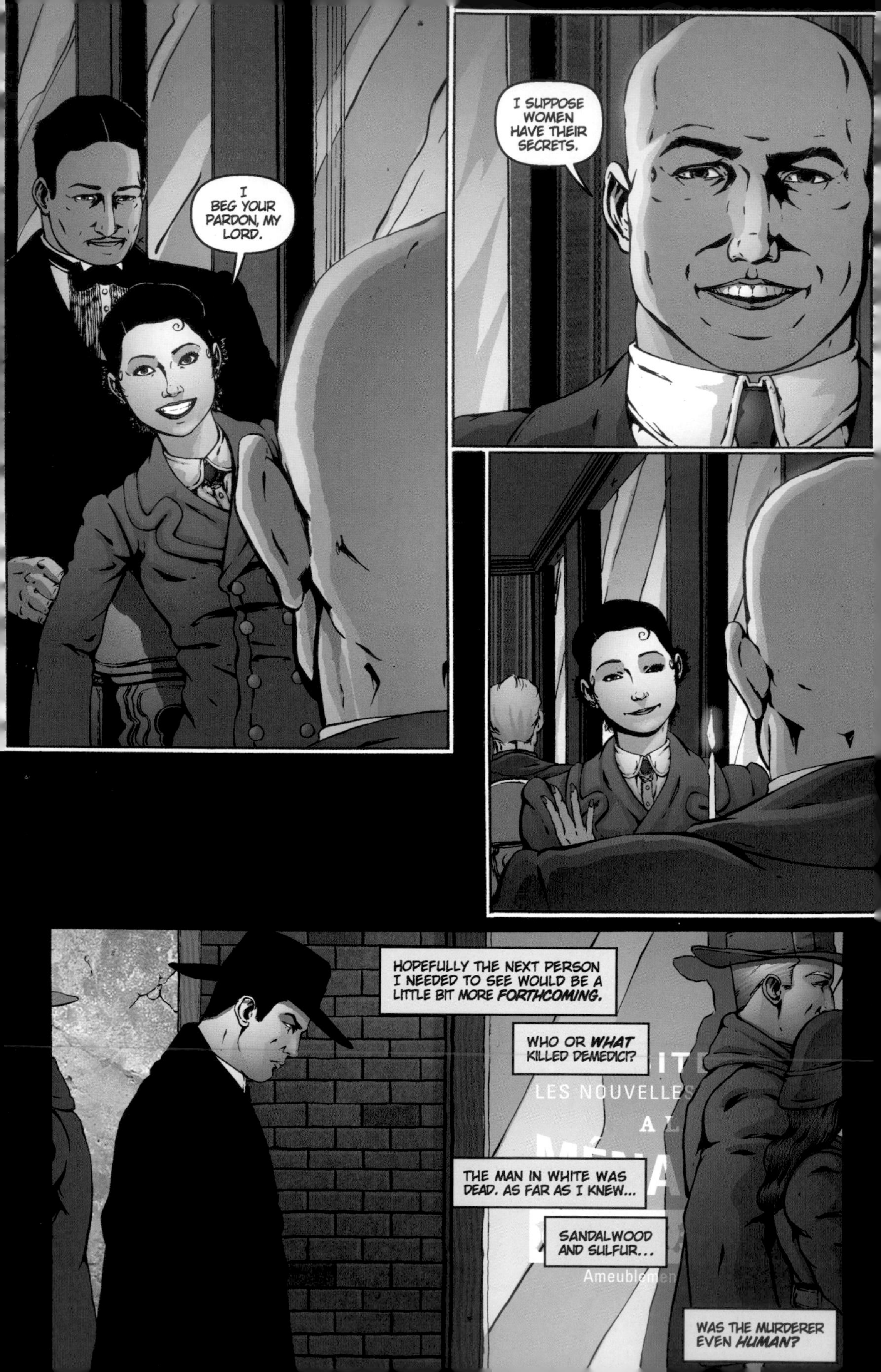
I BEG YOUR PARDON, MY LORD.
I SUPPOSE WOMEN HAVE THEIR SECRETS.
HOPEFULLY THE NEXT PERSON I NEEDED TO SEE WOULD BE A LITTLE BIT MORE *FORTHCOMING.*
WHO OR *WHAT* KILLED DEMEDICI?
LES NOUVELLES
THE MAN IN WHITE WAS DEAD. AS FAR AS I KNEW...
SANDALWOOD AND SULFUR...
WAS THE MURDERER EVEN *HUMAN?*

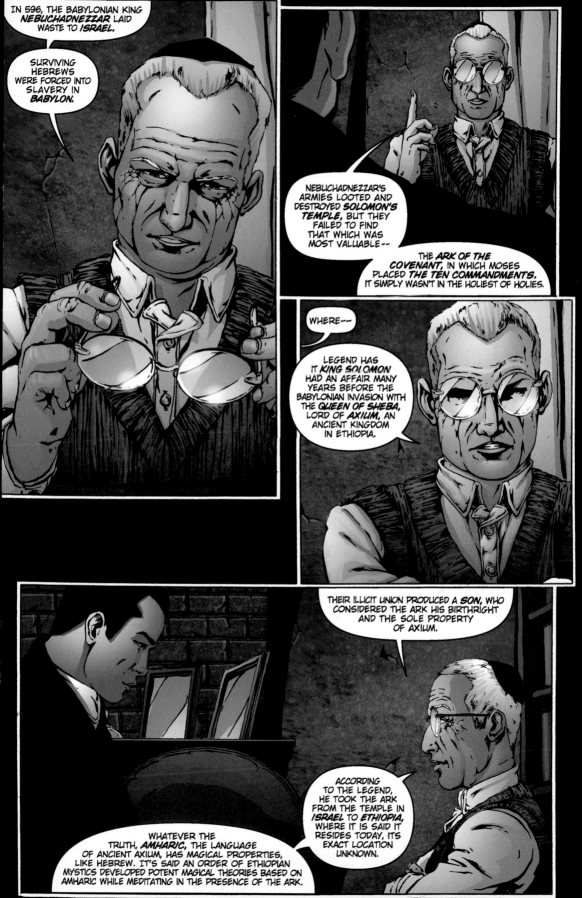

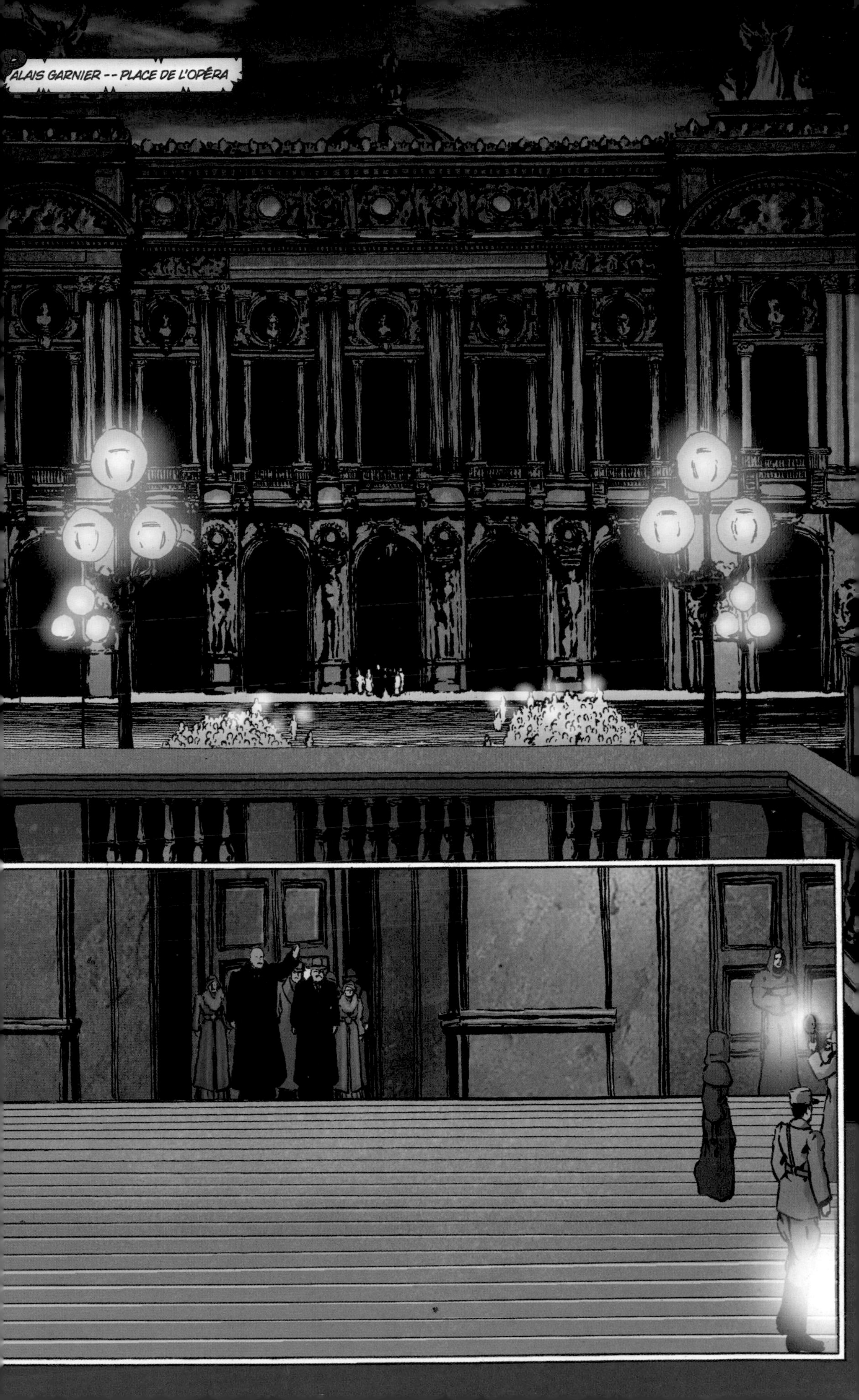

PALAIS GARNIER -- PLACE DE L'OPÉRA

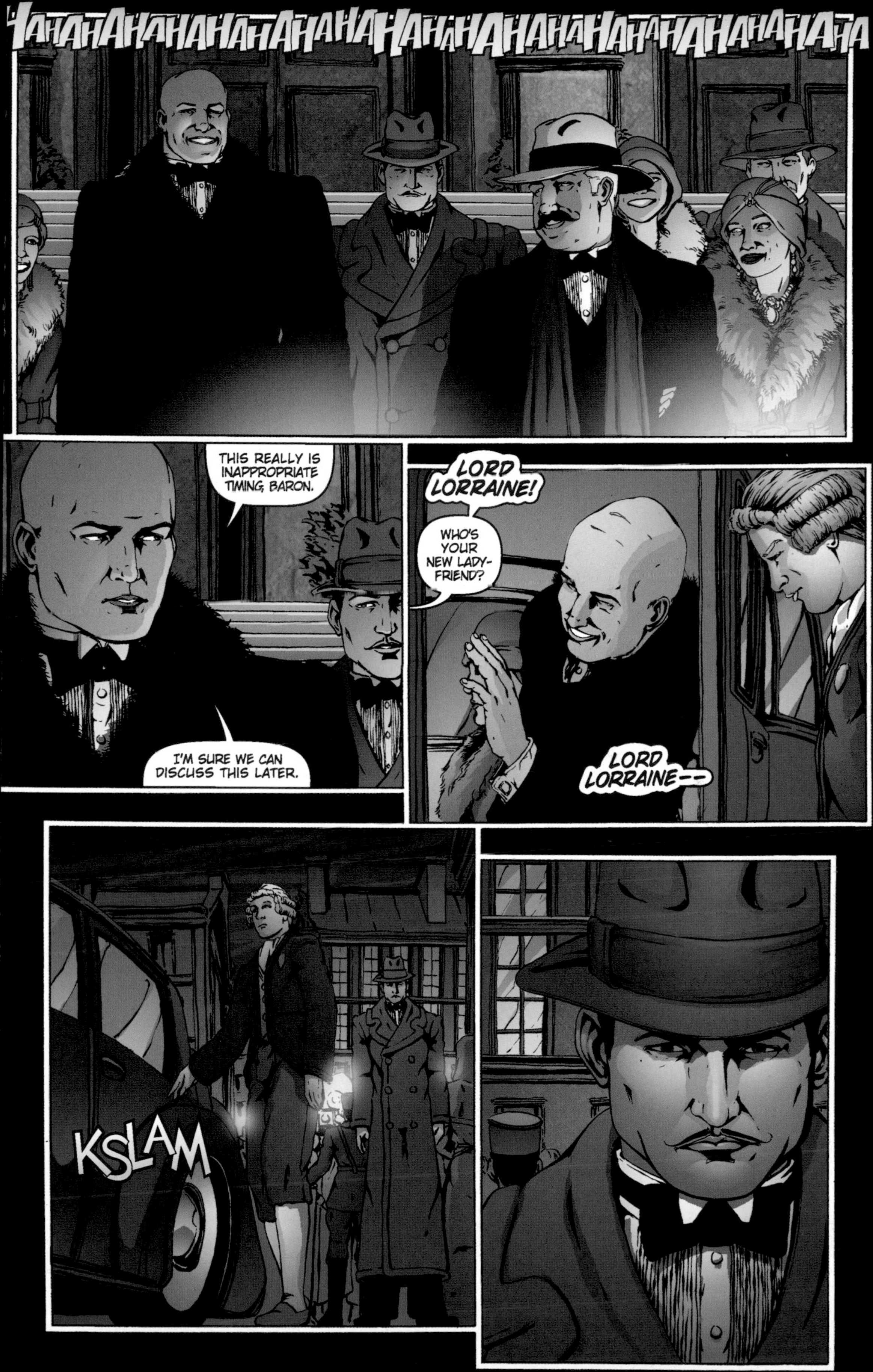
HAHAHAHAHAHAHAHAHAHAHAHAHAHAHAHAHAHAHAHAHAHAHAHAHA
THIS REALLY IS INAPPROPRIATE TIMING, BARON.
I'M SURE WE CAN DISCUSS THIS LATER.
LORD LORRAINE!
WHO'S YOUR NEW LADY-FRIEND?
LORD LORRAINE--
KSLAM

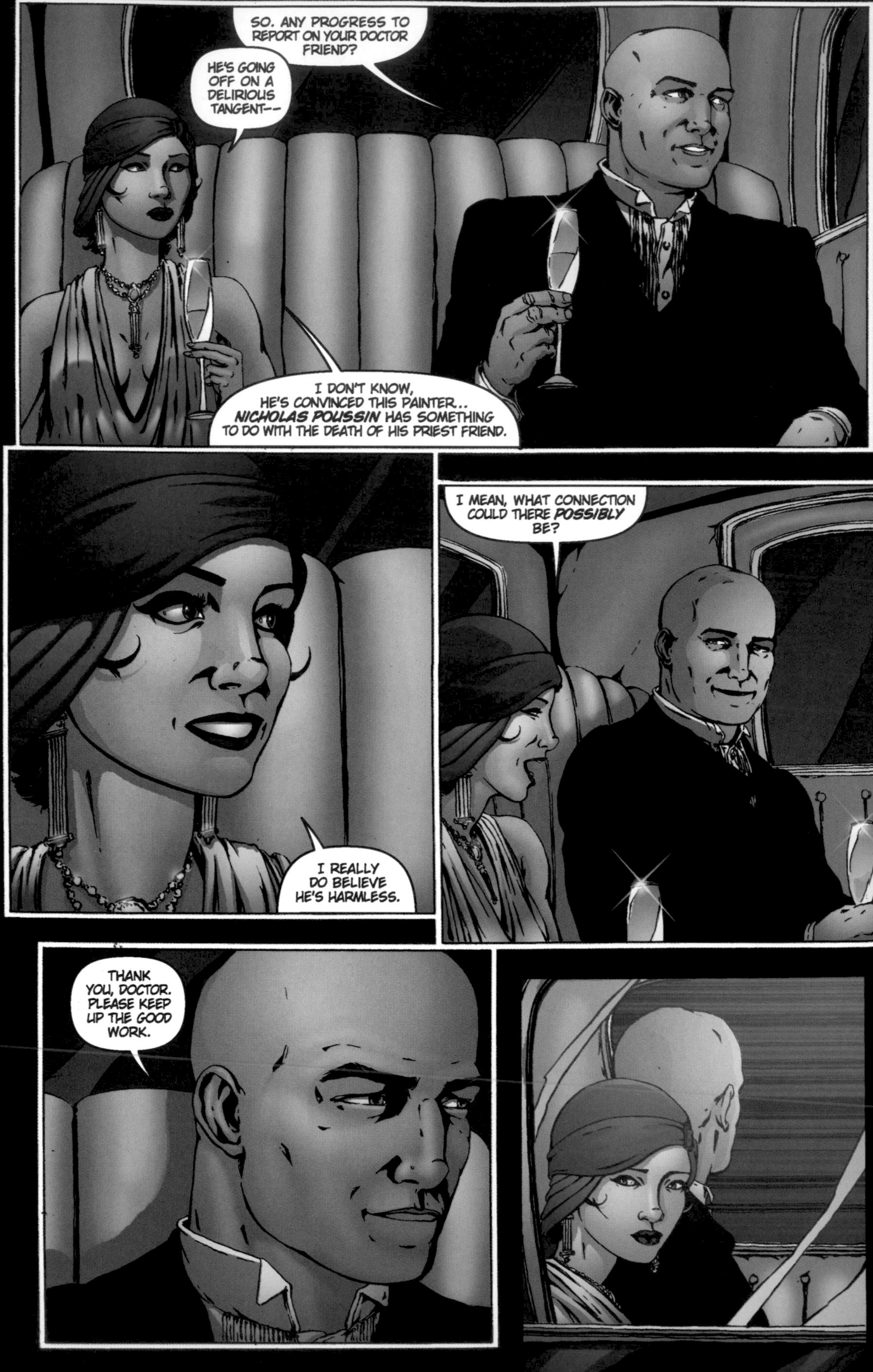
SO. ANY PROGRESS TO REPORT ON YOUR DOCTOR FRIEND?
HE'S GOING OFF ON A DELIRIOUS TANGENT--
I DON'T KNOW, HE'S CONVINCED THIS PAINTER... NICHOLAS POUSSIN HAS SOMETHING TO DO WITH THE DEATH OF HIS PRIEST FRIEND.
I MEAN, WHAT CONNECTION COULD THERE POSSIBLY BE?
I REALLY DO BELIEVE HE'S HARMLESS.
THANK YOU, DOCTOR. PLEASE KEEP UP THE GOOD WORK.

Le Journal de la Liberté

Paris's leading anglophone newspaper • vol. 205, no. 102 • Oct. 25, MCMXXXIII

Editors in Chief: M. Tait Bergstrom, M. Matthew Pasteris. **Story Editor:** M. Arvid Nelson. **Art Editors:** M. EricJ, M. Jeromy Cox. **Photography Editor:** M. Alexander Waldman. **Layout Supervisor:** M. William Kartalopoulos. **Editors Emeritus:** M. Clark A. Smith, M. Howard P. Lovecraft, M. Robert E. Howard. Redacted by the Holy Parisian Inquisition under the direction of His Excellency Archbishop Emile-Jean Ireneaux. Le Journal de la Liberté is printed under the benign auspices of his most puissant majesty KING LOUIS XXII of FRANCE. GOD SAVE THE KING.

Papal Seal

of Approval

DE MEDICI FAMILY HEIR BRUTALLY MURDERED IN DARING LATE-NIGHT HEIST

Inquisition searching for killer of influential Italian merchant prince, denies underworld connection

Quays of the Seine, where Hugo deMedici's much-abused corpse was found. Inquisition officials have not named a suspect but promise "swift justice."

Paris – Hugo deMedici, a powerful figure in the deMedici family financial empire, was found slain in a riverside office building early this morning.

Inquisitors and gendarmerie officers rushed to the scene on a tipoff from an anonymous informant.

DeMedici was pronounced dead on the scene by Antione Laborde, a forensic attaché from the Guild of Physicians.

"He sustained deep lacerations to his limbs, face and torso. The cause of death was shock and blood-loss," Laborde said.

Members of the Inquisition refused to comment on the motivation for the crime beyond simple greed.

"DeMedici was a wealthy man," Grand Inquisitor Moricant, chief representative of the Church on the scene, said. "We are treating this as a robbery-homicide, the work of opportunistic thugs."

Inquisition officials said "significant" amounts of currency and stock certificates had been looted from the office.

Moricant denied a connection to the wave of underworld killings over the past few weeks.

"DeMedici was a regular churchgoer and an outstanding member of the community," he said. "There is no reason to suspect his involvement in illicit activities."

Nonetheless, the wounds described by Dr. Laborde bear a striking similarity to those recently found on the corpses of a number of hoodlums.

Moricant dismissed the connection. "If the circumstances seem similar to murders committed over the past few weeks, it is only because all degenerate and criminal types have a disposition towards excessive violence and rage."

"Right now, our theory is that killer or killers forcibly entered deMedici's office sometime early in the morning. DeMedici resisted, and the intruders became overzealous," a gendarmerie officer said. "The crime scene is in a terrible state. Like a swarm of locusts came through."

Dr. Laborde confirmed that the wounds on deMedici's body were largely defensive in nature.

"He put up a fight, right to the very end, it seems," he said.

Inquisitors said they had no suspects, but that an apprehension was "only a matter of time."

"Crimes such as this, directed at pillars of the community, are nothing less than assaults on our Christian way of life," Moricant said. "We promise swift justice for deMedici and his family. It is our job to show the criminals that Christ rules the streets, not Satan."

Born into a life of privilege, Mr. deMedici nonetheless worked hard to attain the status he enjoyed in the deMedici empire.

"He never took anything in life for granted," his father, Cosimo deMedici, said. "He was a loving son and a vital asset to our organization. His mother, his siblings, myself, we're all in a state of disbelief."

DeMedici began as a humble clerk in a capital investment firm run by his father in Florence, but in a short while he climbed his way to the top of his family's empire. He attributed his success to his "bottom-up" experience in an interview earlier this year.

But deMedici wasn't content simply making money. He became interested in politics at an early age, and was one of the most vocal supporters of the Duke of Lorraine in business circles.

"Lord Lorraine expresses his deep regret and sadness at this sudden an unexplainable loss of life," Baron Robert Teniers, a spokesman for the Duke of Lorraine, said.

Lorraine and deMedici forged
continued on page B1

LORDS OF THE SPANISH MARCHES PROCLAIM SUPPORT FOR DUKE OF LORRAINE

Navarre, Aragon and Castile pledge support for Duke in upset for French Crown

The Spanish Marches – The Marquises of Aragon, Castile and Navarre yesterday proclaimed endorsement of the policy of French territorial expansion in the Iberian peninsula.

"We believe the time has come to turn the tide of Islam back from Europe," Alonzo deGonzaga, a spokesman for the three Lords of the Marches, said. "And we believe Lord Lorraine is the man to do it."

The "Lords of the Marches," as they are known, are feudal landholders on the border between France and the Emirate of Cordova. They enjoy ancient privileges of autonomy from the King of France in return for their steadfast defense against moorish incursions.

Over the centuries the Lords have been the first line of defense against Islam in Western Europe, and as such have enjoyed the gratitude and good will of the French Crown.

Now, that might all be about to change.

"His Majesty King Louis thinks this is a dangerous road to take, and it could jeopardize our mutual interests," Mayor of the Court Charles Martel said.

The Marquises insist they are strengthening the position of the King, not weakening it.

Not so, said Hall of the Robe member Eustache Lambert, a close ally of the King.

"The best person to determine what's best for France is the king, not a group of scruffy Spanish robber-lords."

Lorraine dismissed allegations he was deliberately antagonizing
continued on page A9

LE JOURNAL SPECIAL: THE HOLY HIERARCHY

The lands of St. Peter & environs

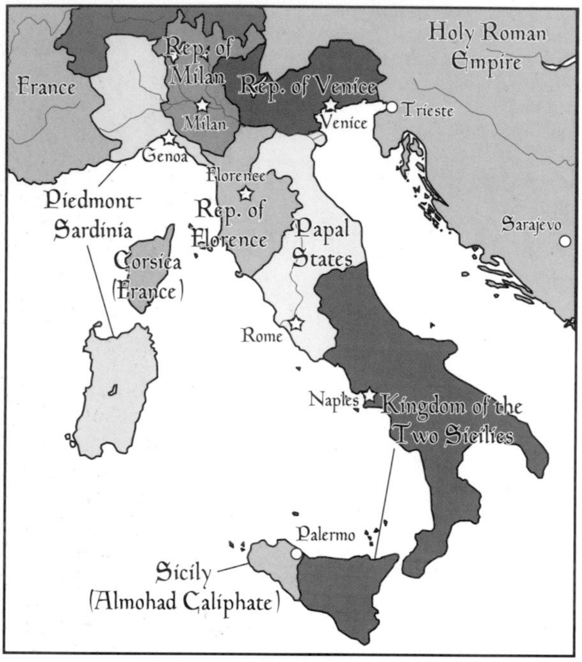
Holy Roman
Empire
Rep. of
Milan
Rep. of Venice
France
Milan
Venice
Trieste
Genoa
Florence
Piedmont-
Sardinia
Rep. of
Florence
Papal
States
Sarajevo
Corsica
(France)
Rome
Naples
Kingdom of the
Two Sicilies
Palermo
Sicily
(Almohad Caliphate)

The Church's holdings are most concentrated in the Italian peninsula, but it also possesses large amounts of land throughout Europe, the result of centuries of charitable donations.

His Holiness Pope John XIV announced yesterday a general convocation of bishops to discuss matters of theology and the future course of the church. Such a meeting, an "ecumenical council," has not occurred in over 350 years.

The term "catholic" means "universal," and no word could better describe the Church. It is the most powerful organization in the world, overseeing the coronations of emperors and providing spiritual guidance to all Christians, like a big brother.

In this special edition of *Le Journal de la Liberté,* we examine the organization of the Church and the civilizing, stabilizing effect it has on humanity as a whole.

"Ego Sum Caesar": The Papacy

"Ego Sum Caesar" – *I am Caesar* in Latin. Thus spoke Pope Boniface VIII in 1302, and in doing so he perfectly summed up the role of the Pope.

"The Holy Father wields an enormous amount of power," said Brother Eugène Lourié, a Carmelite monk and Church historian, said.

"If the Church is Christ's mystical body, then the Pope is the head. Christ ordained St. Peter to be His heir, and this divine right to rule has been passed down unbroken over the centuries to each successive pope."

"In a more mundane sense, the Church is, quite literally, the transubstantiation of the Roman Empire," Brother Eugène said.

As the social and political apparatus of the Roman Empire began to collapse, the Church assumed the mantle of leadership.

"There wasn't anyone else to do the job," Brother Eugène said. "The Church was the only institution with the organizational infrastructure to fill the vacuum of power."

Just as Caesar ruled Rome, so does the Pope rule the Church.

The Pope governs through the institution of the *Curia*, the assembly of ministries that assist him in governing the Holy See.

"Everything flows from the Holy Father," Brother Eugène said. "Every member of the Ecclesiastical hierarchy above a priest is appointed by the Pope."

The Body of the Church

Below pope is the rank of *cardinal.* Cardinals participate directly in the Curia government and advise the Pope on matters spiritual and temporal. When a pope dies, the cardinals conduct a closed door election, called the *Conclave,* to determine the new Pope. Most often, but not always, the successor pope is a member of the College of Cardinals.

"Cardinals seem to make the best Popes because they are attuned to both the spiritual and political needs of the Church," Brother Eugène said. "There have been a few instances in which men of great faith but little experience have been elected to the Throne of St. Peter. These occasions have mostly proved disasters."

The administration of the Church outside the Vatican falls to the next ranks in descending order: *Archbishops* and *Bishops.*

Archbishops rule over a *province*, a large swath of land composed of several *dioceses.* A diocese is the territory under the control of a Bishop. Bishops, in turn, ordain priests who preside over a *parish*, the smallest subdivision of land in the Church hierarchy. Priests perform mass for lay Christians and ensure their souls travel to heaven after death.

"Of course, it's not as simple as all that," Brother Eugène said. "There are many officials within the Church who do not preside over a diocese or a parish. Instead they provide special services. For example, there is the office of a *Papal Nuncio*, an ambassador of the Church, or an appointment as the director of the regional activities of the Holy Inquisition."

Religious Orders - A Body Apart

"Scholars think that when Christianity became the state religion of Rome, people who previously would have sought martyrdom instead became hermits and monks, the most famous of which is St. Anthony," Brother Eugène said. "Who knows? Fifteen hundred years ago instead of wearing these robes I might have been turning on a spit in a Roman dungeon."

Most religious orders were founded in the Middle Ages by men of renown faith and intell
The founder of an order create
rule, a set of guidelines by wh
a person who decides to en
must abide.

Monastic orders, such as
Carmelites, generally require a
of "poverty, chastity and obe
ence," Brother Eugène sa
"Obedience to the head of
order and to Christ."

Other orders, such as t
Jesuits, founded in part in respo
the heresy of Lutheranis
enforce a less strict code of co
duct and do not require co
munal life.

The Inquisition: The Sword of Christ

One order in particular,
Dominicans, serves a very spec
function: members of their or
constitute the majority of t
Holy Inquisition.

Christ said "I am come r
to bring peace but a sword. I
was referring to the Inquisitio
Inquisitor and Dominican fr
Augusto Santiago said.

The Inquisition was found
in the Middle Ages to com
rampant heresy. While this ma
date still obtains, it has also evolv
into a secular police force.

"The problems facing t
Church and Christian society
large are legion," Brother Santia
said. "Witchcraft, heresy, de
worship and organized cri
threaten to destroy our cherish
values. The Inquisition is at w
with the forces of darkness."

Secular law enforceme
according to Brother Santia
is ill-equipped to deal with t
myriad problems.

"We are as hard on ourself
we are on the enemies of Chris
he said. "Secular law enforceme
provides the Inquisition wi
valuable auxiliary support, but t
task of tending Christ's flock m
be left to the shepherds, not t
wolves."

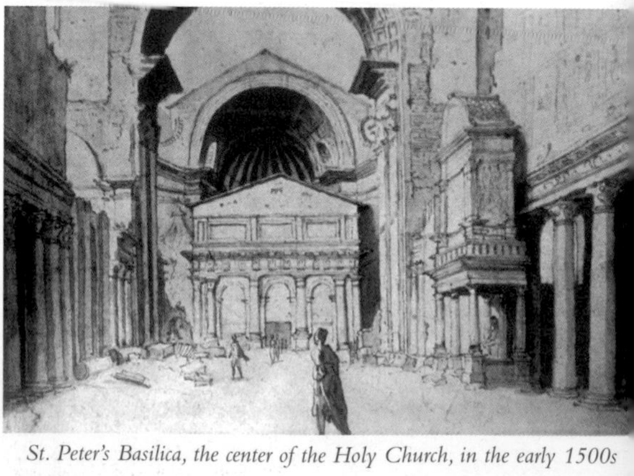

St. Peter's Basilica, the center of the Holy Church, in the early 1500s

CHAPTER FOUR
THE MAN IN THE IRON MASK

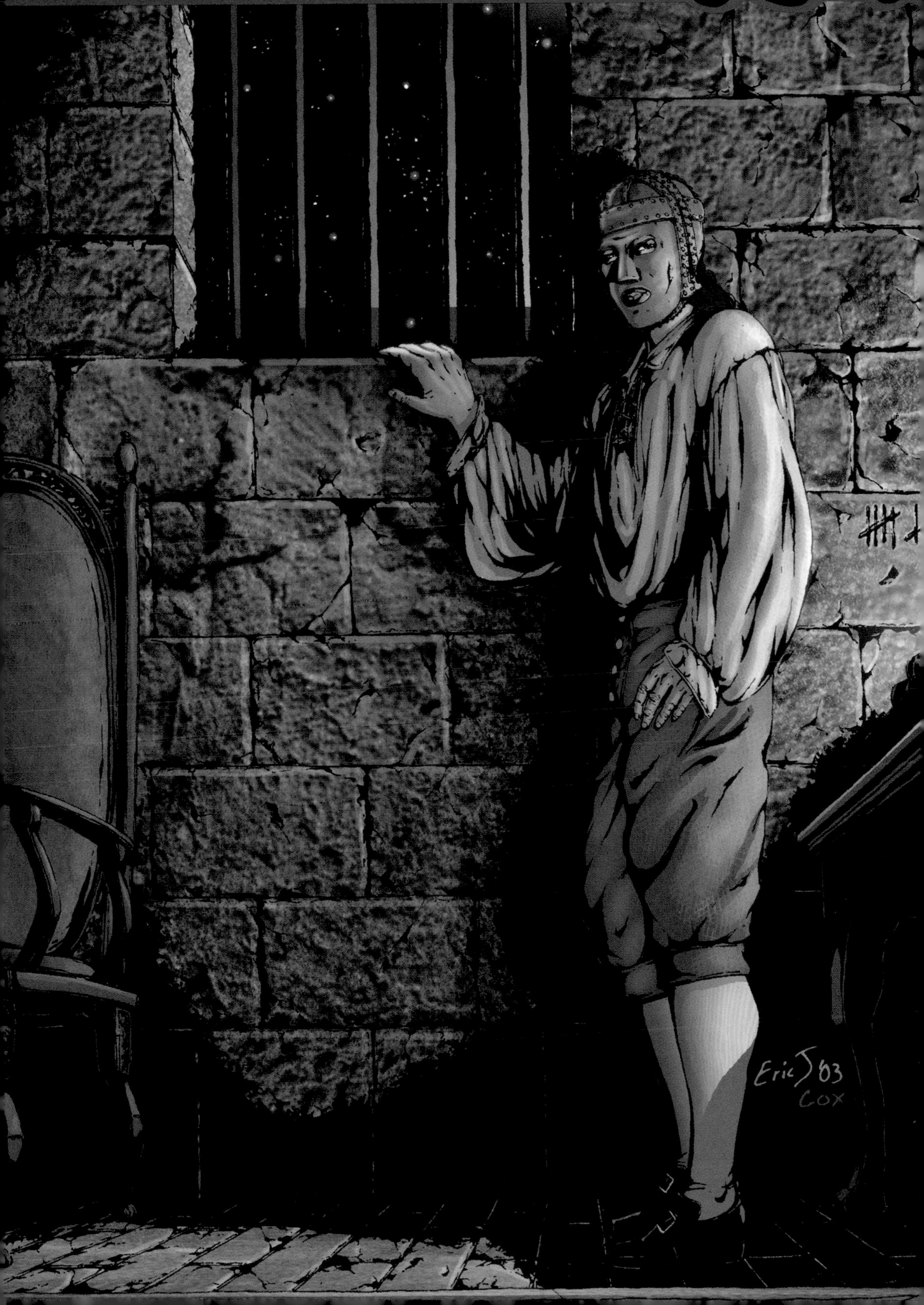
Eric J '03
Cox

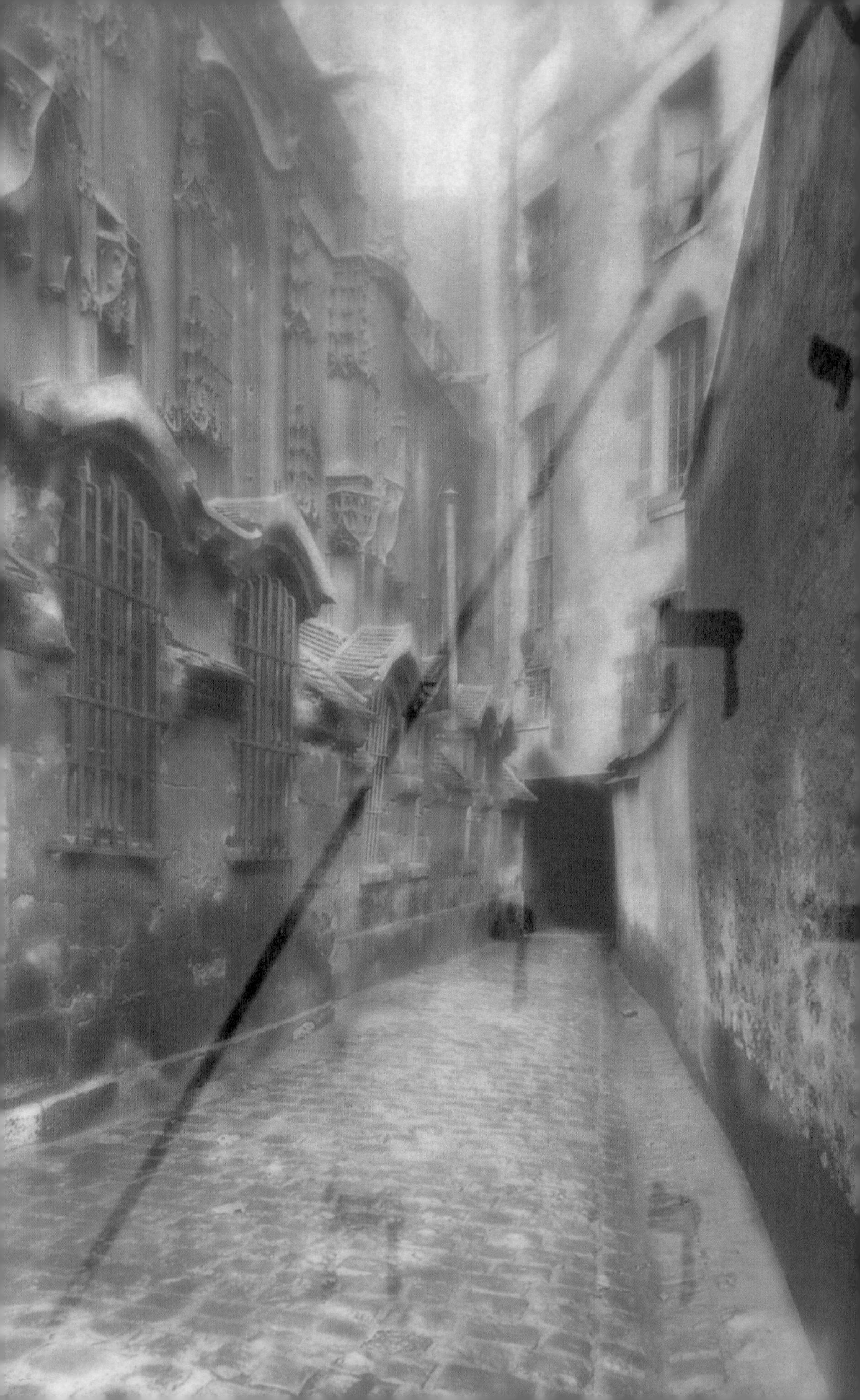

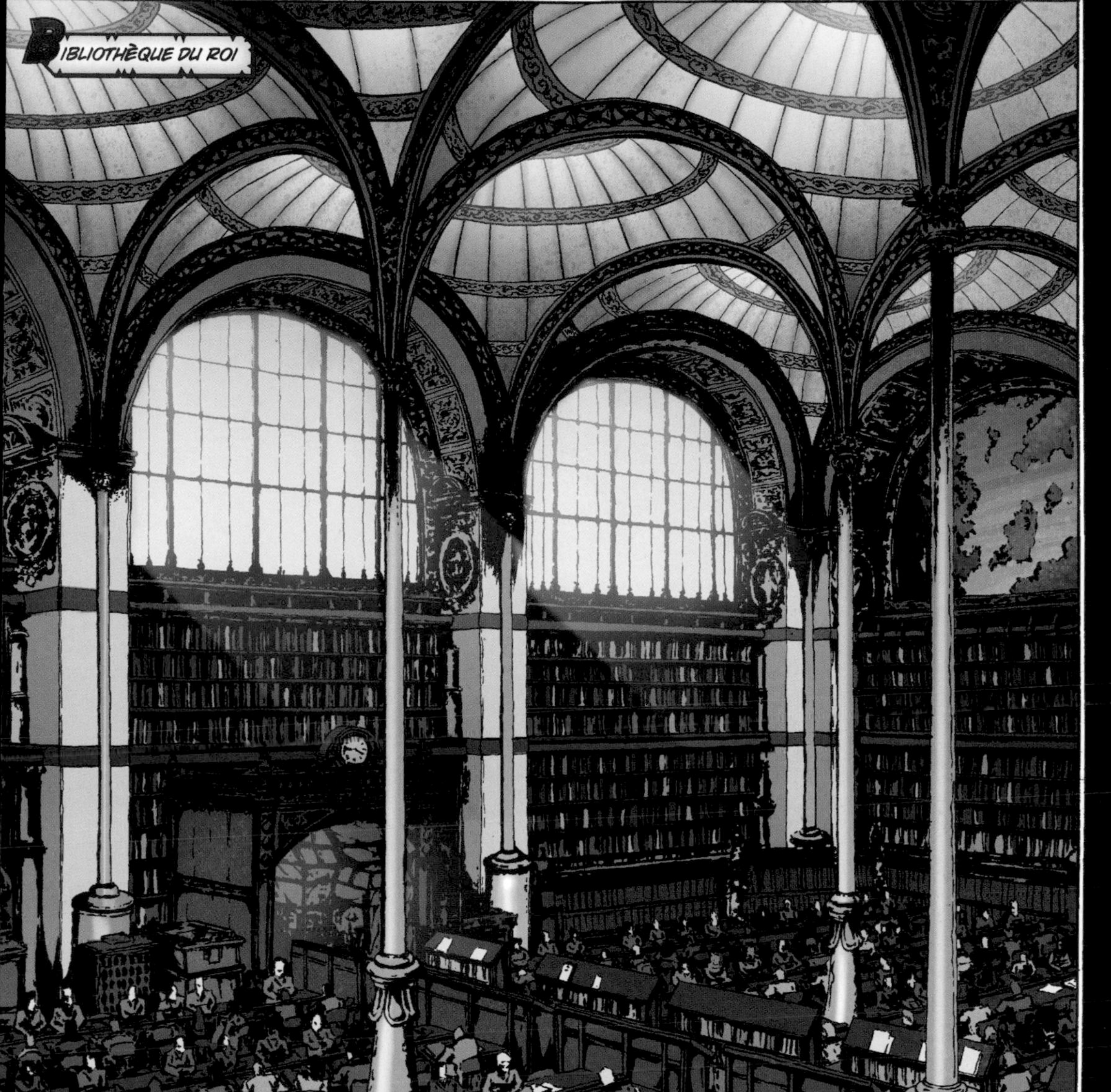
BIBLIOTHÈQUE DU ROI

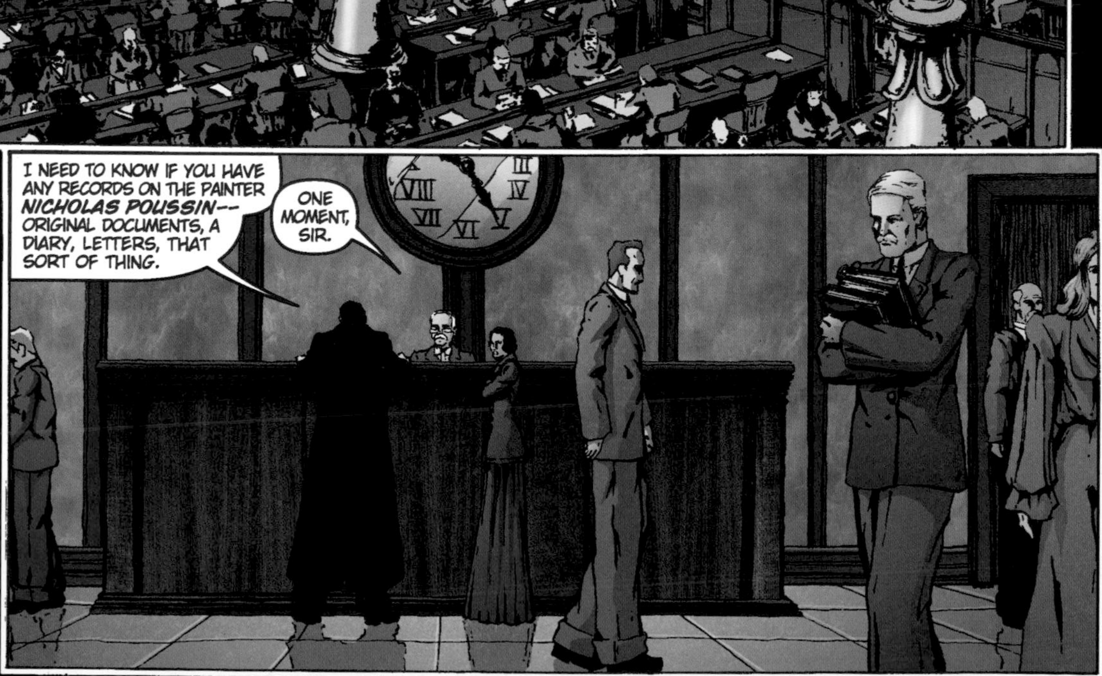
I NEED TO KNOW IF YOU HAVE ANY RECORDS ON THE PAINTER NICHOLAS POUSSIN--ORIGINAL DOCUMENTS, A DIARY, LETTERS, THAT SORT OF THING.
ONE MOMENT, SIR.

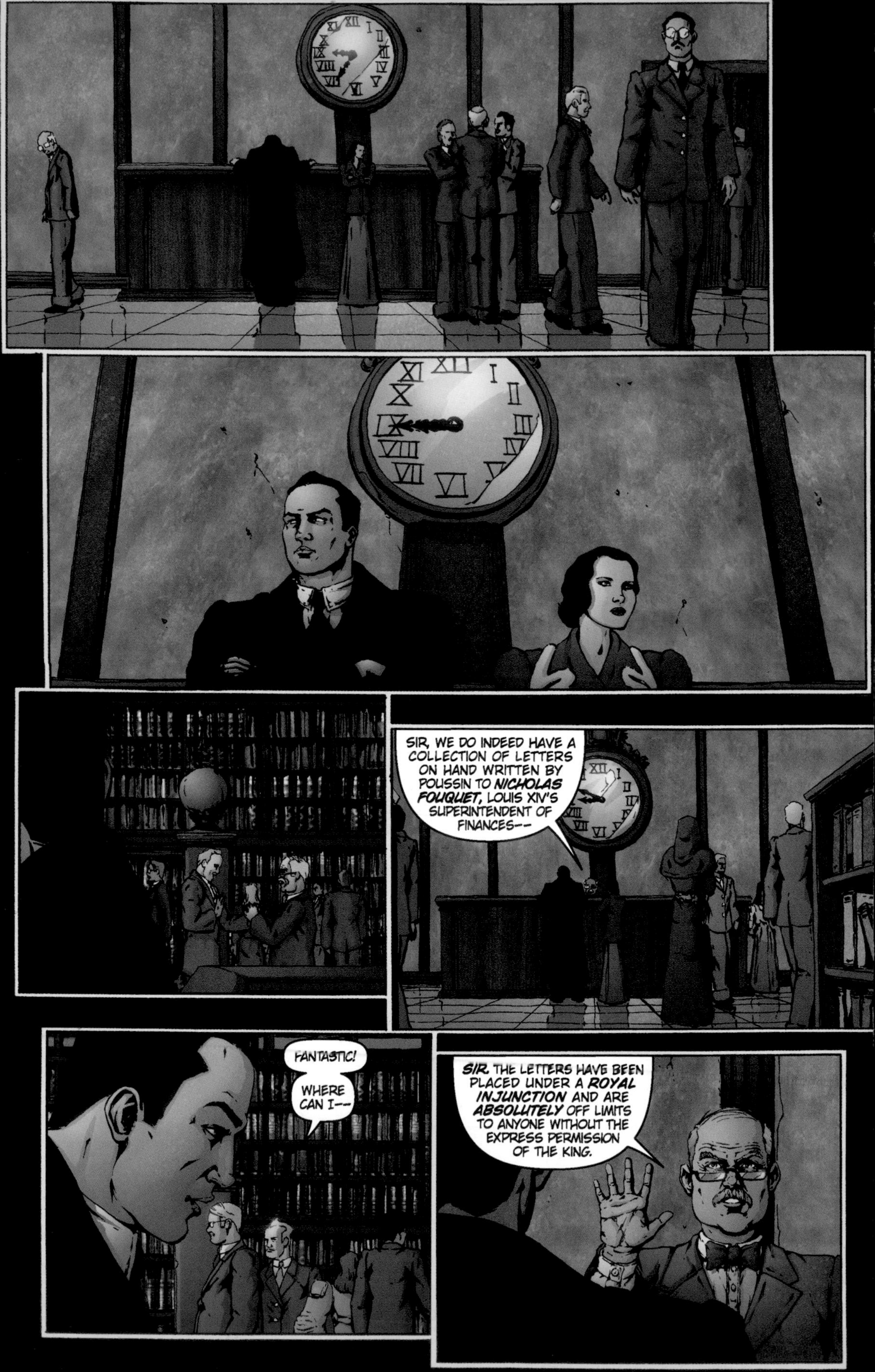
SIR, WE DO INDEED HAVE A COLLECTION OF LETTERS ON HAND WRITTEN BY POUSSIN TO NICHOLAS FOUQUET, LOUIS XIV'S SUPERINTENDENT OF FINANCES--
FANTASTIC!
WHERE CAN I--
SIR. THE LETTERS HAVE BEEN PLACED UNDER A ROYAL INJUNCTION AND ARE ABSOLUTELY OFF LIMITS TO ANYONE WITHOUT THE EXPRESS PERMISSION OF THE KING.

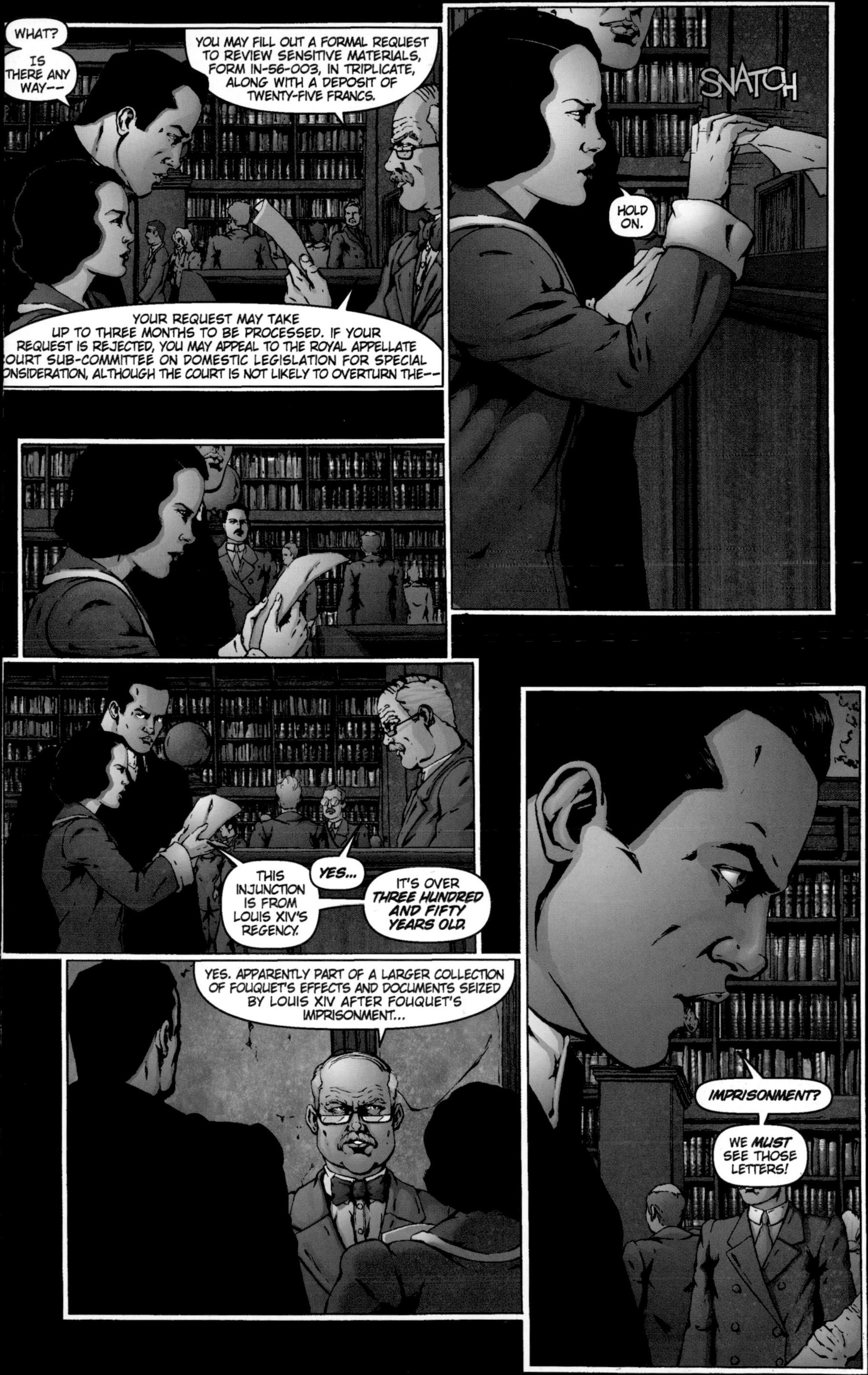
WHAT? IS THERE ANY WAY--
YOU MAY FILL OUT A FORMAL REQUEST TO REVIEW SENSITIVE MATERIALS, FORM IN-56-003, IN TRIPLICATE, ALONG WITH A DEPOSIT OF TWENTY-FIVE FRANCS.
YOUR REQUEST MAY TAKE UP TO THREE MONTHS TO BE PROCESSED. IF YOUR REQUEST IS REJECTED, YOU MAY APPEAL TO THE ROYAL APPELLATE OURT SUB-COMMITTEE ON DOMESTIC LEGISLATION FOR SPECIAL ONSIDERATION, ALTHOUGH THE COURT IS NOT LIKELY TO OVERTURN THE--
SNATCH
HOLD ON.
THIS INJUNCTION IS FROM LOUIS XIV'S REGENCY.
YES...
IT'S OVER THREE HUNDRED AND FIFTY YEARS OLD.
YES. APPARENTLY PART OF A LARGER COLLECTION OF FOUQUET'S EFFECTS AND DOCUMENTS SEIZED BY LOUIS XIV AFTER FOUQUET'S IMPRISONMENT...
IMPRISONMENT?
WE MUST SEE THOSE LETTERS!

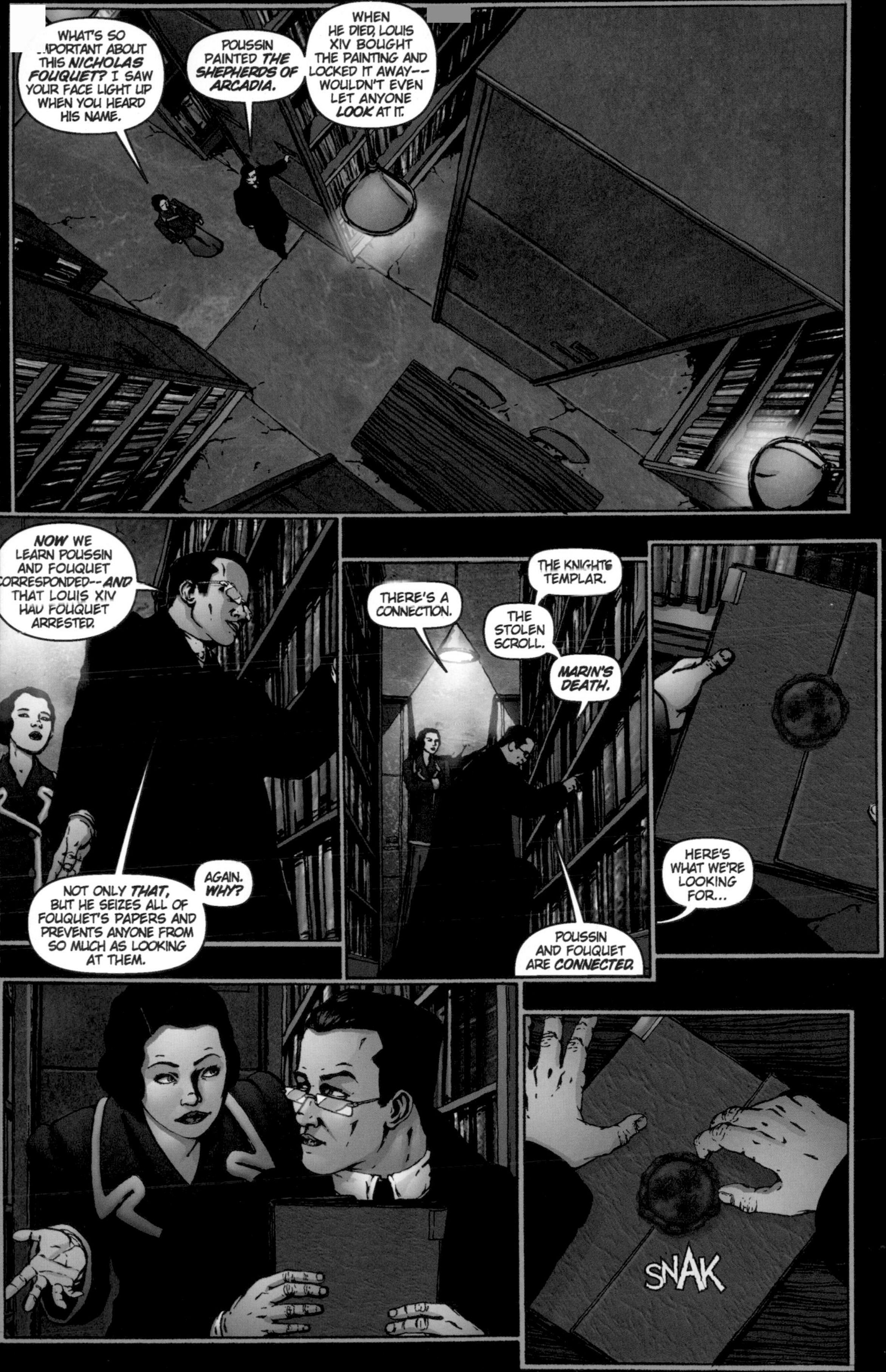
WHAT'S SO IMPORTANT ABOUT THIS NICHOLAS FOUQUET? I SAW YOUR FACE LIGHT UP WHEN YOU HEARD HIS NAME.
POUSSIN PAINTED THE SHEPHERDS OF ARCADIA.
WHEN HE DIED, LOUIS XIV BOUGHT THE PAINTING AND LOCKED IT AWAY-- WOULDN'T EVEN LET ANYONE LOOK AT IT.
NOW WE LEARN POUSSIN AND FOUQUET CORRESPONDED--AND THAT LOUIS XIV HAD FOUQUET ARRESTED.
NOT ONLY THAT, BUT HE SEIZES ALL OF FOUQUET'S PAPERS AND PREVENTS ANYONE FROM SO MUCH AS LOOKING AT THEM.
AGAIN. WHY?
THERE'S A CONNECTION.
THE KNIGHTS TEMPLAR.
THE STOLEN SCROLL.
MARIN'S DEATH.
POUSSIN AND FOUQUET ARE CONNECTED.
HERE'S WHAT WE'RE LOOKING FOR...
SNAK

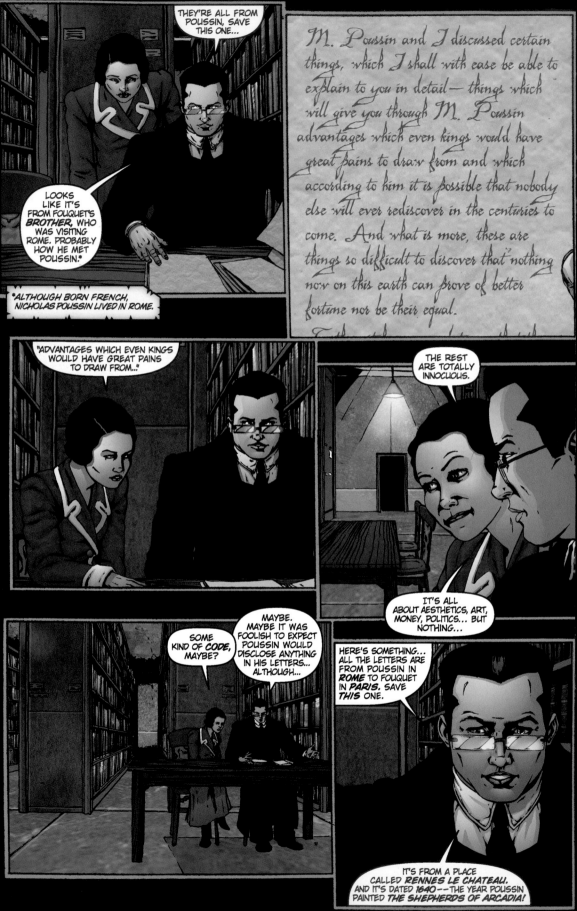

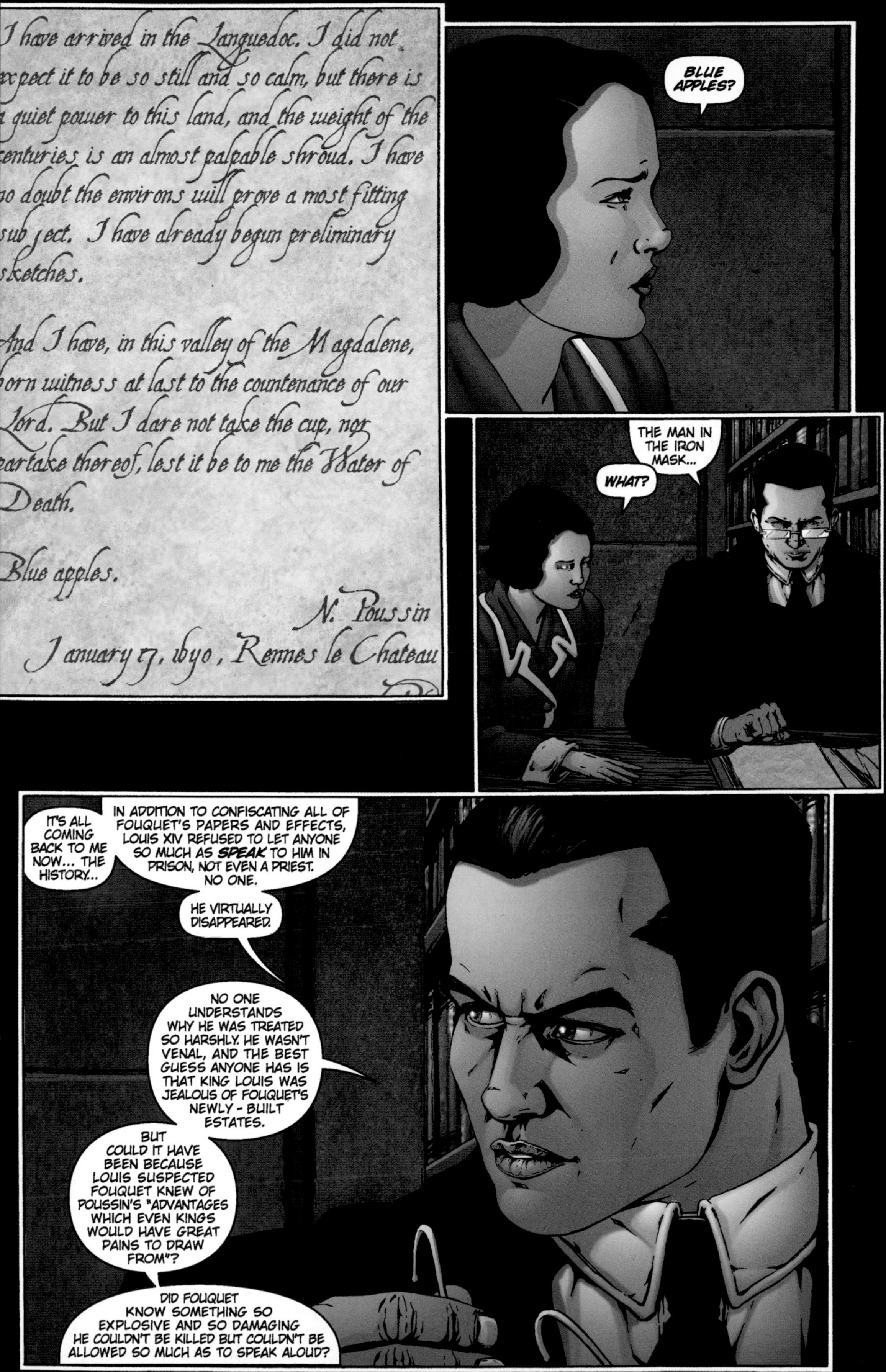
I have arrived in the Languedoc. I did not expect it to be so still and so calm, but there is a quiet power to this land, and the weight of the centuries is an almost palpable shroud. I have no doubt the environs will prove a most fitting subject. I have already begun preliminary sketches.
And I have, in this valley of the Magdalene, born witness at last to the countenance of our Lord. But I dare not take the cup, nor partake thereof, lest it be to me the Water of Death.
Blue apples.
N. Poussin
January 17, 1650, Rennes le Chateau
BLUE APPLES?
THE MAN IN THE IRON MASK...
WHAT?
IT'S ALL COMING BACK TO ME NOW... THE HISTORY...
IN ADDITION TO CONFISCATING ALL OF FOUQUET'S PAPERS AND EFFECTS, LOUIS XIV REFUSED TO LET ANYONE SO MUCH AS SPEAK TO HIM IN PRISON, NOT EVEN A PRIEST. NO ONE.
HE VIRTUALLY DISAPPEARED.
NO ONE UNDERSTANDS WHY HE WAS TREATED SO HARSHLY. HE WASN'T VENAL, AND THE BEST GUESS ANYONE HAS IS THAT KING LOUIS WAS JEALOUS OF FOUQUET'S NEWLY - BUILT ESTATES.
BUT COULD IT HAVE BEEN BECAUSE LOUIS SUSPECTED FOUQUET KNEW OF POUSSIN'S "ADVANTAGES WHICH EVEN KINGS WOULD HAVE GREAT PAINS TO DRAW FROM"?
DID FOUQUET KNOW SOMETHING SO EXPLOSIVE AND SO DAMAGING HE COULDN'T BE KILLED BUT COULDN'T BE ALLOWED SO MUCH AS TO SPEAK ALOUD?

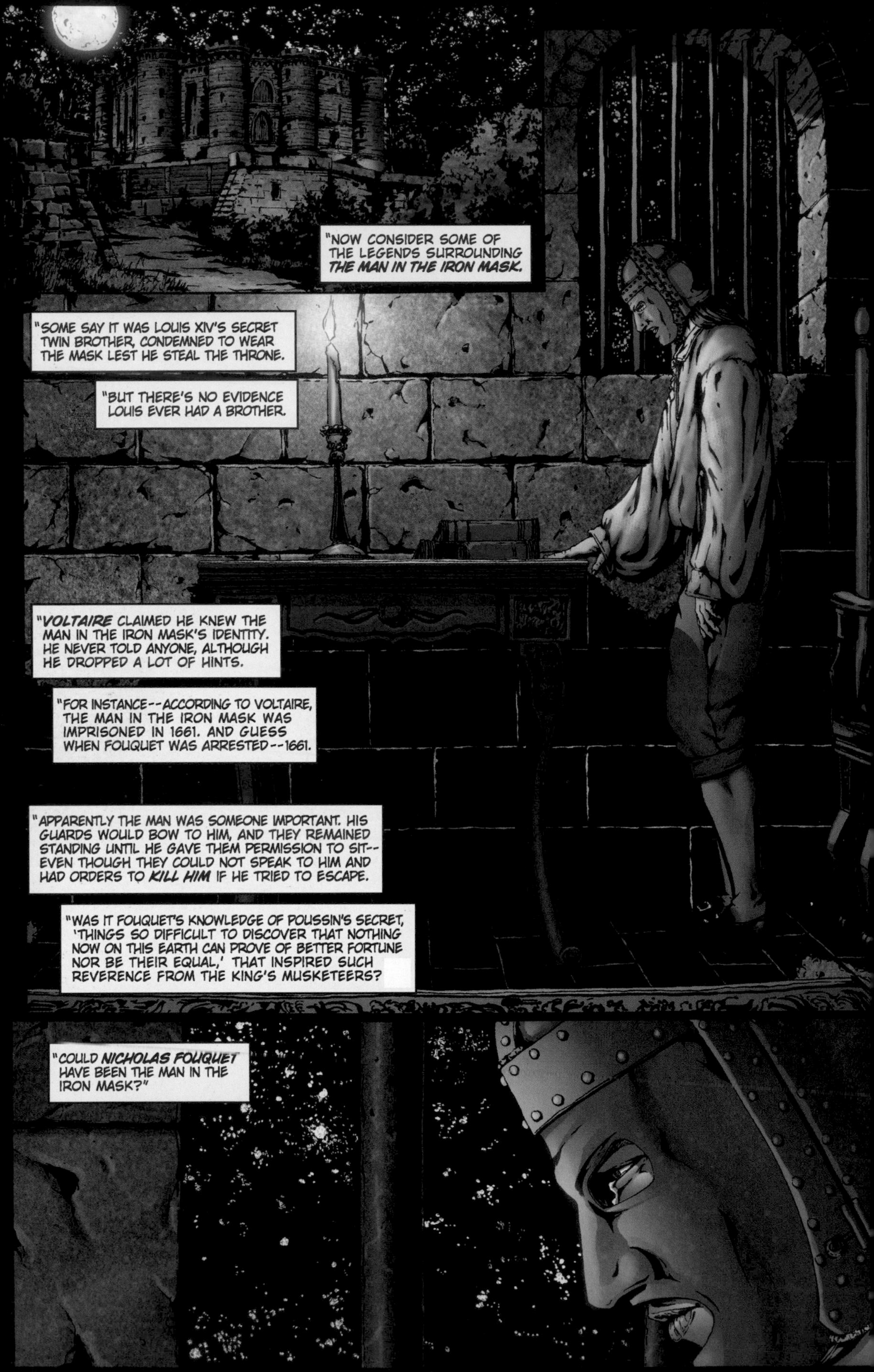
"NOW CONSIDER SOME OF THE LEGENDS SURROUNDING ***THE MAN IN THE IRON MASK.***
"SOME SAY IT WAS LOUIS XIV'S SECRET TWIN BROTHER, CONDEMNED TO WEAR THE MASK LEST HE STEAL THE THRONE.
"BUT THERE'S NO EVIDENCE LOUIS EVER HAD A BROTHER.
"***VOLTAIRE*** CLAIMED HE KNEW THE MAN IN THE IRON MASK'S IDENTITY. HE NEVER TOLD ANYONE, ALTHOUGH HE DROPPED A LOT OF HINTS.
"FOR INSTANCE--ACCORDING TO VOLTAIRE, THE MAN IN THE IRON MASK WAS IMPRISONED IN 1661. AND GUESS WHEN FOUQUET WAS ARRESTED--1661.
"APPARENTLY THE MAN WAS SOMEONE IMPORTANT. HIS GUARDS WOULD BOW TO HIM, AND THEY REMAINED STANDING UNTIL HE GAVE THEM PERMISSION TO SIT--EVEN THOUGH THEY COULD NOT SPEAK TO HIM AND HAD ORDERS TO ***KILL HIM*** IF HE TRIED TO ESCAPE.
"WAS IT FOUQUET'S KNOWLEDGE OF POUSSIN'S SECRET, 'THINGS SO DIFFICULT TO DISCOVER THAT NOTHING NOW ON THIS EARTH CAN PROVE OF BETTER FORTUNE NOR BE THEIR EQUAL,' THAT INSPIRED SUCH REVERENCE FROM THE KING'S MUSKETEERS?
"COULD ***NICHOLAS FOUQUET*** HAVE BEEN THE MAN IN THE IRON MASK?"

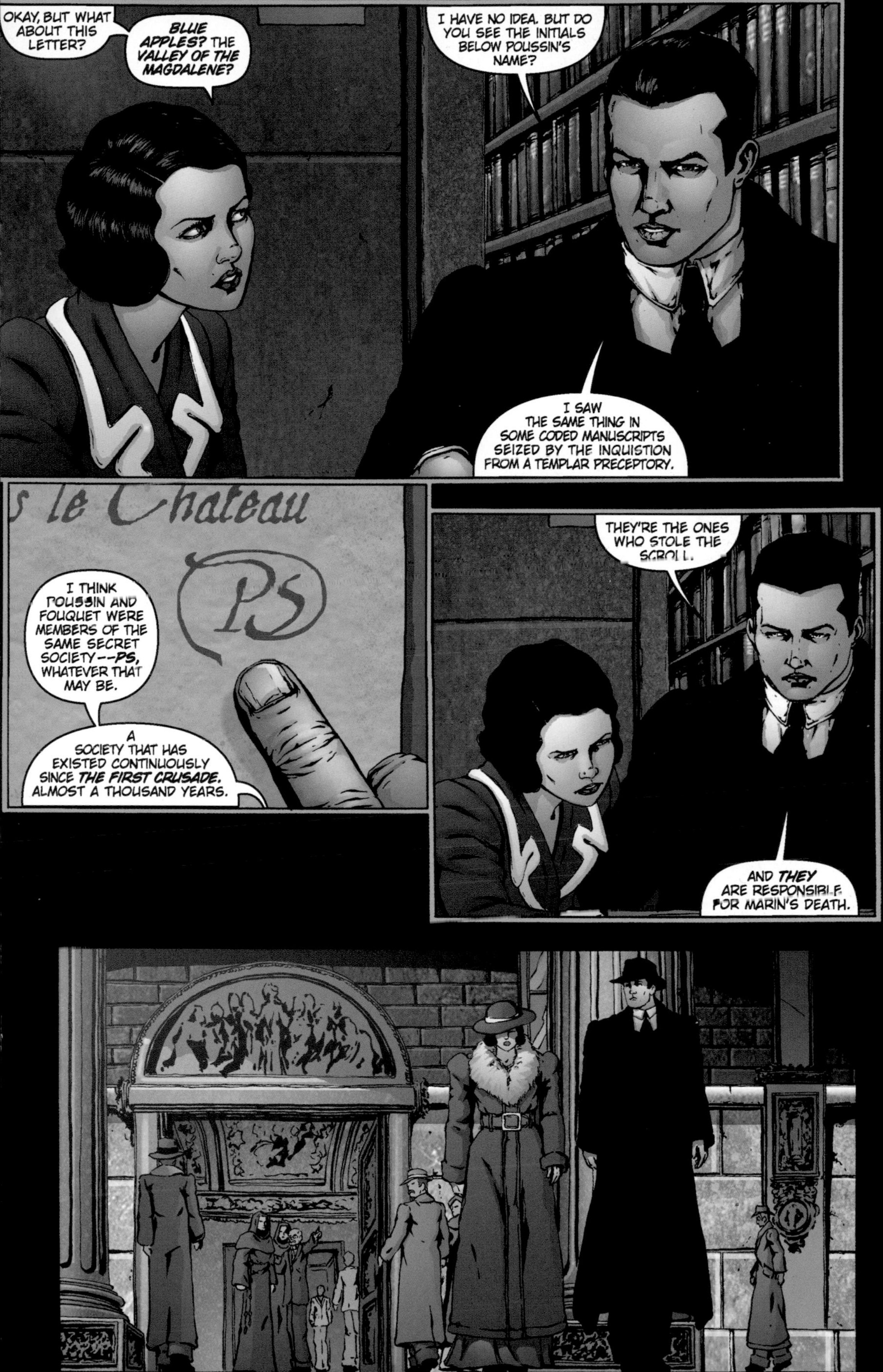

OKAY, BUT WHAT ABOUT THIS LETTER?
BLUE APPLES? THE VALLEY OF THE MAGDALENE?
I HAVE NO IDEA. BUT DO YOU SEE THE INITIALS BELOW POUSSIN'S NAME?
I SAW THE SAME THING IN SOME CODED MANUSCRIPTS SEIZED BY THE INQUISTION FROM A TEMPLAR PRECEPTORY.
s le Chateau
PS
I THINK POUSSIN AND FOUQUET WERE MEMBERS OF THE SAME SECRET SOCIETY--PS, WHATEVER THAT MAY BE.
A SOCIETY THAT HAS EXISTED CONTINUOUSLY SINCE THE FIRST CRUSADE. ALMOST A THOUSAND YEARS.
THEY'RE THE ONES WHO STOLE THE SCROLL.
AND THEY ARE RESPONSIBLE FOR MARIN'S DEATH.

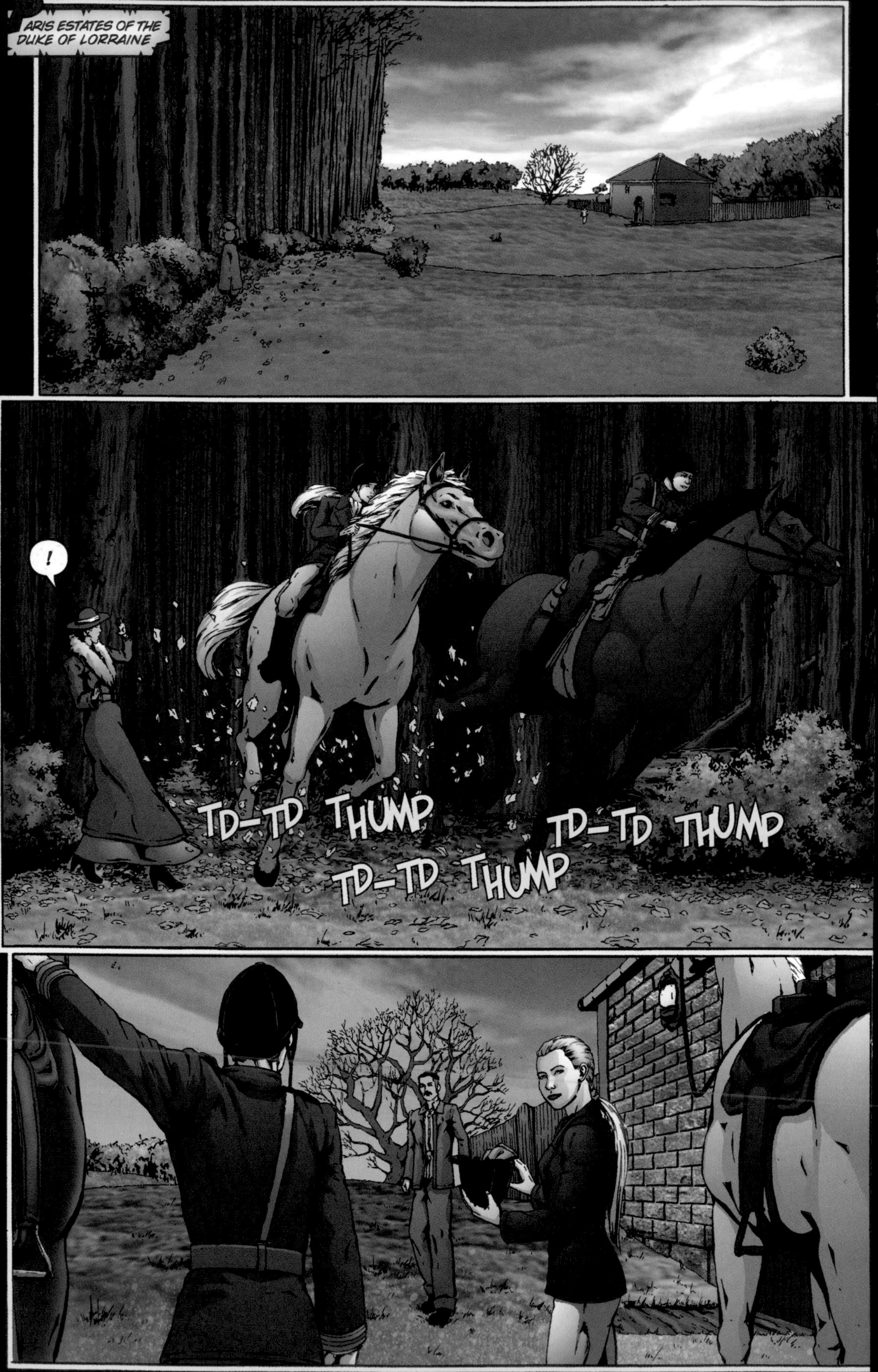
ARIS ESTATES OF THE DUKE OF LORRAINE
!
TD-TD THUMP
TD-TD THUMP
TD-TD THUMP

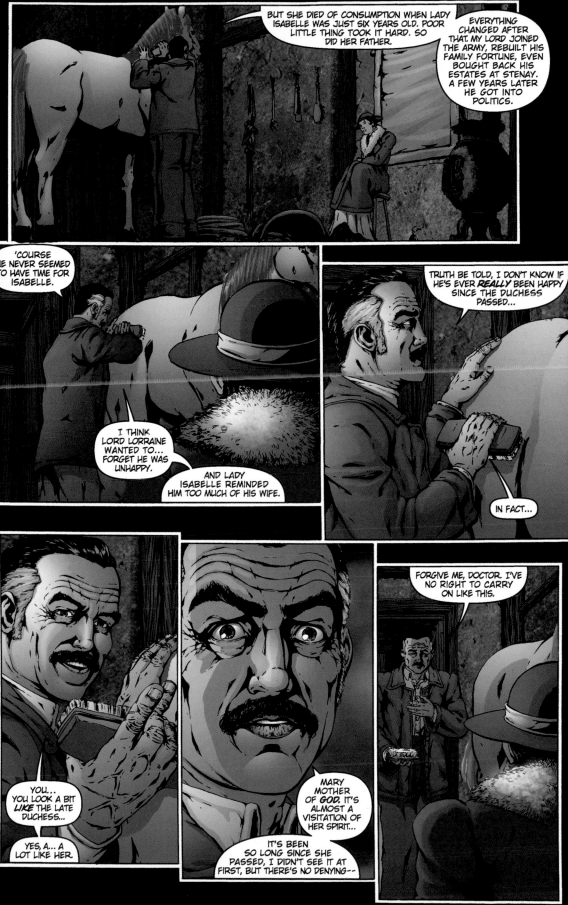

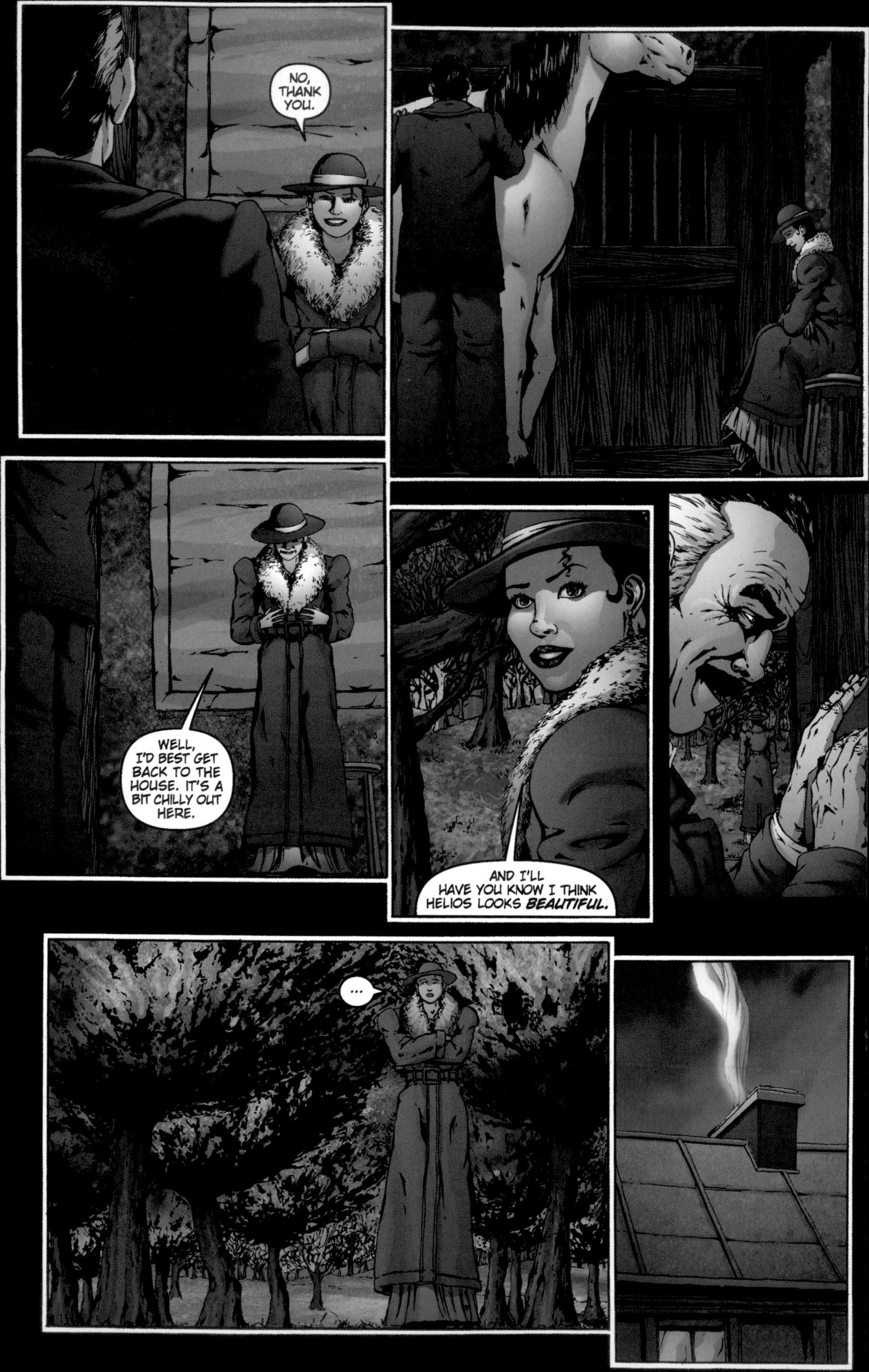
NO, THANK YOU.
WELL, I'D BEST GET BACK TO THE HOUSE. IT'S A BIT CHILLY OUT HERE.
AND I'LL HAVE YOU KNOW I THINK HELIOS LOOKS BEAUTIFUL.
...

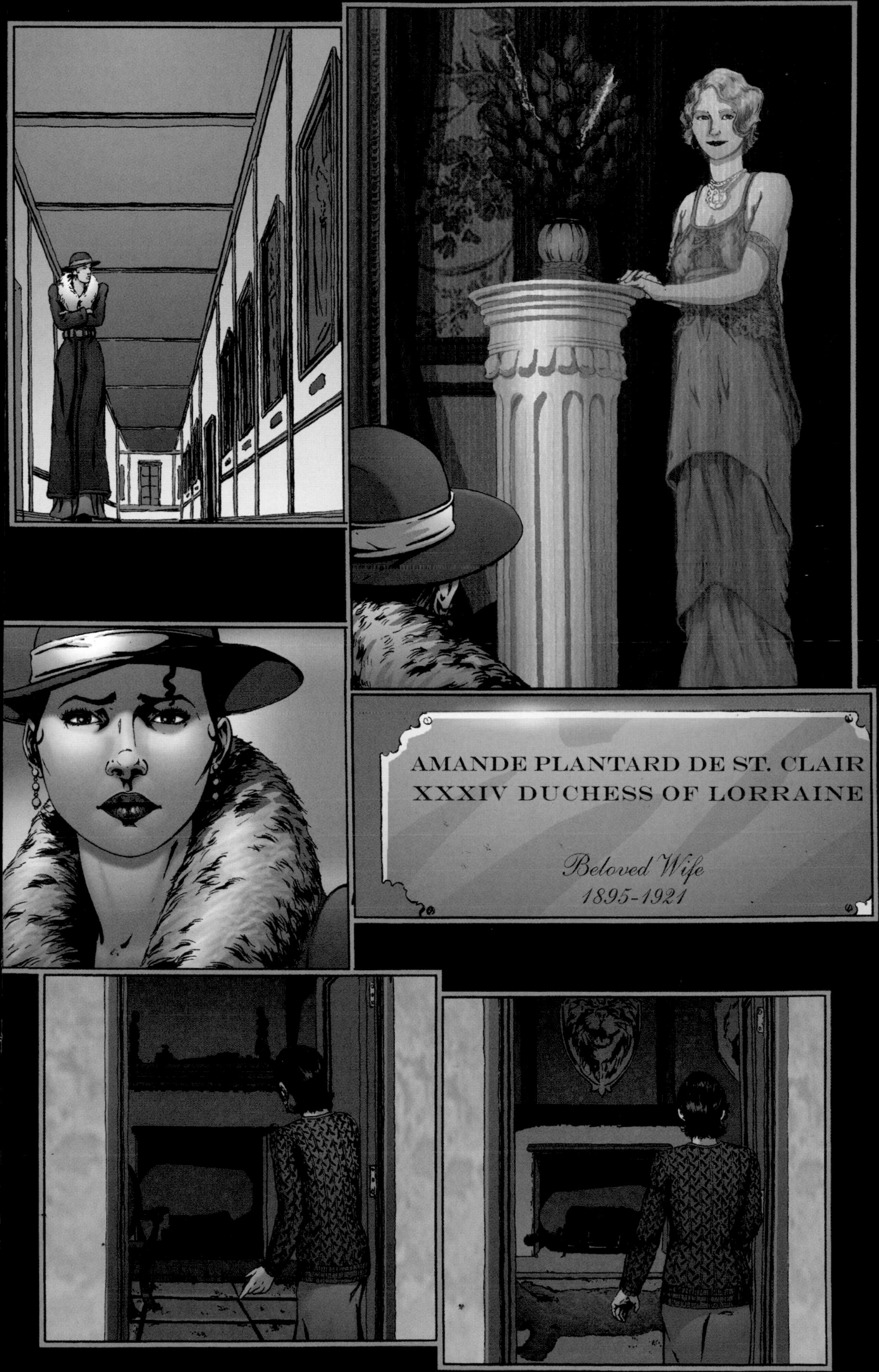
AMANDE PLANTARD DE ST. CLAIR
XXXIV DUCHESS OF LORRAINE
Beloved Wife
1895-1921

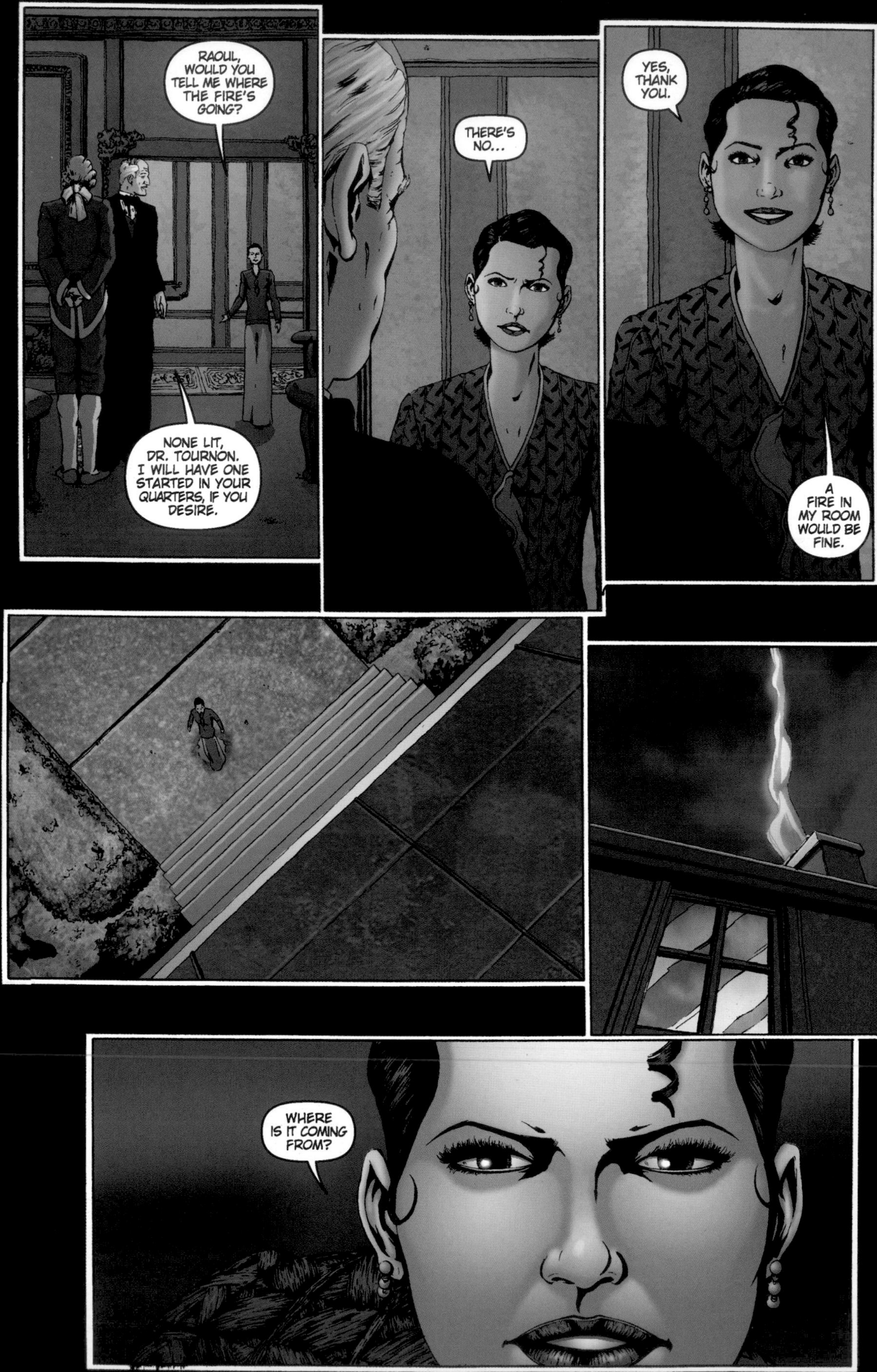
RAOUL, WOULD YOU TELL ME WHERE THE FIRE'S GOING?
NONE LIT, DR. TOURNON. I WILL HAVE ONE STARTED IN YOUR QUARTERS, IF YOU DESIRE.
THERE'S NO...
YES, THANK YOU.
A FIRE IN MY ROOM WOULD BE FINE.
WHERE IS IT COMING FROM?

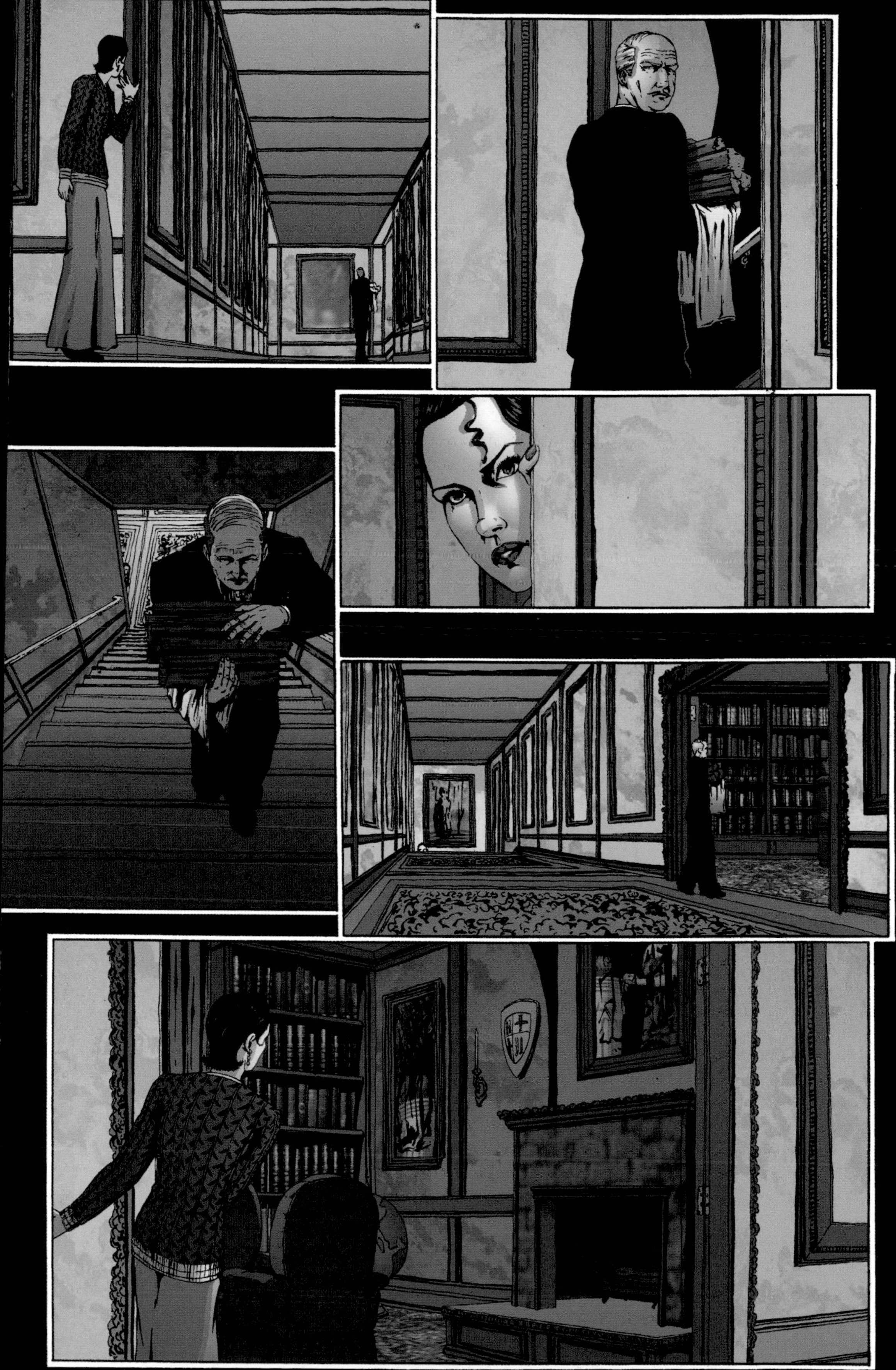

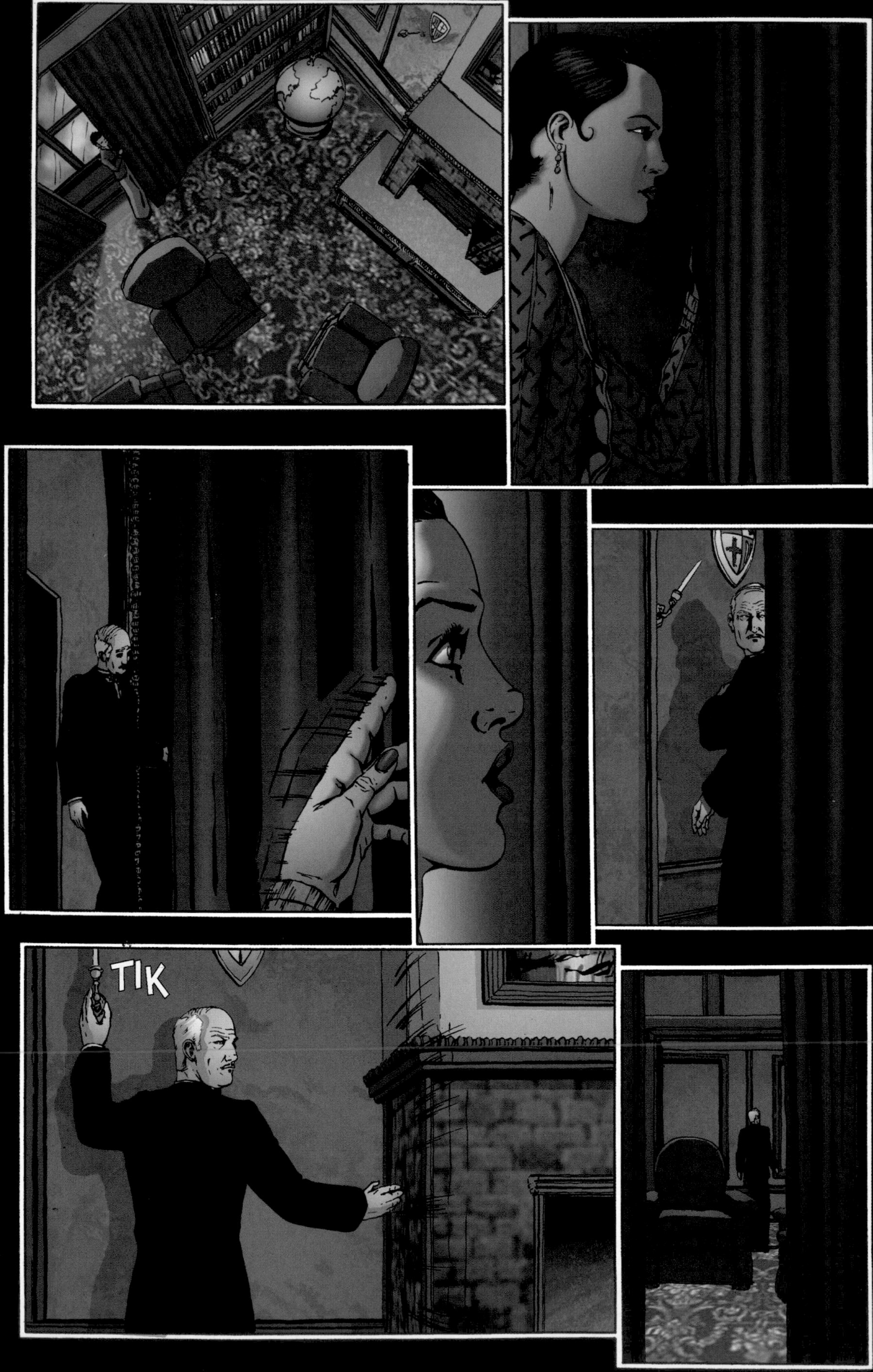
TIK

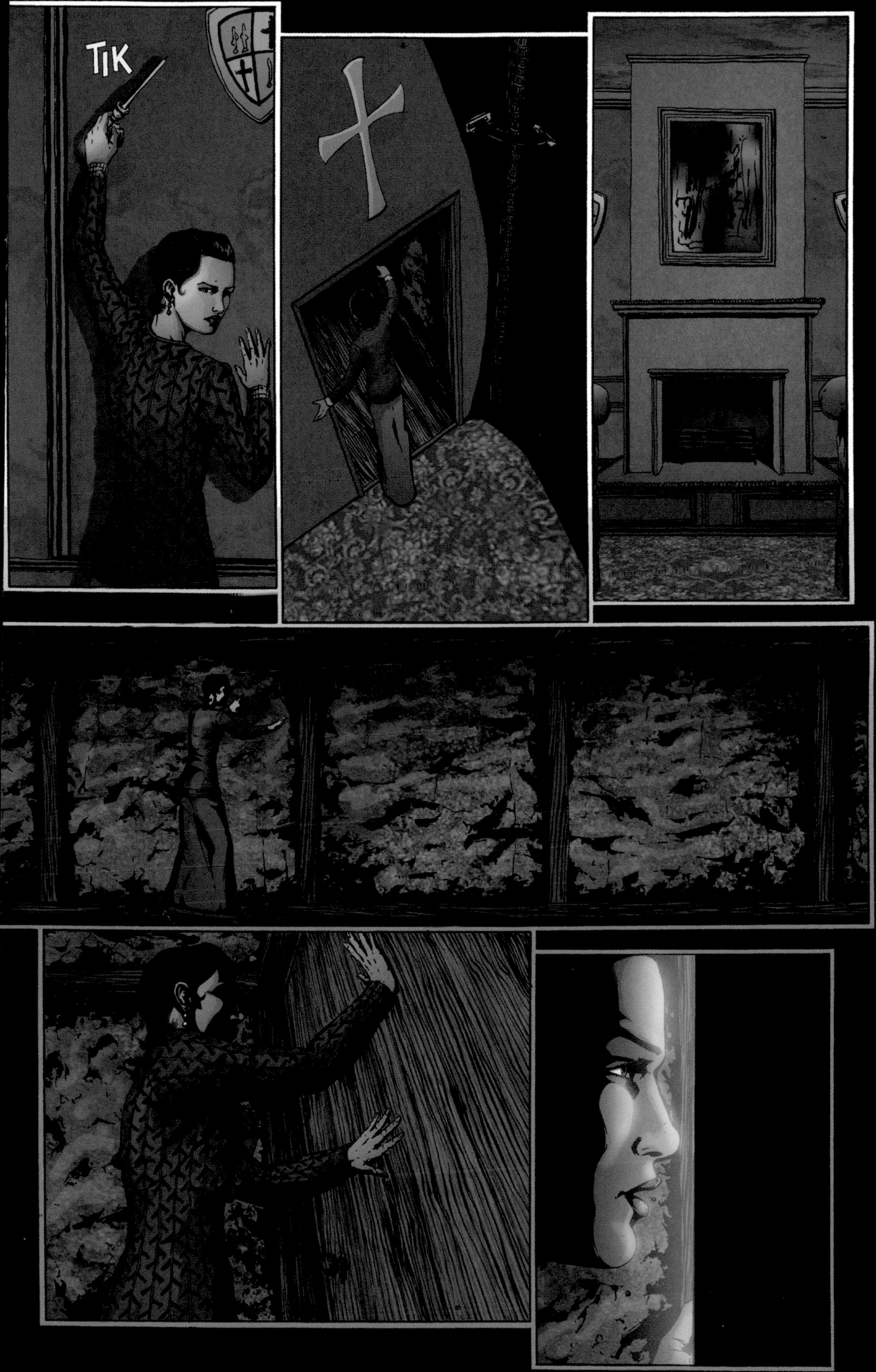
TIK

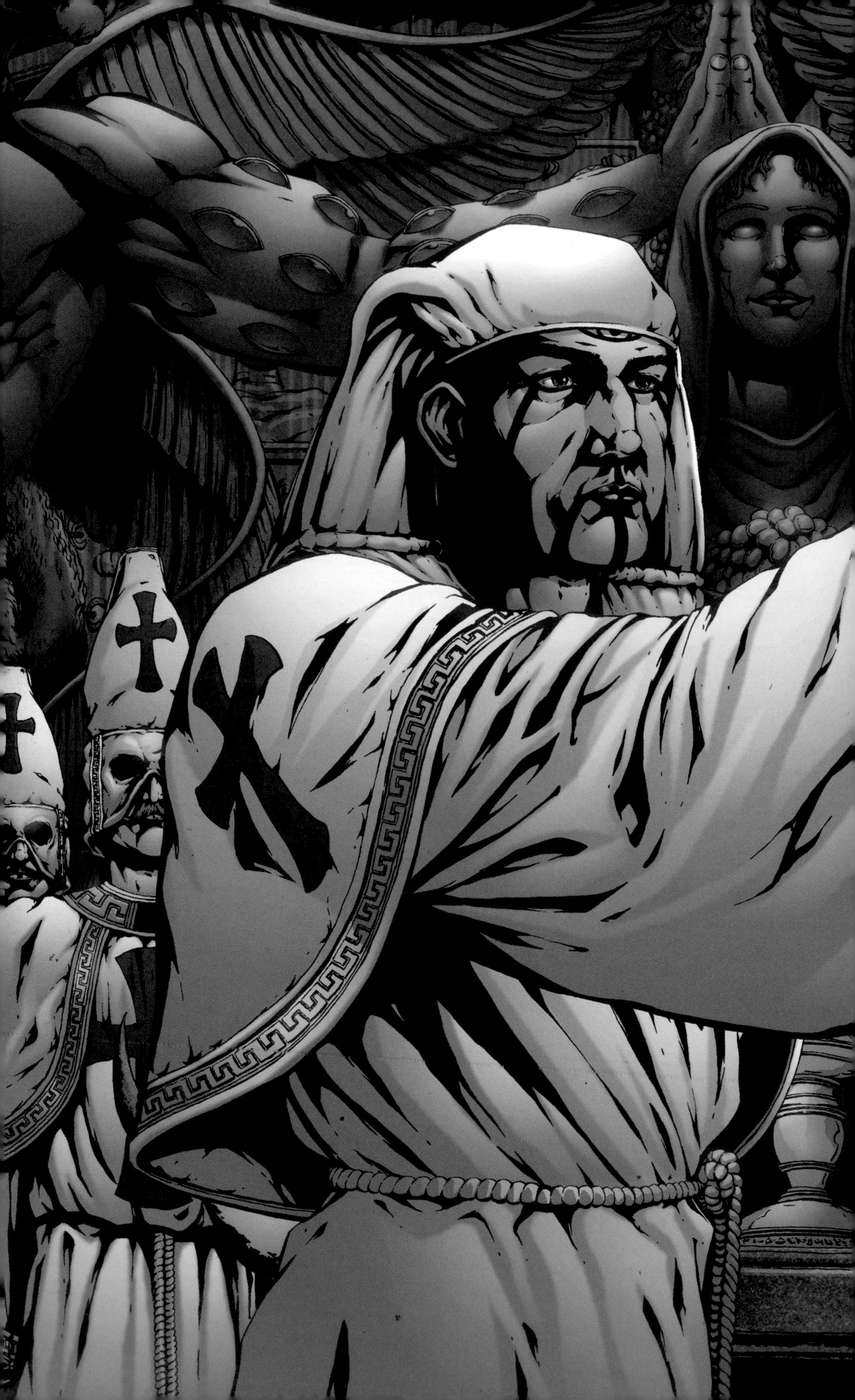

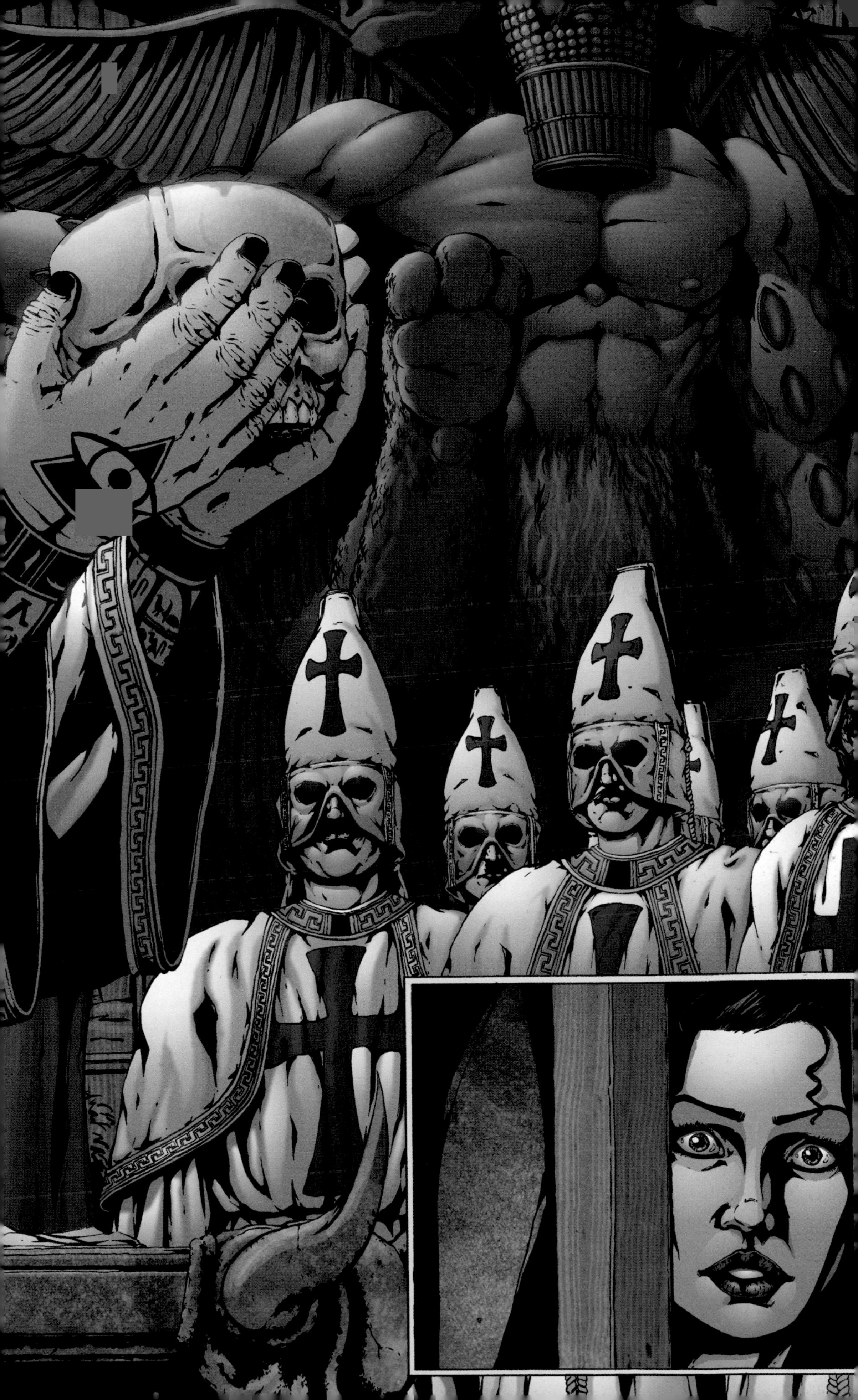

Le Journal de la Libert

Paris's leading anglophone newspaper • vol. 205, no. 103 • Oct. 26, MCMXXXIII

Papal Seal

Editors in Chief: M. Tait Bergstrom, M. Matthew Pasteris. **Story Editor:** M. Arvid Nelson. **Art Editors:** M. EricJ, M. Jeromy Cox. **Photography Editor:** M. Alexander Waldman. **Layout Supervisor:** M. William Kartalopoulos. **Editors Emeritus:** M. Clark A. Smith, M. Howard P. Lovecraft, M. Robert E. Howard. Redacted by the Holy Parisian Inquisition under the direction of His Excellency Archbishop Emile-Jean Ireneaux. Le Journal de la Liberté is printed under the benign auspices of his most puissant majesty KING LOUIS XXII of FRANCE. GOD SAVE THE KING.

of Approval

HALL OF THE ROBE VOTES AGAINST KING ON DOMESTIC LEGISLATION

New law is "innocuous," but political implications might foreshadow a rebellion in Parliament

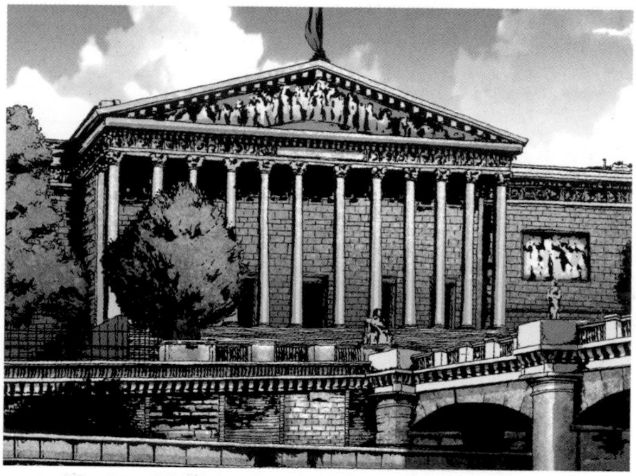

The Assemblé Nationale, sight of the "betrayal" of the Crown.

The bill passed into law yesterday night is hardly worth mentioning. But the way in which it was passed could signal historic changes in France's political landscape.

For the first time ever, both houses of Parliament – the Hall of the Sword and the Hall of the Robe – acted in unison against the will of the King.

King Louis XXII's advisors and spokesmen made it clear they were disappointed by passage of the law, which was introduced by the Count of Toulouse in Hall of the Sword several weeks earlier.

The bill called for an expiration of royal injunctions after 100 years. It passed by a wide margin in the Sword, as was expected.

The broad support for the bill in the Hall of the Robe was not.

According to Jean-Alexis Moncorge, a political advisor to the Hall of the Sword, the Crown has never once lost a fight with Parliament.

"Every time legislation has passed into law under our current system of government, it has either been a three 'yeas', or the Hall of the Robe and the Crown have overpowered the Sword," Moncorge said. "Until now, the Robe has always voted with the King."

This is because the King has the exclusive right to appoint members to the lower house of French parliament, the Hall of the Robe. The King has always stocked the Robe with his most devoted supporters.

But the presumed fealty of the Robe to the King was called into question yesterday.

"This is the first time the Robe has voted against the King," Moncorge said. "What this does is dim the halo of invincibility surrounding the Crown."

Members of the Hall of the Robe played down the significance of the event.

"This is a very small piece of legislation, intended to make our increasingly unmanageable bureaucracy more efficient," said Baronet Aristide deMandeville, Speaker of the Robe. "It should in no way be regarded as an attack on Robe's time-honored tradition of loyalty to the King."

Members of King Louis XXII's court saw a broader context of defiance.

"This is betrayal, pure and simple," said a source close to the king. "The actions of the Hall of the Robe border on treason. His Majesty has been stabbed in the back, plain and simple."

But Lord DeMandeville doesn't think there's any need for concern on the Crown's part.

"We ensured the bill was modified in a number of ways before it was brought to a vote," Lord deMandeville said.

"For instance, the king may renew injunctions as he sees fit once the 100 year time limit is up."

Members of the Hall of the Sword seemed cautiously o mistic about the prospect more power for their historic marginalized Hall.

"France's great houses h been disorganized and apath for many years, but the Duke Lorraine turned that all arour a member of the Hall of Sword said.

"And now we've shown t the Robe has the courage stand up to the King, too. It's precedent that's important h not the passage of the bill itse

Moncorge was inclined agree.

"It's too early to say for s but this could very well signa new era of political significance the Hall of the Robe," he said.

This idea was troublesome advisors close to the king.

"Certain members of the H of the Sword have been b ting around entirely too mu militaristic rhetoric," Char Martel, Louis XXII's Mayor the Court, said.

"If the Sword is poised gain influence, I hope it w be to extend a hand of frien ship to our neighbors, but have my doubts. France and Christendom could be headi off a precipice."

Royal injunctions are issu at the sole discretion of the ki Only the king may view a roya enjoined document.

Leads in deMedici Murder Scarce; Markets Plunge at News of Financier's Death

Inquisitors are still baffled as to the identity of Hugo deMedici's killer twenty-four hours after his death.

Mr. deMedici was the heir-apparent to the vast deMedici family financial empire.

"The individual responsible for this horrific act was particularly clever," Inquisitor Moricant, lead investigator on the case, said. "While our leads are few, they are promising, and we are following them diligently."

In particular, Inquisitors are questioning three members of the Guild of Stevedores near the scene of the murder around the time it occurred.

Officials did not list the three men as suspects but potential witnesses of suspicious activity.

Inquisitor Moricant declined to give the names of the three men or comment further on the case.

An elderly woman who lives in the neighborhood told *Journal* she saw a "man dress in black" walking around t premises of the deMedici offic late that night.

"I was up late at night kn ting stockings when I saw hi He went right into the deMedi building," she said.

Inquisitors declined to com ment on the woman's testimony

Meanwhile, markets reacted

continued on page I

INSIDE

Plus opinion pieces by eds. A. Nelson and EricJ

❧ Society Pages ❧

...o Is the Mysterious Woman ...the Arm of the Duke of ...rraine?

...e's beautiful, she's stylish, she's a doctor. She's ...hottest thing in Paris. Who wouldn't fall for ...lovely Dr. Tournon?

...ase, ladies, no weeping: France's most ...gible — and most elusive — bachelor may ...off limits. Lots of women have been seen ...nging off Lord Lorraine's arm over the ...rs, but never for more than a few nights ...a row. Seems like Lorraine, the man who ...ves beyond a doubt that bald can be sexy, ...es to play it fast and easy.

...til now. For the past two months, Lorraine ...attended every party with the same ...nale companion.

...o months? Practically a lifetime for ...e nubile lord! Lorraine's new flame is a ...rking girl, a member of the Guild of ...ysicians. The young doctor, Genevieve ...urnon, has risen quickly through the ...nks of the Guild. In recent months she has ...come something of a sensation in Paris ...ciety with her boyish good looks, wit and ...peccable couture.

...scretion, too, may be one of her charms: ...cording to her, she and the Duke are "just ...od friends." Our diagnosis: this relationship ...a lot hotter than she's letting on!

...weetness, I Was Only Joking

...hoops! Just three hours after a hasty wed-...ng ceremony, young Baroness Brittany ...uillère has petitioned the Papacy for an ...nulment of her marriage.

...he Baroness, who scandalized her family by ...oosing the life of a professional singer, wed ...untitled young man whom she has known ...ince childhood." Rumor has it the young ...an was a servant of her family.

...new record for shortest marriage? A public-...y stunt for the baroness's upcoming recital? ...ur dedicated reporters are on the beat!

Paris is Burning

Months after the scandal and there's still no let-up for poor Paris. No, we don't mean our fair city, we mean the now-infamous Paris Huguet-Renoir, heir to her father's sprawling hotel-and-casino empire.

In case you've been living in a Siberian convent, we'll fill you in on the gory details. Paris and a Roumanian count (whose name escapes us) had a secret tryst four months ago — or so they had hoped! Paris and the dashing count, who is twice her age, decid-ed to memorialize the event with a Lumière motion-camera.

Apparently, foresight and intelligence are not among the many gifts God bestowed upon the wealthy socialites.

It seems a member of the Count's entourage, a camera enthusiast, overheard the lovebirds' plan and secretly made a print from the negatives of the two in the act.

Although Pope John XIV has threatened excommunication for anyone caught show-ing or distributing the film, underground salons all over Europe have been playing cop-ies of the reel incessantly.

The event has scandalized the Huguet-Renoir family. At a dinner party last night, Henrietta Dobson, the wife of a wealthy American banker known for his social slip-ups, confessed her "deepest sympathy" to Paris's mother Beatriz. Appalled by the gaffe, Paris's mother expressed her "deepest sympa-thy" that Mme Dobson lacked the "etiquette and social grace of a reptile".

Most recently, beautiful-if-not-overtly-inter-esting-aside-from-the-scandal Paris has been consoling herself modeling the clothes of haute-couture designers with her beloved chihuahua Fifi.

"She's a real professional, considering what she's been through," a photographer said of her. Frankly, we couldn't agree more.

Barely Worth Mentioning

Visiting dignitaries from the Confederate States of America received a terrible shock at yesterday's Rugby World Championships.

During a "half-time" performance, famed performer Janet Témerson bared one of her breasts, causing an uproar amongst the Southerners. The wife of one of the diplo-mats shrieked and threatened to faint.

A French count nearby reportedly told the shocked Americans, "It's only a breast. We have lots of those around here."

A Night at the Opera

David-Louis Plantard de St. Clair, better known to us mortals as the Duke of Lorraine, has done the unthinkable: he's made the Le Journal Society Pages twice on the same day!

Lorraine is flying high with his new "good friend" Dr. Genevieve Tournon. And he made a prodigious splash last night at the Palais Garnier opera house, where his production of *The Marriage of Figaro* debuted to wide acclaim from critics and opera-goers.

But surely his majesty King Louis XXII's feathers were ruffled by the Duke's choice of *The Marriage of Figaro*. Written by Mozart, the opera was banned in France until ten years ago because of its "seditious and per-fidious content."

It is also said that Mozart, a Freemason, hid references to Masonic institutions and rituals in his works. Church and crown have brand-ed the secretive Freemason movement as "a grave threat to Christian civilization."

Clearly this did not deter the Duke. He was in attendance last night with his usual entourage of political supporters: Dominique Lourié-Modot, Count of Toulouse, and Baron Robert Teniers.

Lord Toulouse was overheard ridiculing Baron Teniers outside the Palais Garnier, but the young Baron took the slight coolly.

Men about town: Lords Lorraine and Toulouse exit the Palais Garnier yesterday eve-ning after the premiere of The Marriage of Figaro. *Between them is Lord Lorraine's close confidant, Baron Robert Teniers. Why so glum, Baron? Too many secrets to hide?*

LES ARMES DES SATAN

et in arcadia ego...

...TER NOSTER QVI EST IN COELI...

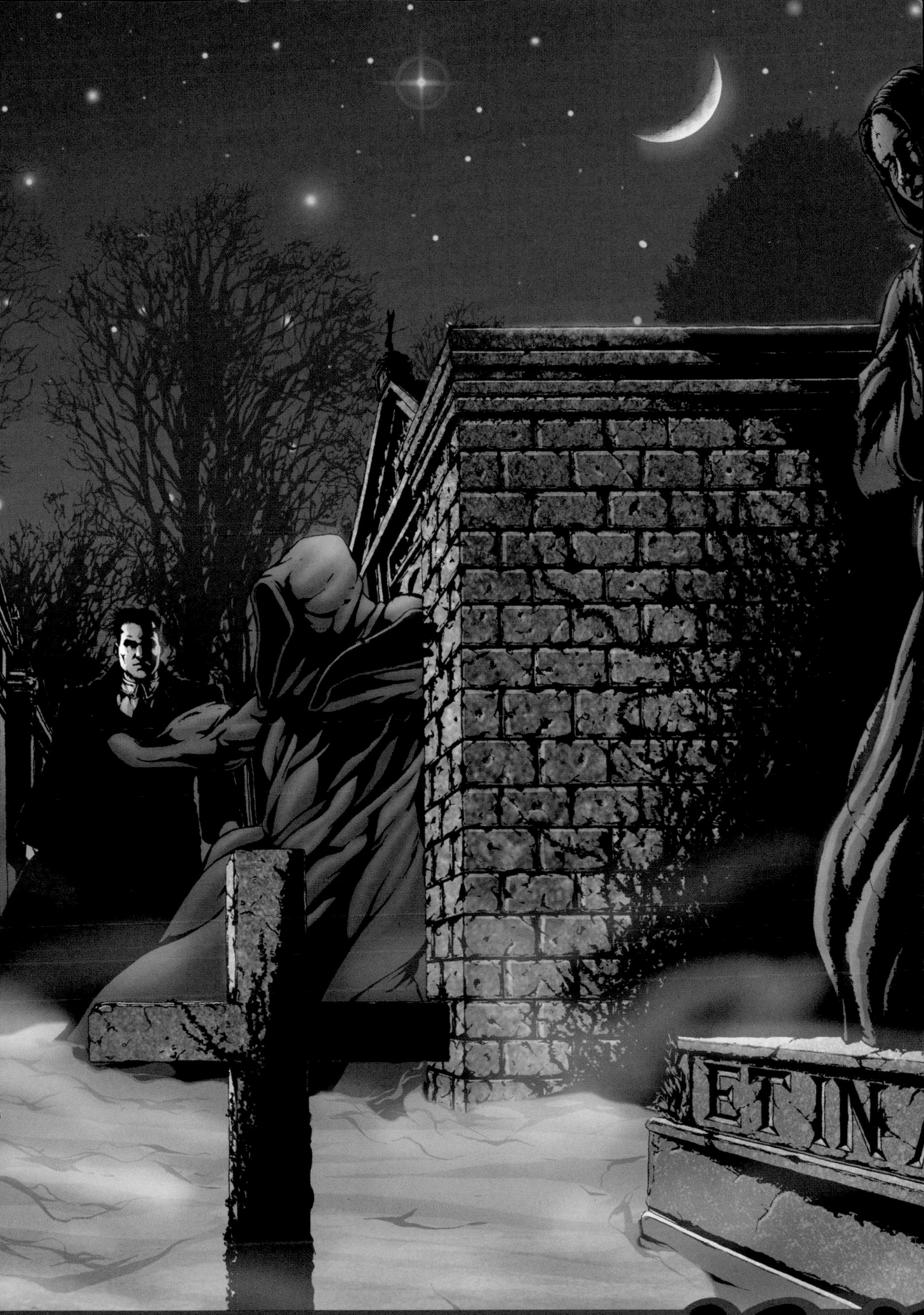
ET IN A

CHAPTER FIVE

THE RIVER UNDERGROUND

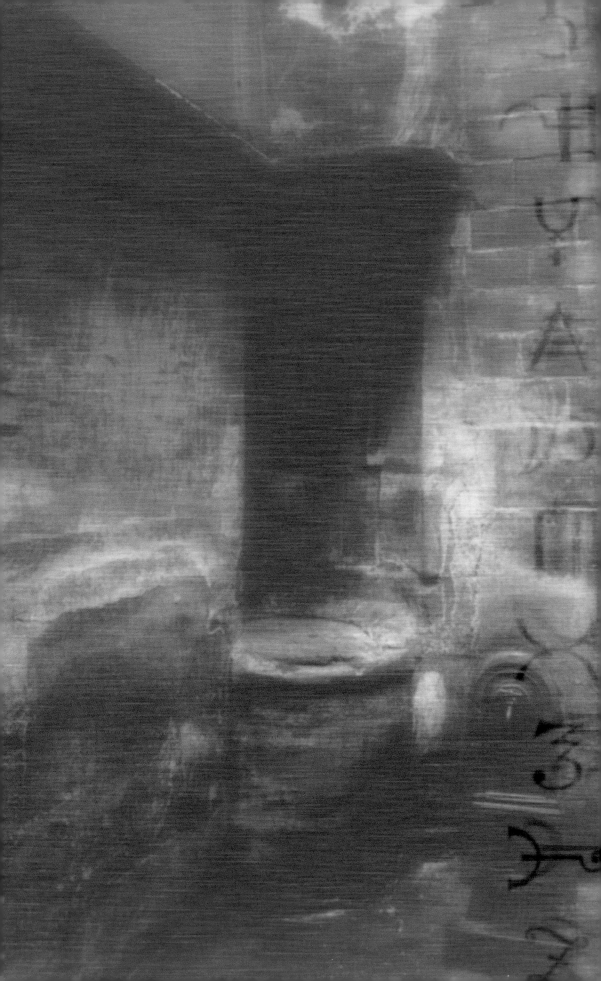

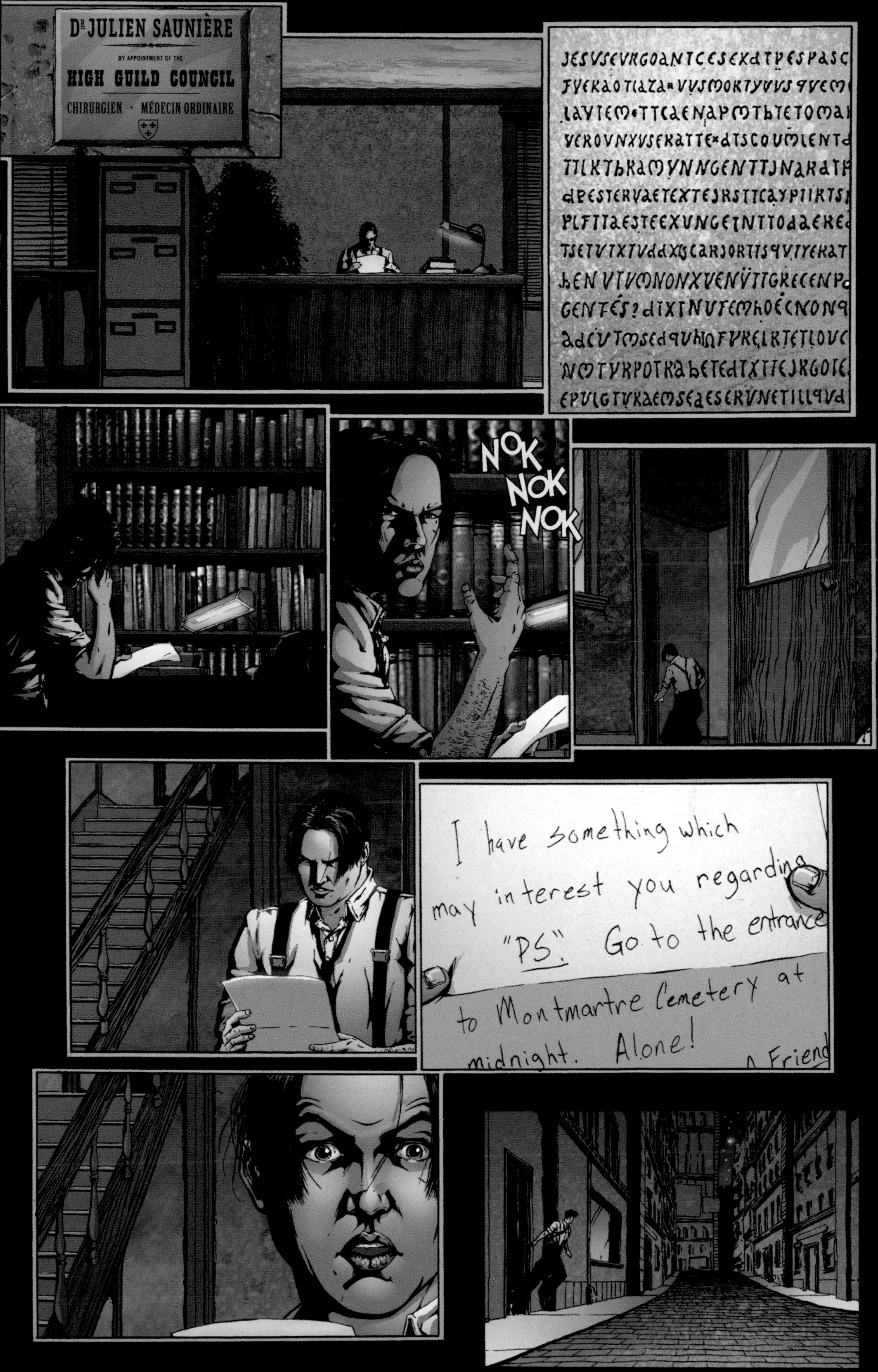

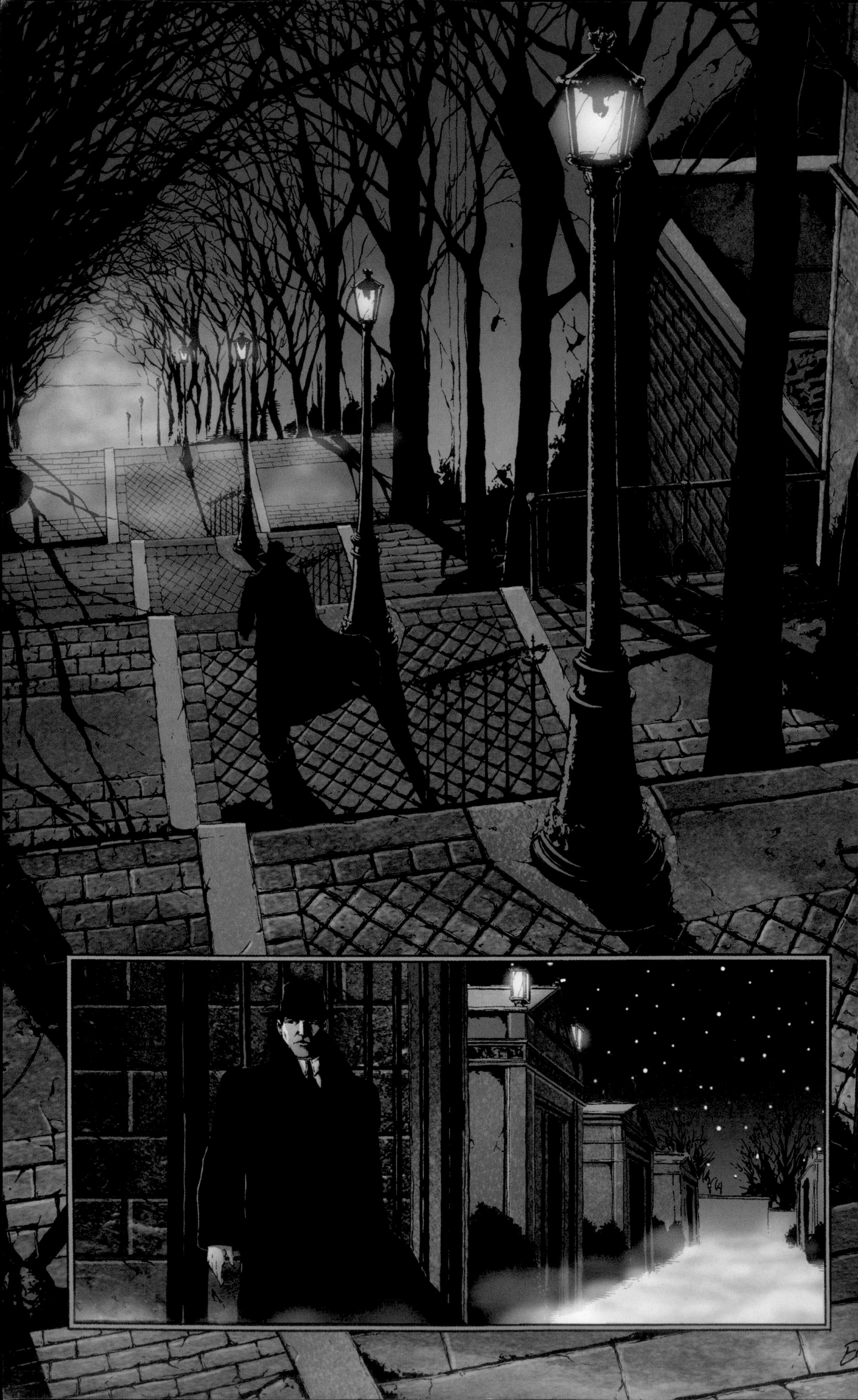

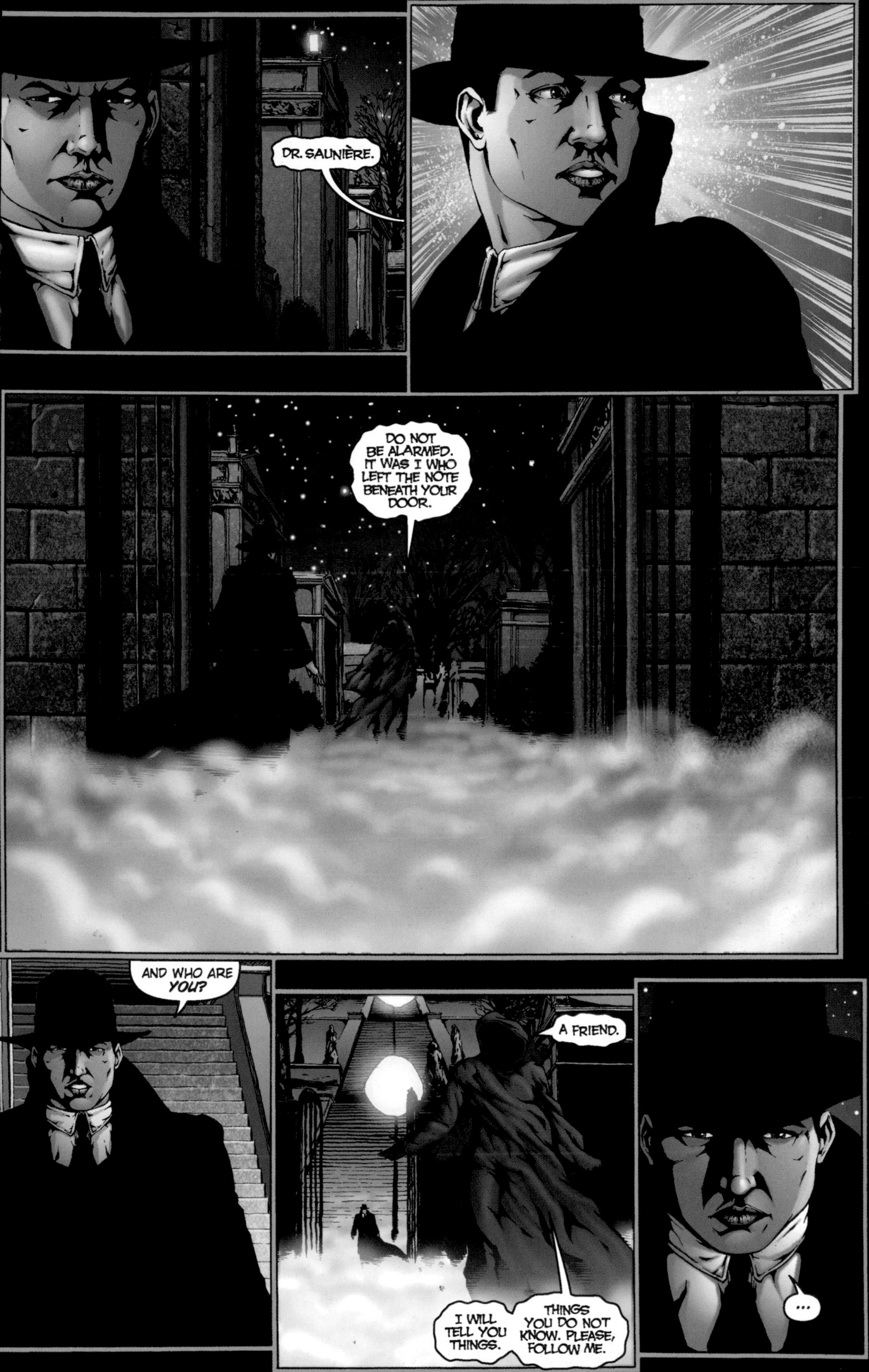
DR. SAUNIÈRE.
DO NOT BE ALARMED. IT WAS I WHO LEFT THE NOTE BENEATH YOUR DOOR.
AND WHO ARE YOU?
A FRIEND.
I WILL TELL YOU THINGS.
THINGS YOU DO NOT KNOW. PLEASE, FOLLOW ME.
...

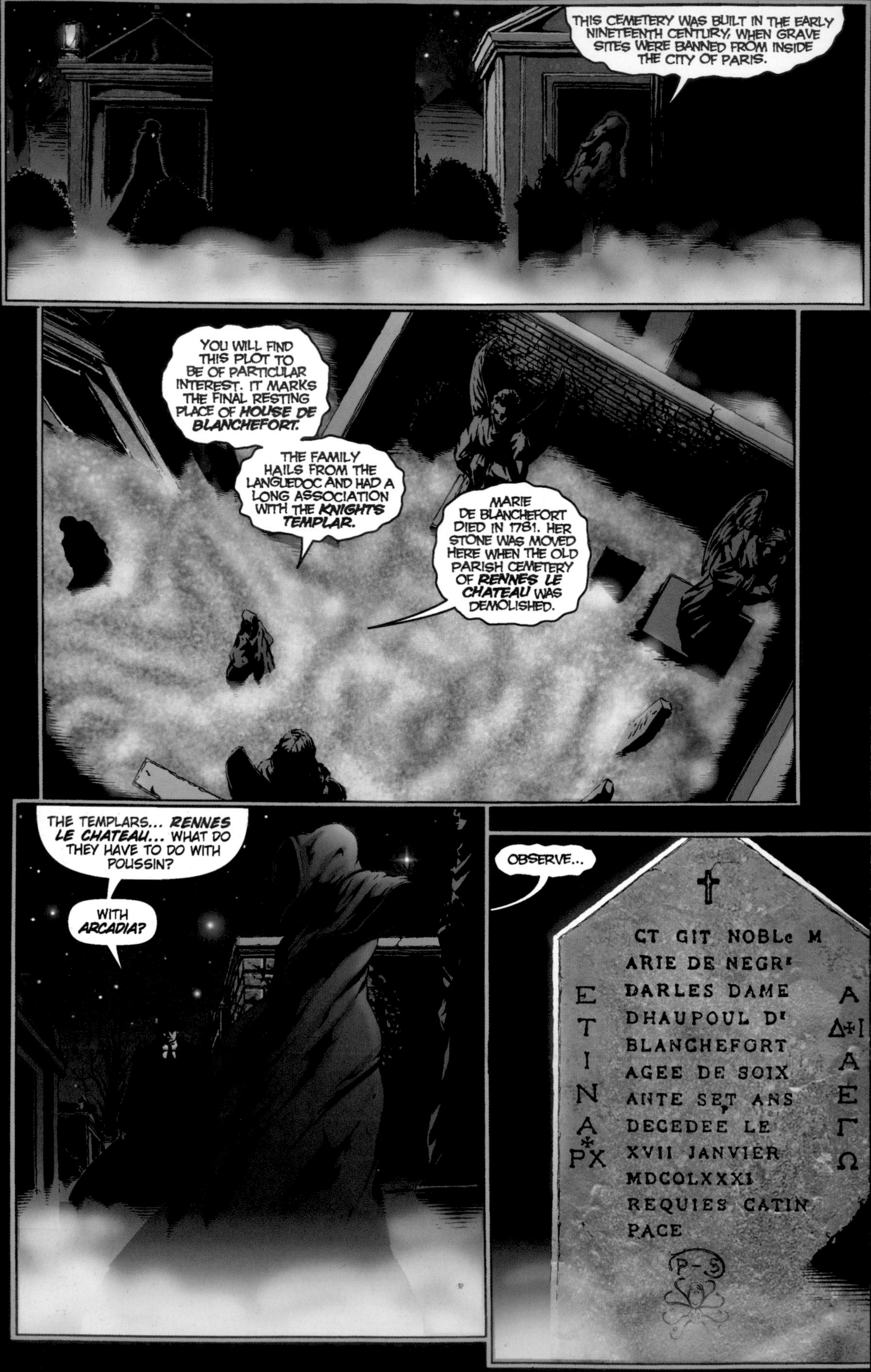
THIS CEMETERY WAS BUILT IN THE EARLY NINETEENTH CENTURY, WHEN GRAVE SITES WERE BANNED FROM INSIDE THE CITY OF PARIS.
YOU WILL FIND THIS PLOT TO BE OF PARTICULAR INTEREST. IT MARKS THE FINAL RESTING PLACE OF HOUSE DE BLANCHEFORT.
THE FAMILY HAILS FROM THE LANGUEDOC AND HAD A LONG ASSOCIATION WITH THE KNIGHTS TEMPLAR.
MARIE DE BLANCHEFORT DIED IN 1781. HER STONE WAS MOVED HERE WHEN THE OLD PARISH CEMETERY OF RENNES LE CHATEAU WAS DEMOLISHED.
THE TEMPLARS... RENNES LE CHATEAU... WHAT DO THEY HAVE TO DO WITH POUSSIN?
WITH ARCADIA?
OBSERVE...
CT GIT NOBLe M
ARIE DE NEGRE
DARLES DAME
DHAUPOUL DE
BLANCHEFORT
AGEE DE SOIX
ANTE SET ANS
DECEDEE LE
XVII JANVIER
MDCOLXXXI
REQUIES CATIN
PACE
P-S

HOUSE LORRAINE HAS ATTEMPTED TO SIEZE THE THRONE OF FRANCE MANY TIMES THROUGHOUT HISTORY.

"*KING PHILIP IV* DISCOVERED THE TRUE NATURE OF THE TEMPLARS AND PUT THEM TO THE STAKE IN 1307.

MOST OF THE KNIGHTS WERE IGNORANT OF THE PRIORY'S EXISTENCE, AND OF THE EXISTENCE OF THE GRAIL.

"THEY DIED BELIEVING THEIR ORDER WAS TRULY INNOCENT OF WITCHCRAFT OR PLOTTING AGAINST THE CROWN."

REQUIEM AETERNAM, DONA EIS DOMINE...

"AND KING PHILIP COULD NOT DESTROY THAT WHICH NEVER OFFICIALLY EXISTED-- *THE PRIORY ITSELF.*

IT TOOK THE PRIORY CENTURIES TO REGROUP FROM THE DISASTER. IT WOULD NOT BE READY TO STRIKE AGAIN FOR NEARLY 300 YEARS.

IN THE SIXTEENTH CENTURY THE HOUSES OF *LORRAINE* AND *GUISE,* A CADET BRANCH OF LORRAINE, ATTEMPTED TO TAKE THE THRONE.

"THEY WAGED A BRUTAL CAMPAIGN OF ASSASSINATION AND INTRIGUE AGAINST THE *VALOIS* KINGS.

"BUT BY THE TIME THE VALOIS WERE EXTINCT, HOUSE LORRAINE HAD BEEN SO DEPLETED BY POLITICAL MURDERS IT COULD NOT PRODUCE AN HEIR FOR THE THRONE.

THE GRAIL WAS RESPONSIBLE FOR THE DARKEST ATROCITIES OF THE *FRENCH REVOLUTION*.

"THE TURMOIL WAS INCITED BY A SECRET SOCIETY CALLED THE *FREEMASONS,* WHO WORKED IN SECRET FOR A CENTURY TO BRING THEIR REVOLUTION TO FRUITION.

"JUST AS THE TEMPLARS, THE MASONS WERE BUT AN EXTENSION OF THE *PRIORY OF SION.*

"THE REAL AIM OF THE REVOLUTION WAS NOT *LIBERTY, EQUALITY AND BROTHERHOOD* BUT THE INSTALLATION OF HOUSE LORRAINE ON THE THRONE OF FRANCE THROUGH THE ERADICATION OF THE BOURBON DYNASTY.

"BUT FOR ALL THEIR PLANNING, THE MASONS QUICKLY LOST CONTROL OF THE TERROR THEY SET LOOSE. MASS CHAOS AND MOB RULE ENSUED. MANY OF FRANCE'S BEST MILITARY OFFICERS DIED IN THE MADNESS.

"A YOUNG CORSICAN NAMED *NAPOLEON BONAPARTE* DIED OF TUBERCULOSIS WHILE IMPRISONED FOR CONTUMACY.

KEF KEF

"SION'S BID FOR POWER *FAILED.* ROYALIST TROOPS RESTORED THE HOUSE OF BOURBON, ALBEIT WITH THE FORMATION OF A CONSTITUTIONAL MONARCHY.

"THUS WERE BORN *THE HALL OF THE ROBE* AND *THE HALL OF THE SWORD,* THE TWO BODIES OF FRENCH PARLIAMENT."

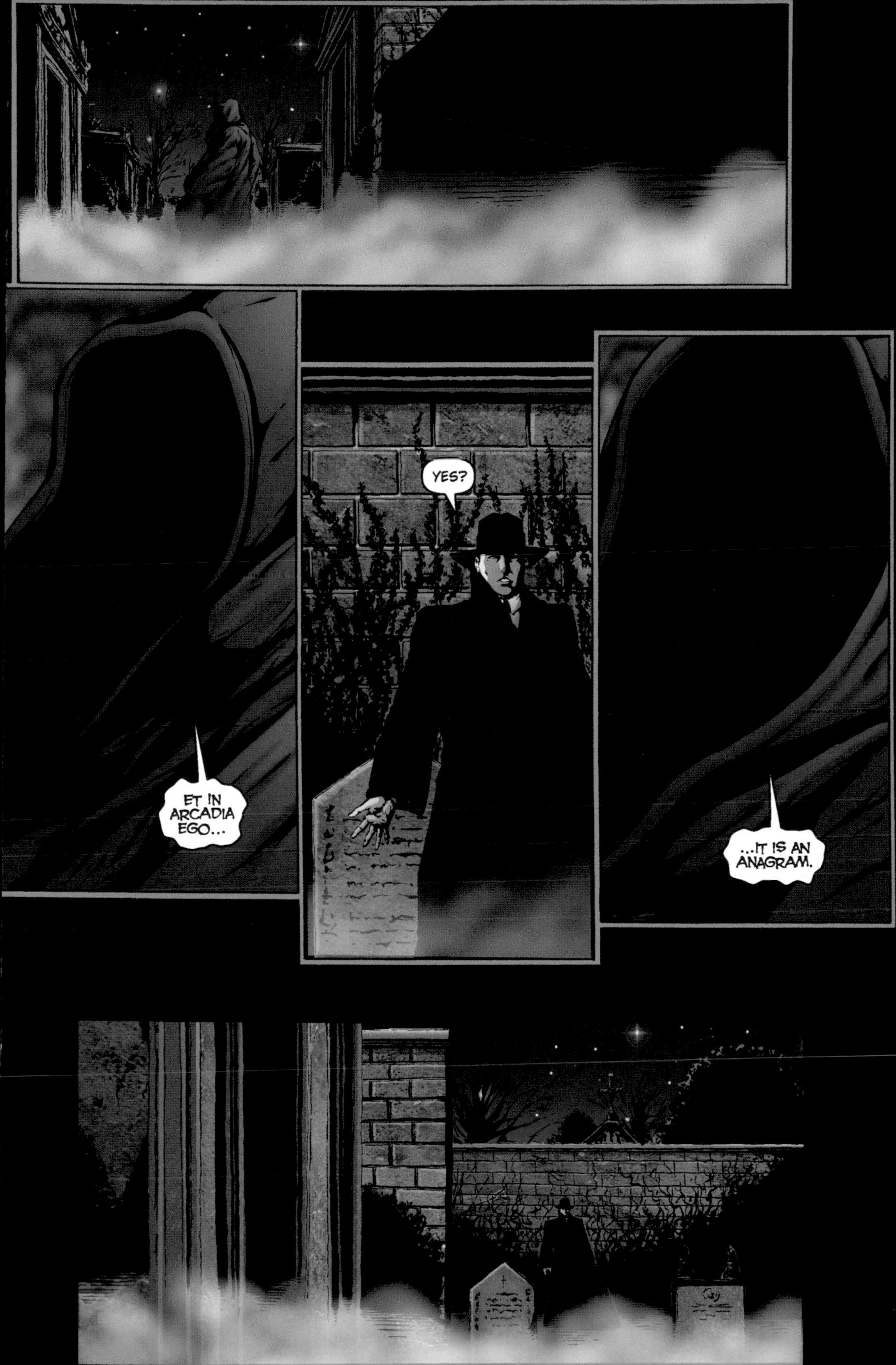
ET IN ARCADIA EGO...
YES?
...IT IS AN ANAGRAM.

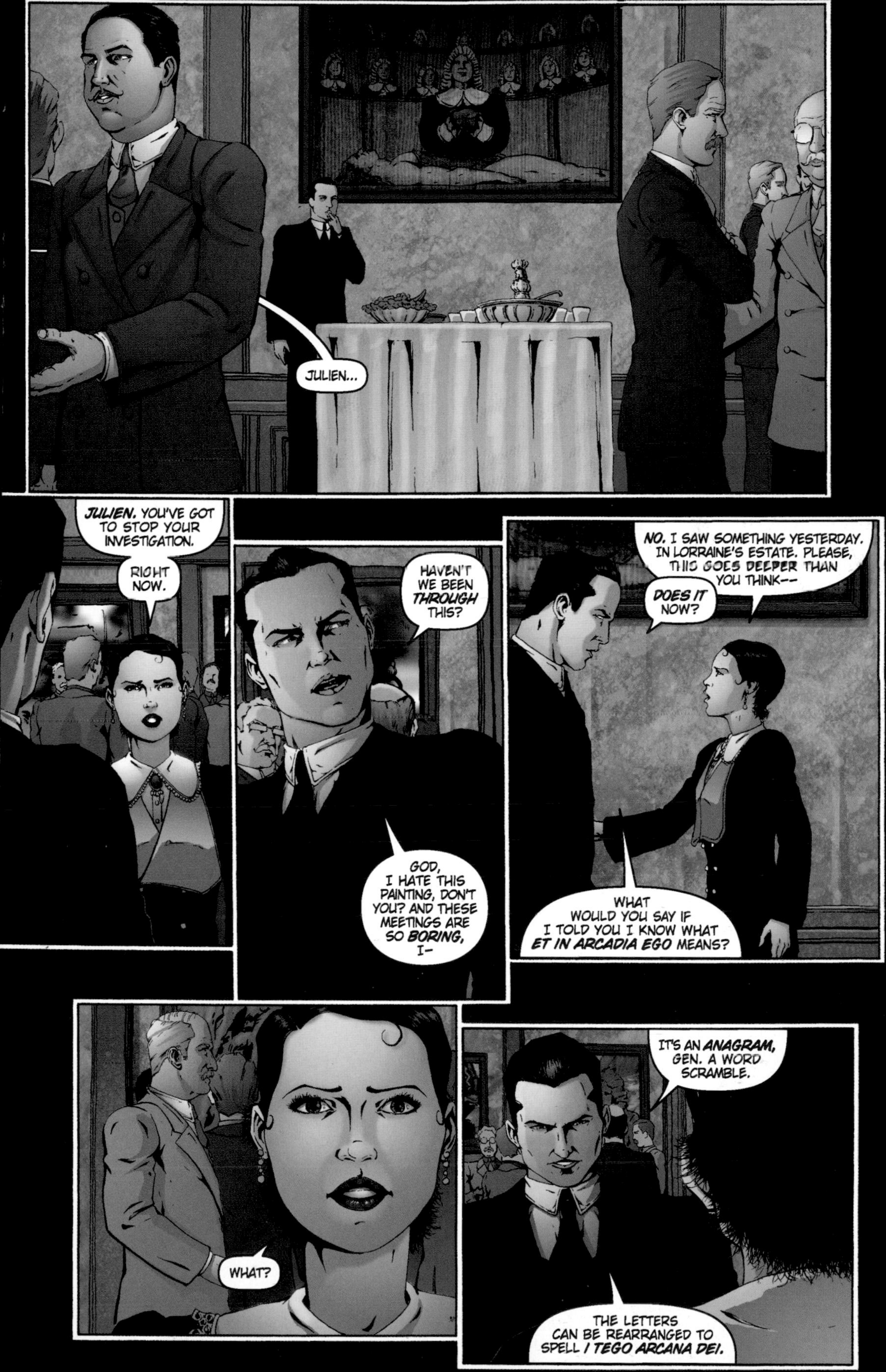

JULIEN...
JULIEN. YOU'VE GOT TO STOP YOUR INVESTIGATION.
RIGHT NOW.
HAVEN'T WE BEEN THROUGH THIS?
GOD, I HATE THIS PAINTING, DON'T YOU? AND THESE MEETINGS ARE SO BORING, I-
NO. I SAW SOMETHING YESTERDAY. IN LORRAINE'S ESTATE. PLEASE, THIS GOES DEEPER THAN YOU THINK--
DOES IT NOW?
WHAT WOULD YOU SAY IF I TOLD YOU I KNOW WHAT ET IN ARCADIA EGO MEANS?
WHAT?
IT'S AN ANAGRAM, GEN. A WORD SCRAMBLE.
THE LETTERS CAN BE REARRANGED TO SPELL I TEGO ARCANA DEI.

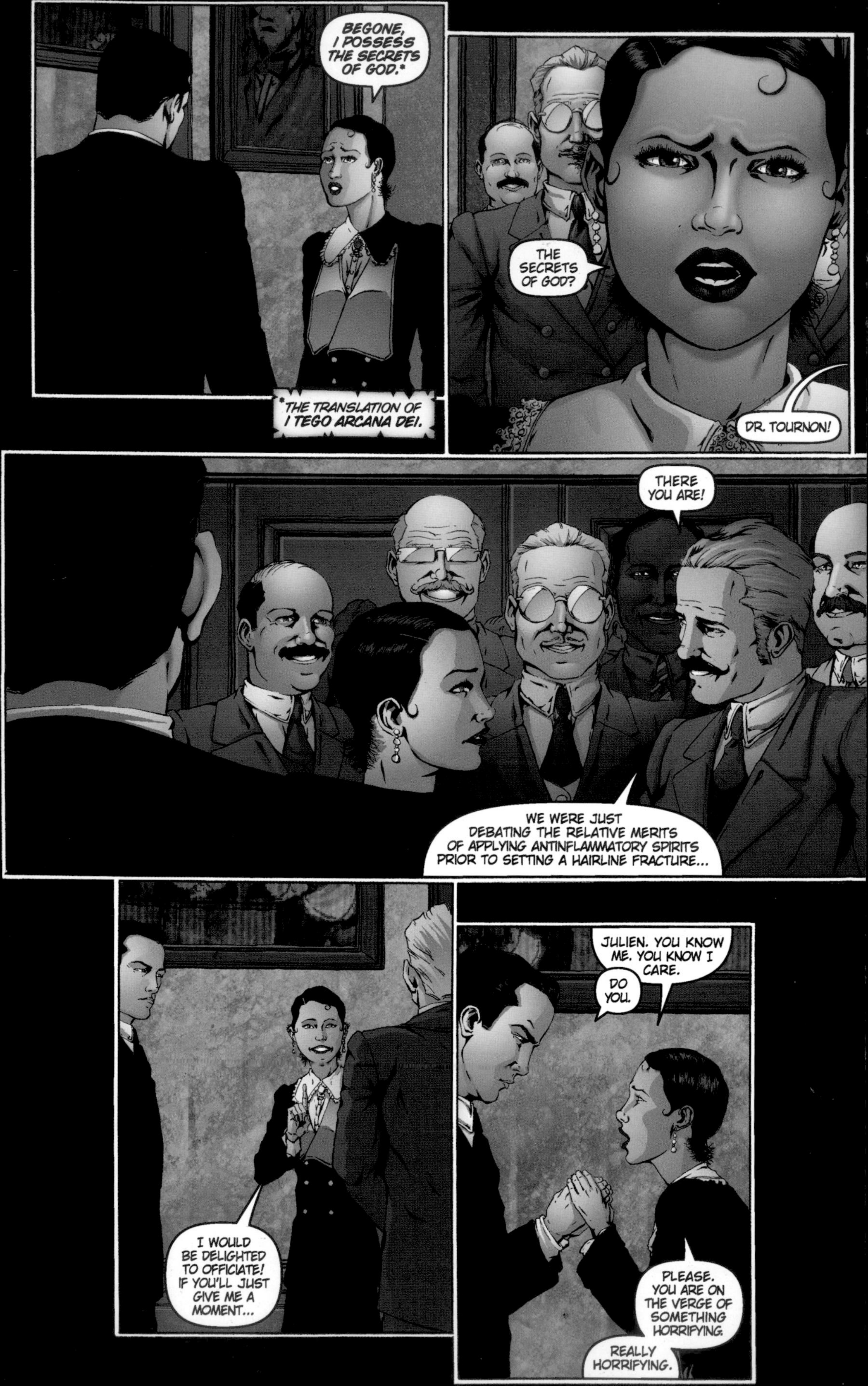
BEGONE, I POSSESS THE SECRETS OF GOD.*
*THE TRANSLATION OF I TEGO ARCANA DEI.
THE SECRETS OF GOD?
DR. TOURNON!
THERE YOU ARE!
WE WERE JUST DEBATING THE RELATIVE MERITS OF APPLYING ANTINFLAMMATORY SPIRITS PRIOR TO SETTING A HAIRLINE FRACTURE...
I WOULD BE DELIGHTED TO OFFICIATE! IF YOU'LL JUST GIVE ME A MOMENT...
JULIEN. YOU KNOW ME. YOU KNOW I CARE.
DO YOU.
PLEASE. YOU ARE ON THE VERGE OF SOMETHING HORRIFYING.
REALLY HORRIFYING.

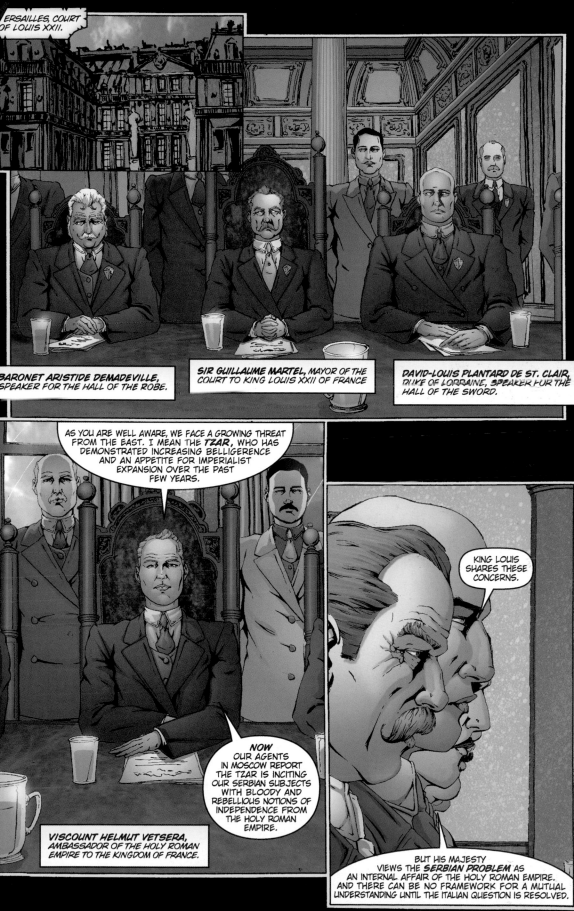

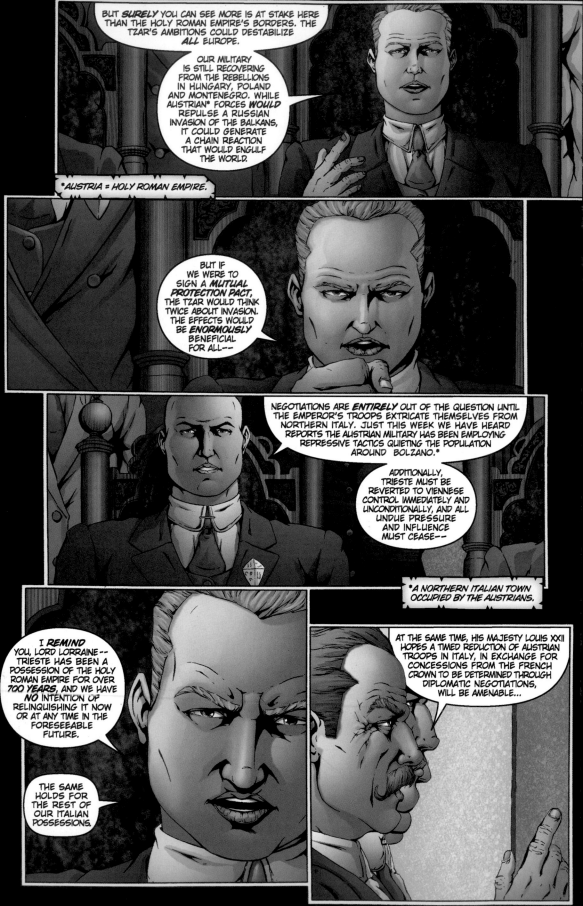

BUT **SURELY** YOU CAN SEE MORE IS AT STAKE HERE THAN THE HOLY ROMAN EMPIRE'S BORDERS. THE TZAR'S AMBITIONS COULD DESTABILIZE **ALL** EUROPE.

OUR MILITARY IS STILL RECOVERING FROM THE REBELLIONS IN HUNGARY, POLAND AND MONTENEGRO. WHILE AUSTRIAN* FORCES **WOULD** REPULSE A RUSSIAN INVASION OF THE BALKANS, IT COULD GENERATE A CHAIN REACTION THAT WOULD ENGULF THE WORLD.

*AUSTRIA = HOLY ROMAN EMPIRE.

BUT IF WE WERE TO SIGN A **MUTUAL PROTECTION PACT**, THE TZAR WOULD THINK TWICE ABOUT INVASION. THE EFFECTS WOULD BE **ENORMOUSLY** BENEFICIAL FOR ALL--

NEGOTIATIONS ARE **ENTIRELY** OUT OF THE QUESTION UNTIL THE EMPEROR'S TROOPS EXTRICATE THEMSELVES FROM NORTHERN ITALY. JUST THIS WEEK WE HAVE HEARD REPORTS THE AUSTRIAN MILITARY HAS BEEN EMPLOYING REPRESSIVE TACTICS QUIETING THE POPULATION AROUND BOLZANO.*

ADDITIONALLY, TRIESTE MUST BE REVERTED TO VIENNESE CONTROL IMMEDIATELY AND UNCONDITIONALLY, AND ALL UNDUE PRESSURE AND INFLUENCE MUST CEASE--

*A NORTHERN ITALIAN TOWN OCCUPIED BY THE AUSTRIANS.

I **REMIND** YOU, LORD LORRAINE-- TRIESTE HAS BEEN A POSSESSION OF THE HOLY ROMAN EMPIRE FOR OVER **700 YEARS**, AND WE HAVE **NO** INTENTION OF RELINQUISHING IT NOW OR AT ANY TIME IN THE FORESEEABLE FUTURE.

THE SAME HOLDS FOR THE REST OF OUR ITALIAN POSSESSIONS.

AT THE SAME TIME, HIS MAJESTY LOUIS XXII HOPES A TIMED REDUCTION OF AUSTRIAN TROOPS IN ITALY, IN EXCHANGE FOR CONCESSIONS FROM THE FRENCH CROWN TO BE DETERMINED THROUGH DIPLOMATIC NEGOTIATIONS, WILL BE AMENABLE...

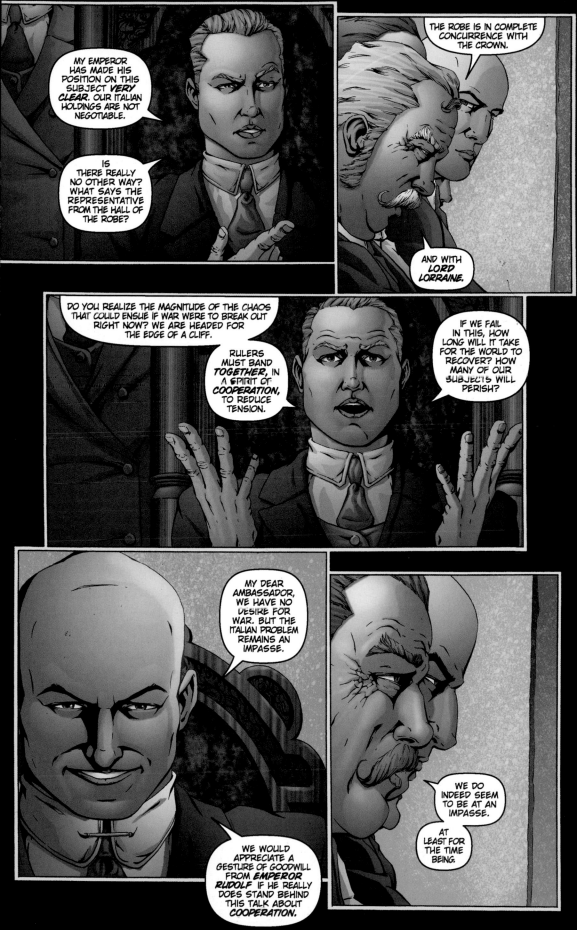

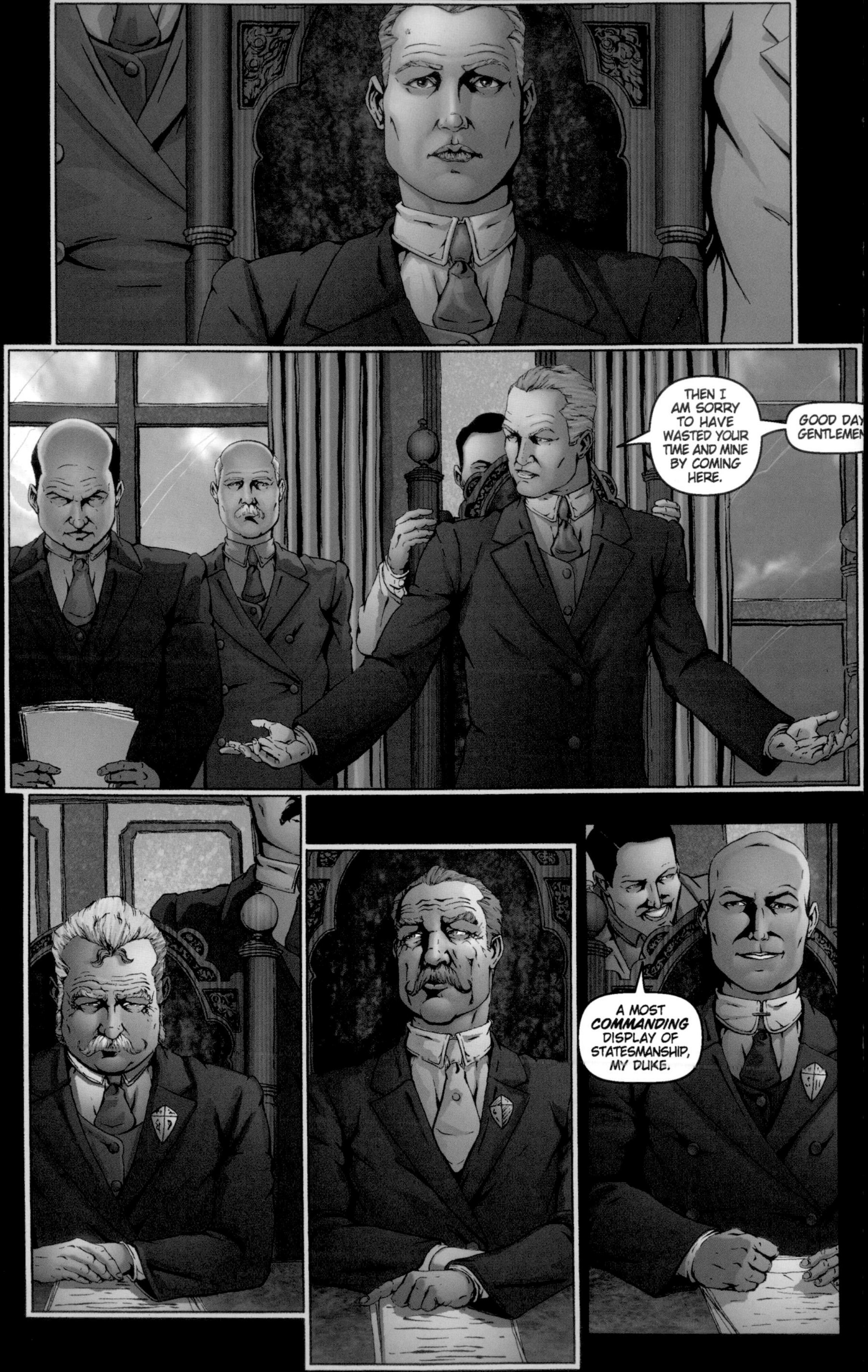
THEN I AM SORRY TO HAVE WASTED YOUR TIME AND MINE BY COMING HERE.
GOOD DAY GENTLEMEN
A MOST *COMMANDING* DISPLAY OF STATESMANSHIP, MY DUKE.

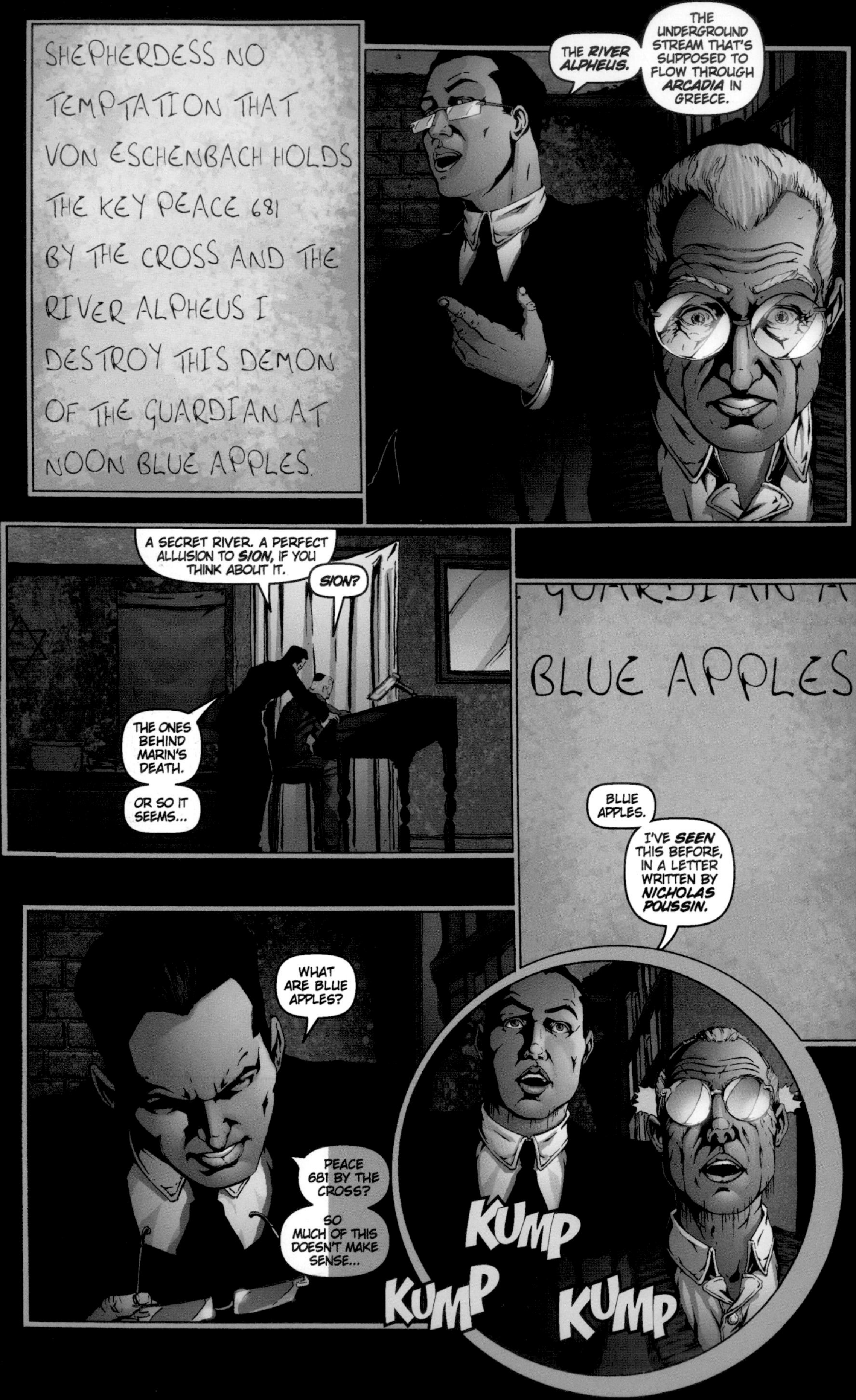

SHEPHERDESS NO TEMPTATION THAT VON ESCHENBACH HOLDS THE KEY PEACE 681 BY THE CROSS AND THE RIVER ALPHEUS I DESTROY THIS DEMON OF THE GUARDIAN AT NOON BLUE APPLES.
THE RIVER ALPHEUS.
THE UNDERGROUND STREAM THAT'S SUPPOSED TO FLOW THROUGH ARCADIA IN GREECE.
A SECRET RIVER. A PERFECT ALLUSION TO SION, IF YOU THINK ABOUT IT.
SION?
THE ONES BEHIND MARIN'S DEATH.
OR SO IT SEEMS...
BLUE APPLES
BLUE APPLES.
I'VE SEEN THIS BEFORE, IN A LETTER WRITTEN BY NICHOLAS POUSSIN.
WHAT ARE BLUE APPLES?
PEACE 681 BY THE CROSS?
SO MUCH OF THIS DOESN'T MAKE SENSE...
KUMP
KUMP
KUMP

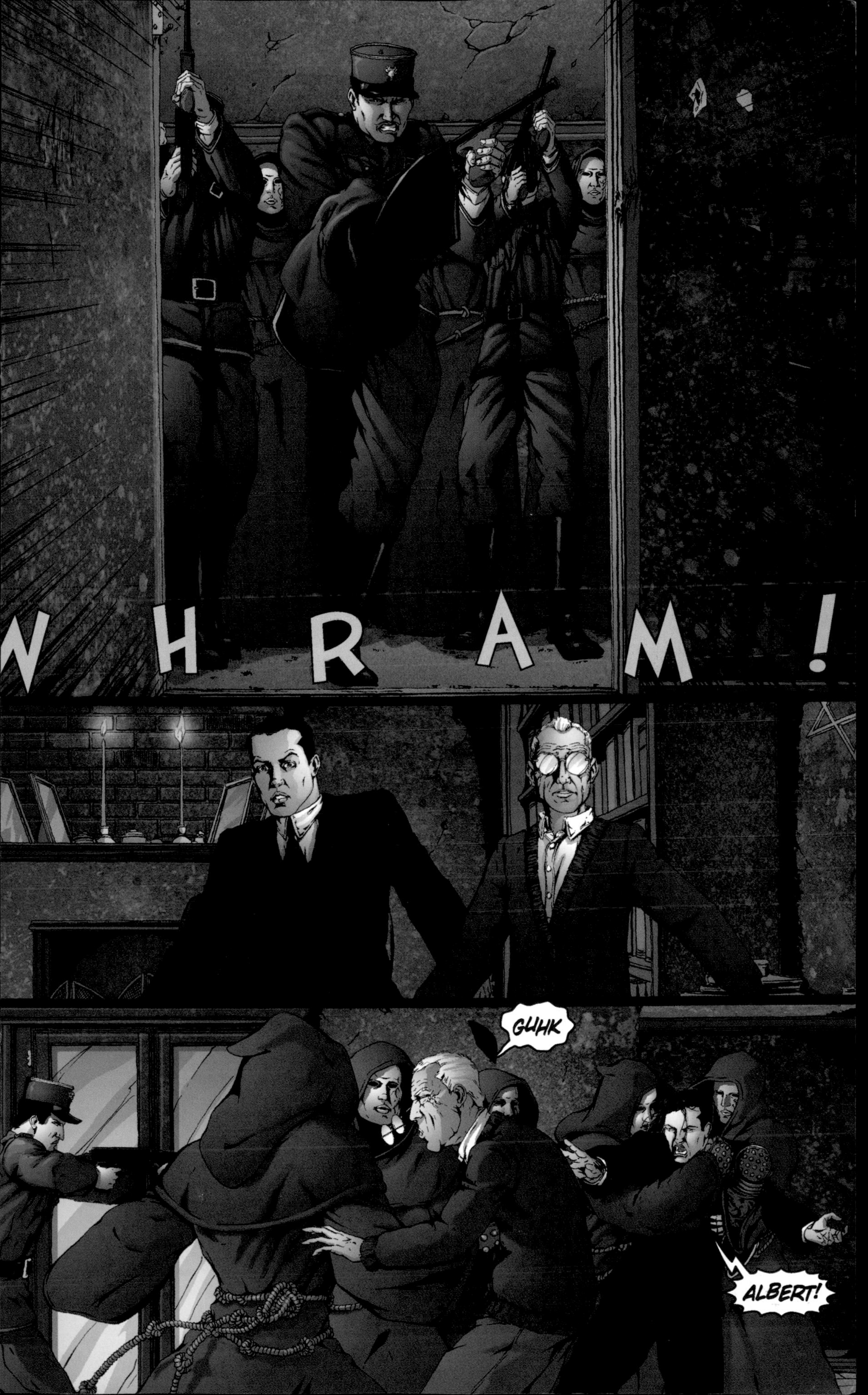
WHRAM!
GUHK
ALBERT!

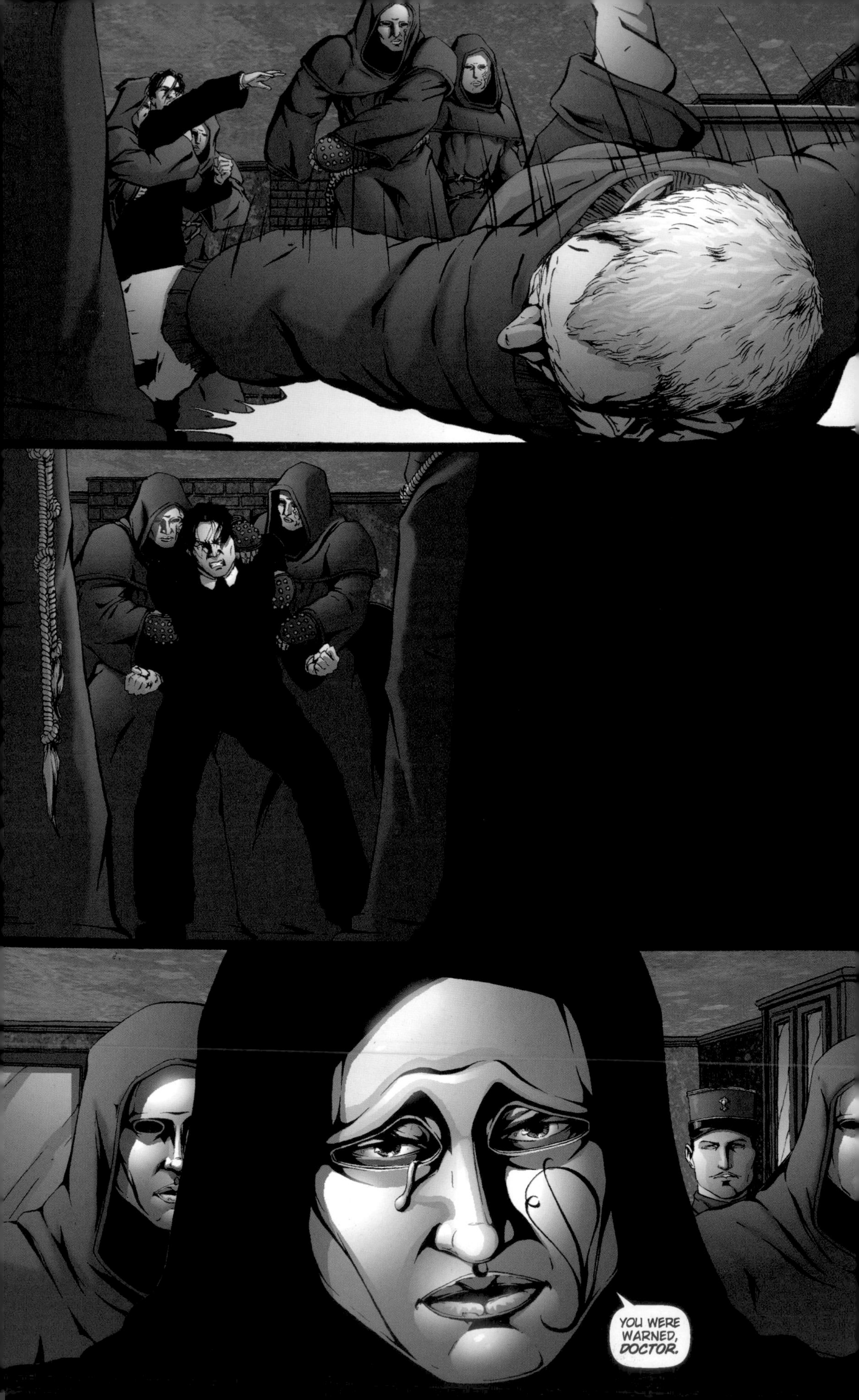
YOU WERE WARNED, DOCTOR.

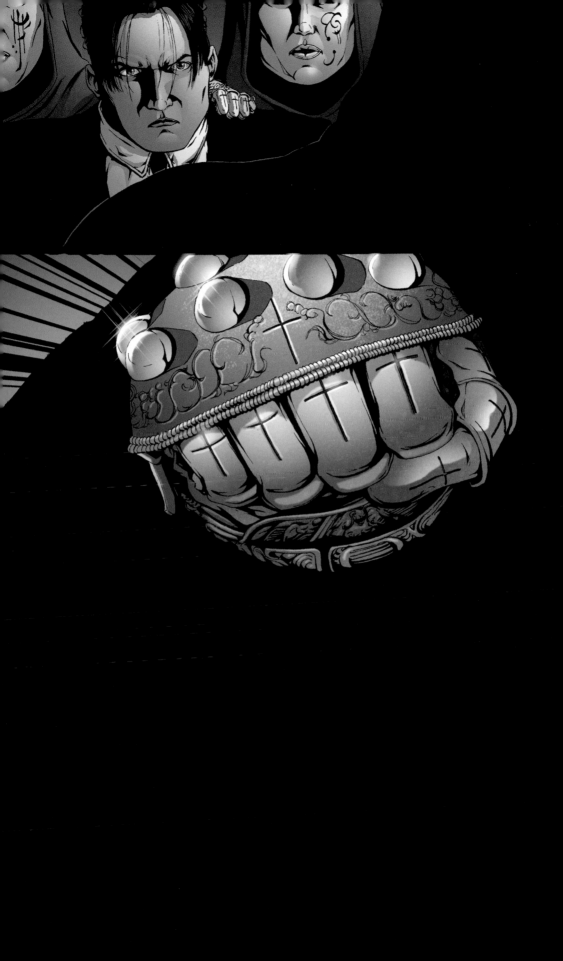

Le Journal de la Libert

Paris's leading anglophone newspaper • vol. 205, no. 97 • Oct. 27, MCMXXXIII

Editors in Chief: M. Tait Bergstrom, M. Matthew Pasteris. **Story Editor:** M. Arvid Nelson. **Art Editors:** M. EricJ, M. Jeromy Cox. **Photography Editor:** M. Alexander Waldman. **Layout Supervisor:** M. William Kartalopoulos. **Editors Emeritus:** M. Clark A. Smith, M. Howard P. Lovecraft, M. Robert E. Howard. Redacted by the Holy Parisian Inquisition under the direction of His Excellency Archbishop Emile-Jean Ireneaux. Le Journal de Liberté is printed under the benign auspices of his most puissant majesty KING LOUIS XXII of FRANCE.

GOD SAVE THE KING.

Papal Seal

of Approv

SUPPORT FOR KING'S POLICIES ERODING IN PARLIAMENT

King's advisors express concern, dismay over recent defections in Hall of the Robe but remain confident

Versailles, Paris – The rank-and-file members of the Hall of the Robe, Louis XXII's bastion of support, continue to defect to Lord Lorraine, the crown's most vocal opponent.

Publicly, the crown's spokesmen remain dismissive. But private anxieties over the king's evaporating political base are surfacing.

"I think it's safe to say we're looking at a trend now," said a member of Louis's court. "It's impossible to say what the effect will be, but it's a cause of some concern."

The political shake-up started earlier this week, when Baron Aristide deMandeville, leading member of the Hall of the Sword and the King's close ally, announced a dramatic policy reversal.

While he once condemned Lord Lorraine's policies and "warmongering and myopic," deMandeville now calls Lorraine's

aggressive foreign stance "a clarion call for the French Kingdom."

"France had only two options, global supremacy or abject servitude as an Arab or German satrapy," deMandeville said in his floor speech announcing his changed intentions four days ago. DeMandeville has not been available for comment since his abrupt shift.

"Baron deMandeville is entitled to his opinions, but King Louis find his reversal most dishonorable," crown spokesman Sir Jean Dasté said.

"We welcome any addition to our ranks," Baron Robert Teniers, a spokesman for the Duke of Lorraine, said. "It's occurring to more and more people that the path to security for France lies in strength, not weakness."

Whatever his reasons, deMandeville's disavowal of the King has triggered a small but

growing number of defections in the Hall of the Robe. Such a move would have been unthinkable before. So far, a dozen Robe members have changed allegiances.

"DeMandeville gave courage to those of us in the Robe who were uncomfortable with the King's policies," junior Robe member and recent defector Count Ralph Perou Weigand said.

Yesterday, this newfound independence was felt dramatically when the Robe voted against the King's wishes on a bill – the first time since its inception in 1802.

While the king has the powe appoint members to the Hall of Robe, under France's constitut only the Robe may expel its ow

"I can't see the Robe voting a member because of this, at l not for the time being. But if th get much worse, action might taken," loyalist Robe member J Claude Dhien said. The King v have the last word on the subj according to him.

"Let's not forget the majo of the Robe still supports the K We will consult him on any is concerning His kingdom."

Versailles, Court of Louis XXII. The tranquility of the gardens belies growi turmoil as King Louis faces an insurrection in Parliament.

FRA President Franklin Delano Roosevelt Announces Detention of Alleged English Spies; Edward VIII Expresses "Outrage"

Washington, DC, FRA – Five British nationals have been detained by Bureau of Investigation (BOI) agents on charges they illegally obtained "top secret information vital to the security of the Federal Republic of America," according to BOI spokesman J. Edgar Hoover.

The men, whose identities have not been released, allegedly worked through the British Embassy in Washington, D.C.

President Roosevelt announced the arrests jointly with Hoover in a press conference on the White House Lawn yesterday afternoon.

Roosevelt praised Hoover for his diligence in tracking down "foreign nationals who seek to compromise the safety of American citizens."

"It is no secret that a vast network of underground English royalists is at work in Washington, trying to undermine the very fabric of our societal values," Hoover said.

He would not comment on the nature of the secrets allegedly stolen, save to say that the arrests concern "fortifications and defenses on the Mason-Dixon line."

The Mason-Dixon line separates the Federal Republic of America and the Confederate States of America. Each side is wary of a surprise invasion by the other.

"We have sent a clear message to the Confederates and their allies: their attempts to undermine our way of life will fail," Roosevelt said.

The English crown was quick to condemn the move.

"These charges are scurrilous
continued on page A13

High-Level French Officials to Discuss Territoria Disputes, Instability with Austrian Ambassador

Versailles, Paris – Relations between the Holy Roman Empire and France have been frosty for several generations. However, a shift towards friendlier footing may be imminent.

In a potentially historic gesture, Austrian Ambassador Viscount Helmut Von Vetsera has extended an invitation to the French political establishment, hoping, in his words, "to establish a mutual framework of trust and cooperation."

In attendance at the talks scheduled for today will be Vetsera himself, Lord Lorraine, Speaker for the Sword, the King's spokesman Sir Charles Martel, and Baron Aristide deMandeville, Speaker for the Robe.

Lorraine is openly mistrustful of the Austrians, a fact reflected in his voting record, while Martel is a

strong advocate of greater coope tion amongst Christian monarch

Attention is therefore focu on Lord deMandeville, who di theatrical about-face on the fl of the Hall of the Robe four d ago. Once a staunch ally of K Louis, he declared support Lord Lorraine, his former polit arch-rival.

"It mystified a lot of people member of the Hall of the Sw said. "So this is a touchstone for recent change of heart. We'll se he means it or not."

Security and international s bility are expected to be high Ambassador Vetsera's agenda. recent years, the Austrian army been severely strained suppress rebellions in its outlying provin It now faces external threats fr
continued on page

E JOURNAL SPECIAL: The Holy Roman Empire

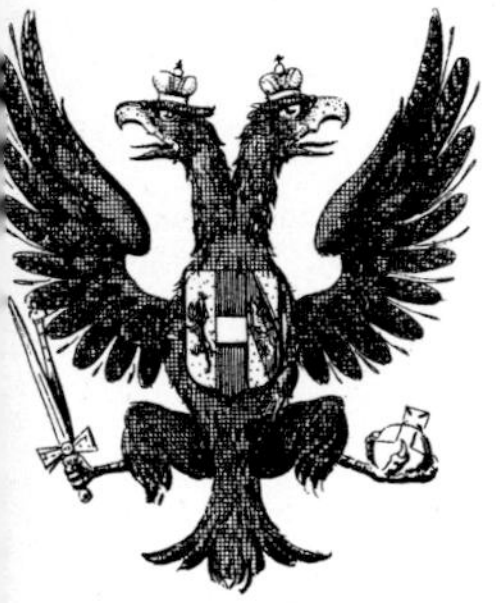

e two-headed eagle, symbol of Holy Roman Empire and the bsburg dynasty.

he Holy Roman Empire (HRE) is one of the oldest despotisms in inuous existence. Although the bsburgs have had a firm grip on this wling, polyglot empire for over t hundred years, recent events have many wondering about its future. his special section of Le Journal de iberté, *we take a look at the his- of the HRE, at its current state of irs, and what it all means to the rage Parisian citizen.*

Origins of the Empire

Voltaire famously said the HRE neither Holy, nor Roman, nor Empire." A more common name the Habsburg domains is the *stro-Hungarian Empire*, since the most prominent ethnic popu- ons of the empire, the Magyars Hungary and the Germans of stria, are its virtual masters.

The name "Holy Roman pire" was coined during the gn of Charlemagne, crowned ovus Constantinus" by Pope II in the year 800 AD. arlemagne was seen as a new ristian Emperor in the tradition Constantine the Great, and the ellation Holy Roman Empire med an appropriate description his lands.

The character and dimensions the HRE have changed since dieval times, but the Habsburg nasty, considered the heirs to arlemagne's legacy, have provid- a thread of continuity through- the empire's turbulent history.

House of Habsburg-Lothringen

The venerable House of bsburg-Lothringen has an illus- ous past. "Their pedigree has duced more monarchs than any er," according to Sir Jean-Marc ayette, Royal Herald of the nch College of Arms.

Over the years, the Habsburgs have ceded some political power to provincial councils and the *Reichsrat*, the national legislative council.

But none should question who really commands the empire.

"Control over military and foreign affairs is the sole domain of the Emperor," Viscount Helmut Von Vetsera, Ambassador of the Holy Roman Empire to the Kingdom of France, said.

Emperor Rudolf: The Prodigal Son

Rudolf von Habsburg-Lothringen is the current Emperor. He was unusually old before he ascended to the throne; his father Franz-Josef took the title at the age of eighteen. Rudolf was obliged to wait to wait until his father abdicated in 1906. He was 64 years old at the time.

The Emperor had a difficult relationship with his father; Franz Josef was strictly conservative, while young Rudolf was liberally minded. Rumors abounded that the young Rudolph, then an archduke, tried to kill himself in 1889 at an imperial hunting lodge in Mayerling, Austria.

However, Rudolf's anticlerical and anti-social opinions mellowed later on in life, and now he champions the causes closest to his late father's heart.

"...Nor an Empire"

Although the Habsburgs consider themselves German Emperors, their subjects include Ukrainians, Poles, Italians, Roumanians, Slavs, Magyars, Ruthenes, and Bohemians, to name a few. This mixture of ethnicities is "extremely volatile," according to Lord Vetsera.

The many ethnic groups of the empire are prone to unrest and outright rebellion when they feel the yoke of Habsburg rule is too heavy.

"Our Emperor must carefully balance the concerns of all His subjects. Granting too much freedom to one minority may cause resentment amongst others," Vestera said. "But at its core, the Holy Roman Empire is a German Empire. This is what provides us with stability."

Some believe this attitude of German superiority actually adds to the chronic unrest within the Empire. Not all the Emperor's subjects are happy to be ruled by what they consider a foreign power.

"It's simply not tenable," Hall of the Robe member Sir Jean-Paul Gartier said. "Emperor Rudolf's father nearly caused a civil war by announcing he would be coronated King of Bohemia. Rudolf won't dare make the same mistake. And they have made so many recent concessions to the Hungarians that the other minorities are extremely unhappy."

According to some, the divisions amongst the myriad ethnic groups can be considered an asset to the Emperor.

"They bicker intensely with one another, so there's no impetus for a collective movement against the Habsburgs," said a source within the Imperial Ministry of State.

Indeed, politics in the empire are a noisy, contentious affair. Members of the Reichsrat are even known to bang on drums and blast trumpets during the speeches of opposition party members.

But no one argues the revolutionary, nationalist tendencies amongst the HRE's subjects promote the empire's stability.

The Keystone of Europe

"Our internal differences are a natural result of geography. We are at the crossroads of the world," Baron Lajos Ferenczy, a member of the Hungarian Parliament, said. "To our east lie the Ottomans. To the north, Russia, and to the west Italy and Prussia. This is why the two-headed eagle is our symbol: we must be vigilant in all directions."

Tension electrifies every one of the HRE's frontiers. Serbian nationalists in the east are widely believed to have the support of Tzar Nicholas II. To the west, the Austrian occupation of northern Italy engenders ill will amongst the monarchs of France and England, particularly in regard to Adriatic port of Trieste.

Austro-Hungarian officials see this disharmony as a direct threat to the whole of Europe.

"We are the keystone of Europe," Ambassador Vetsera said. "We are the Christian vanguard against the Mohammedan threat of the Turks. If we fall, so does all Europe." Charles Martel, mayor of the court to King Louis XXII, is inclined to agree.

"Austria-Hungary must not be allowed to disintegrate, or all the nations of Europe risk exposing themselves to a conflict beyond anyone's power to contain. The time has never been more critical."

But a growing chorus of French politicians disagree with this point of view.

"The problems faced by Austria-Hungary are of its own making," Lord Lorraine, Speaker for the Hall of the Sword, said. "We cannot be held accountable for their bad management."

Whatever the case, most agree the Holy Roman Empire is in a position of unprecedented weakness.

"Over the last decade, the Austrian army has been sorely taxed suppressing rebellions in Croatia, Galicia and Hungary. We came close to the precipice, and we're only inching away very slowly," a source within the Hofburg palace said. "One sharp tug could send the Holy Roman Empire over the edge."

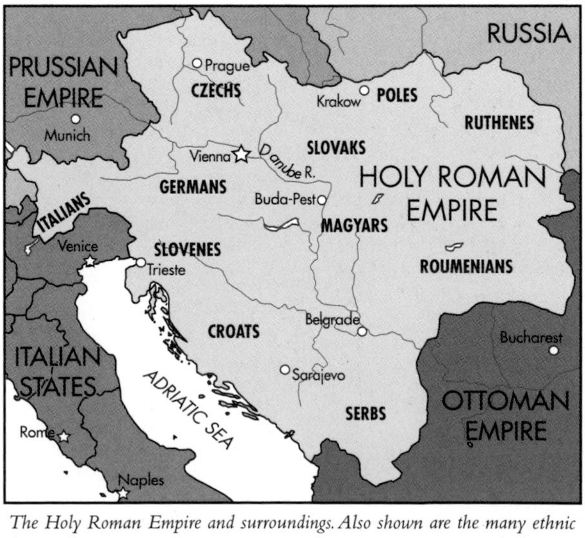
RUSSIA
PRUSSIAN EMPIRE
Prague
CZECHS
Krakow
POLES
RUTHENES
Munich
SLOVAKS
Vienna
Danube R.
HOLY ROMAN EMPIRE
GERMANS
Buda-Pest
MAGYARS
ITALIANS
Venice
SLOVENES
Trieste
ROUMENIANS
Belgrade
CROATS
Bucharest
ITALIAN STATES
Sarajevo
ADRIATIC SEA
SERBS
OTTOMAN EMPIRE
Rome
Naples

The Holy Roman Empire and surroundings. Also shown are the many ethnic groups within the Empire. "A volatile mix," according to Ambassador Vetsera.

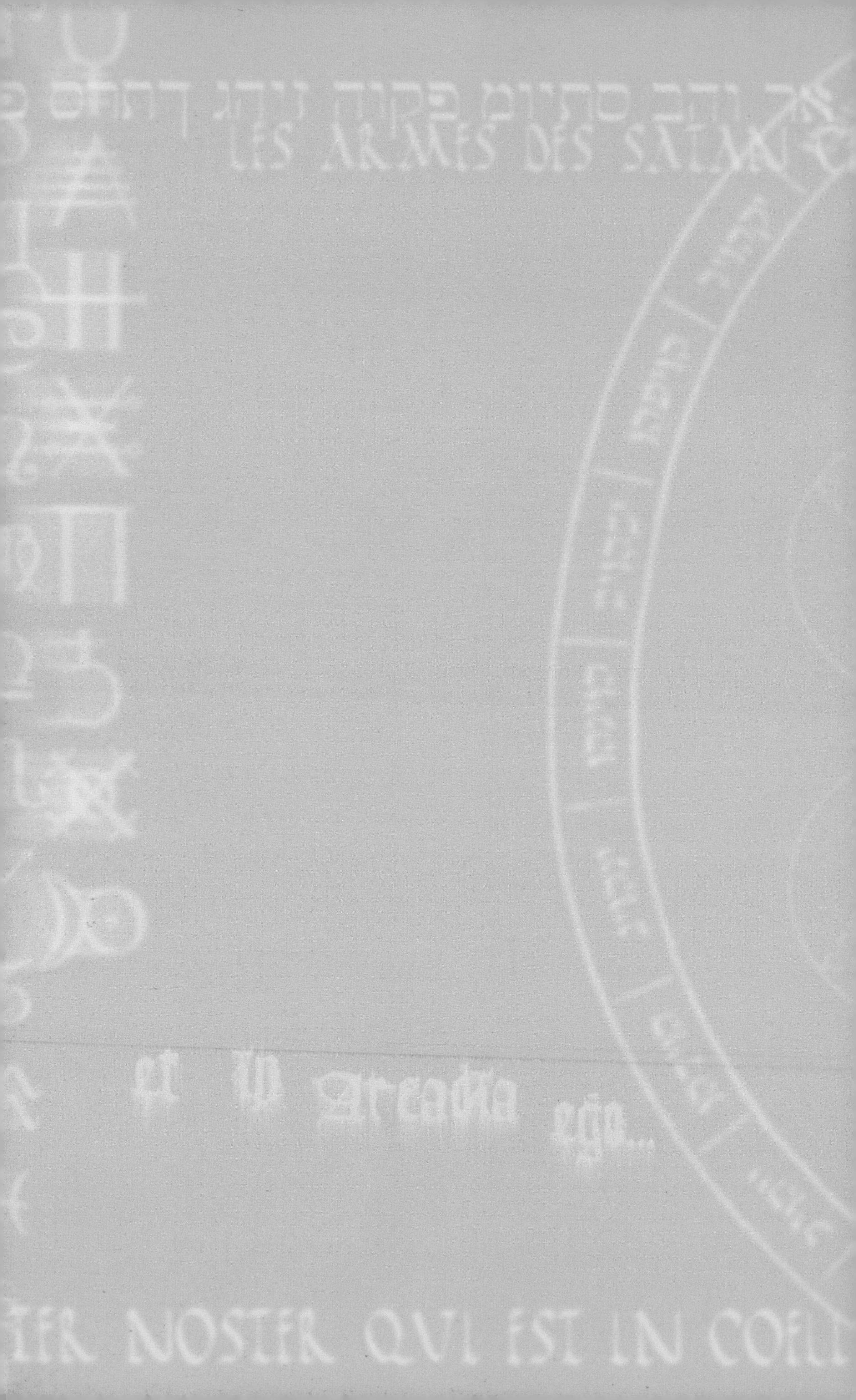
LES ARMES DES SATAN
et in Arcadia ego...
TER NOSTER QVI EST IN COELI

CHAPTER SIX
THE TREASURE OF THE TEMPLE

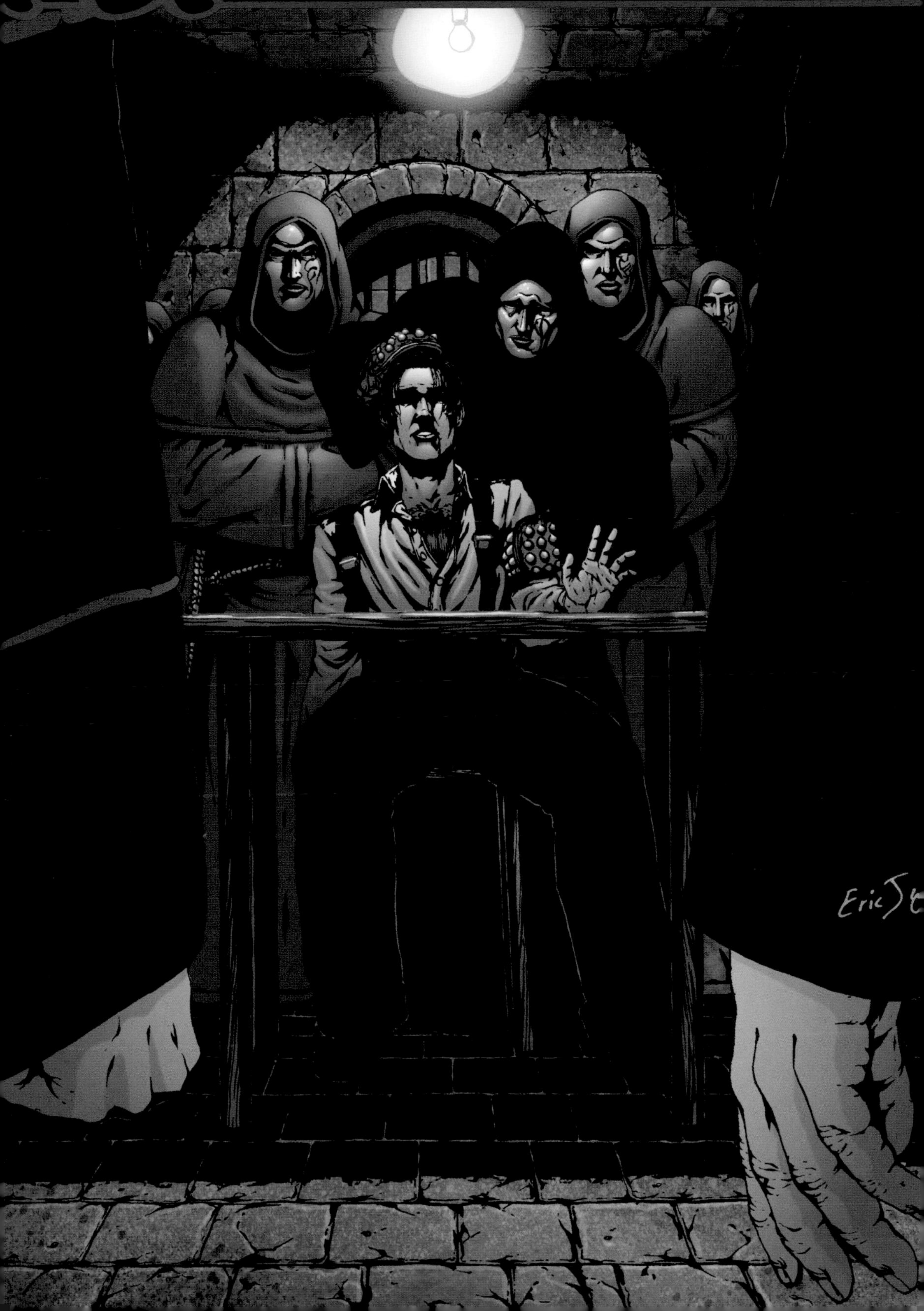

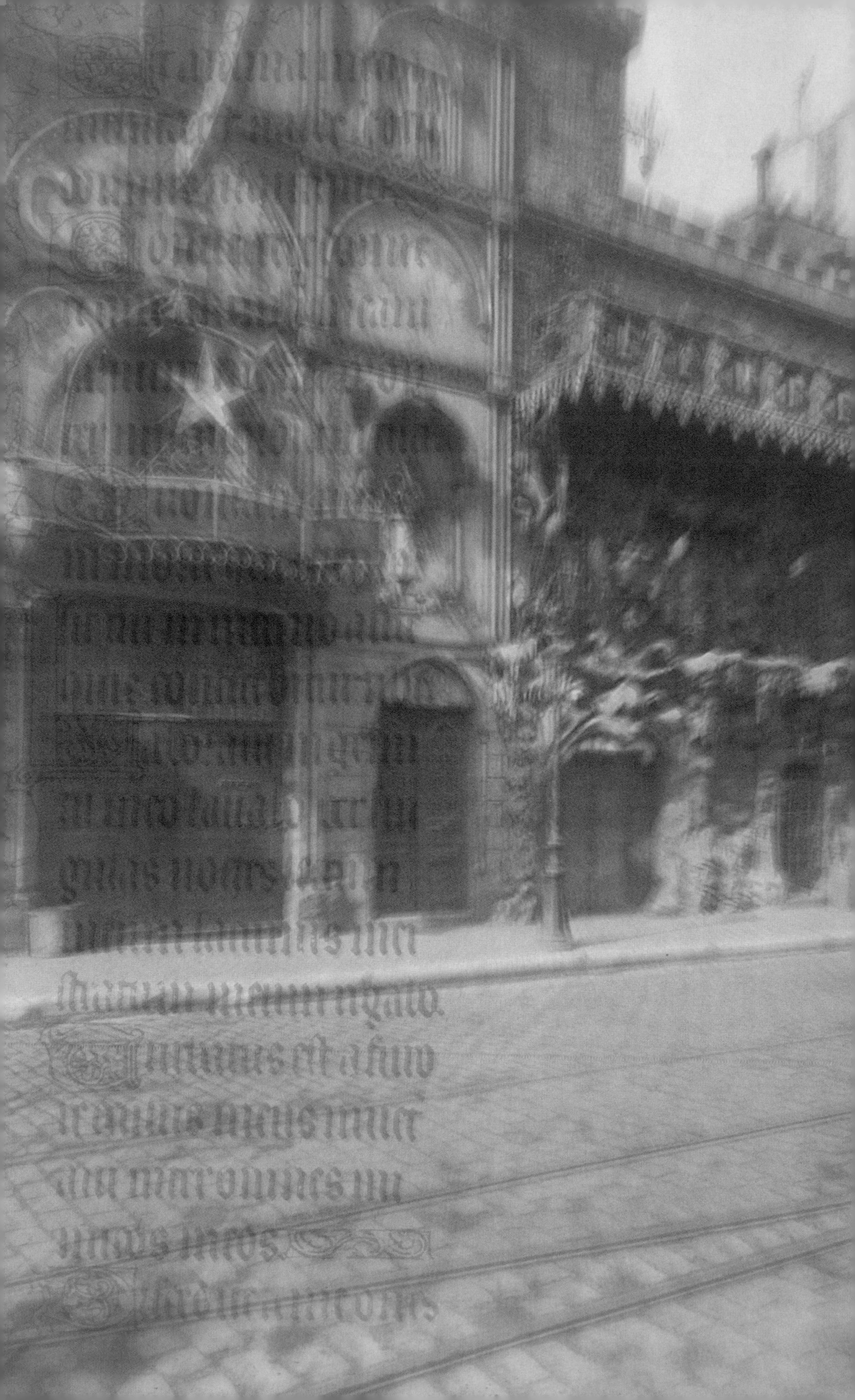

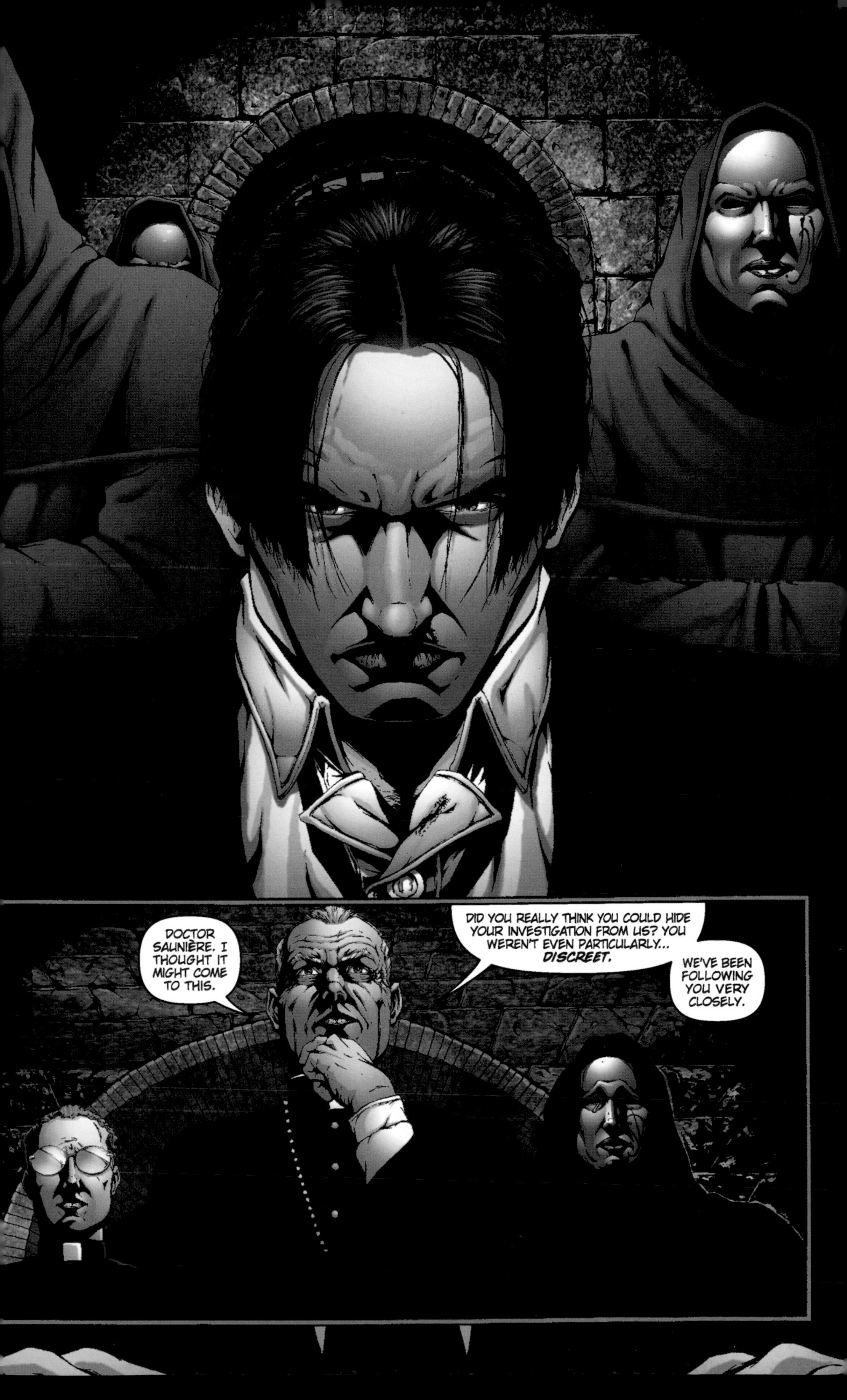
DOCTOR SAUNIÈRE. I THOUGHT IT MIGHT COME TO THIS.
DID YOU REALLY THINK YOU COULD HIDE YOUR INVESTIGATION FROM US? YOU WEREN'T EVEN PARTICULARLY... DISCREET.
WE'VE BEEN FOLLOWING YOU VERY CLOSELY.

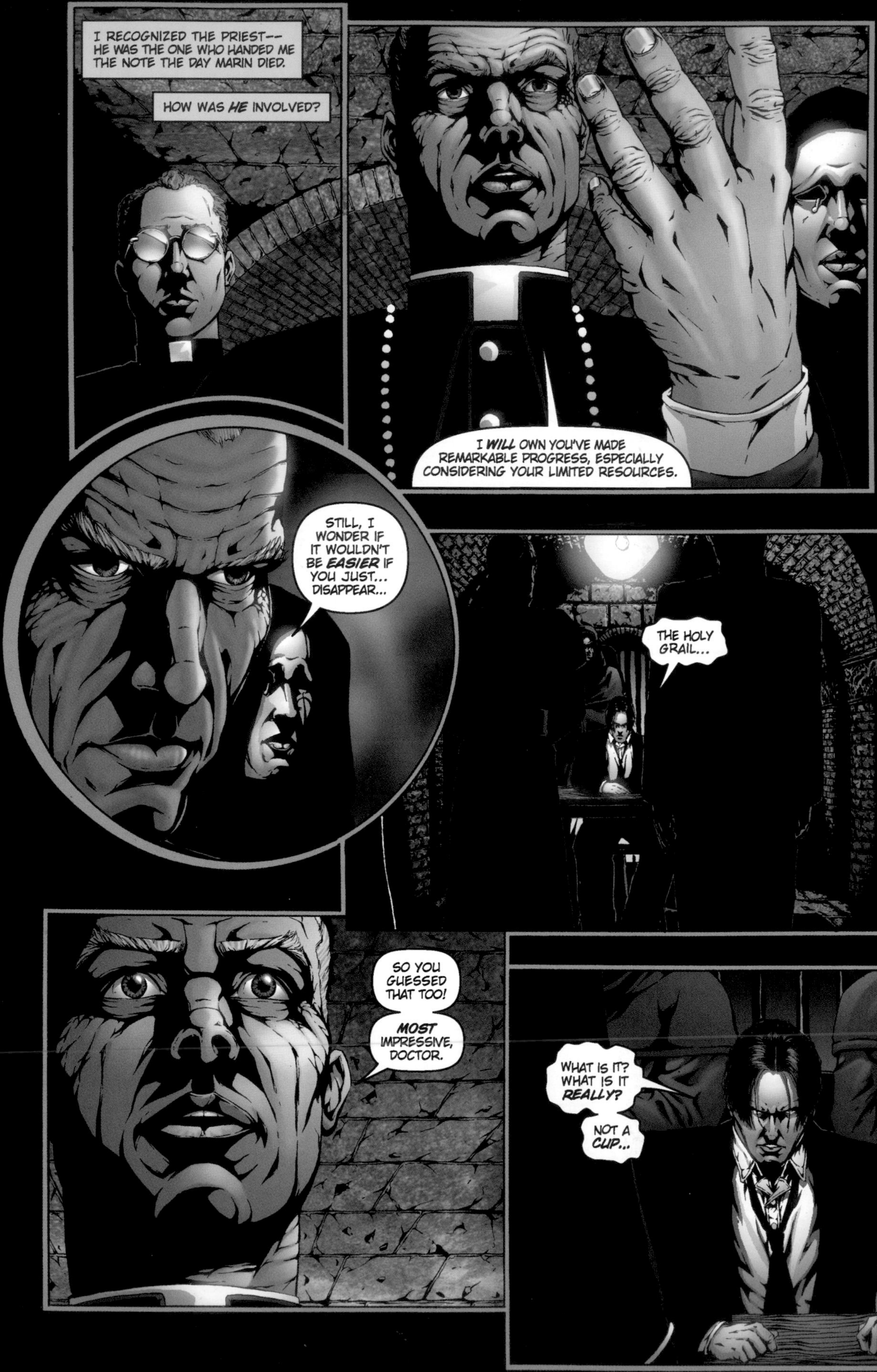
I RECOGNIZED THE PRIEST-- HE WAS THE ONE WHO HANDED ME THE NOTE THE DAY MARIN DIED.
HOW WAS HE INVOLVED?
I WILL OWN YOU'VE MADE REMARKABLE PROGRESS, ESPECIALLY CONSIDERING YOUR LIMITED RESOURCES.
STILL, I WONDER IF IT WOULDN'T BE EASIER IF YOU JUST... DISAPPEAR...
THE HOLY GRAIL...
SO YOU GUESSED THAT TOO!
MOST IMPRESSIVE, DOCTOR.
WHAT IS IT? WHAT IS IT REALLY?
NOT A CUP...

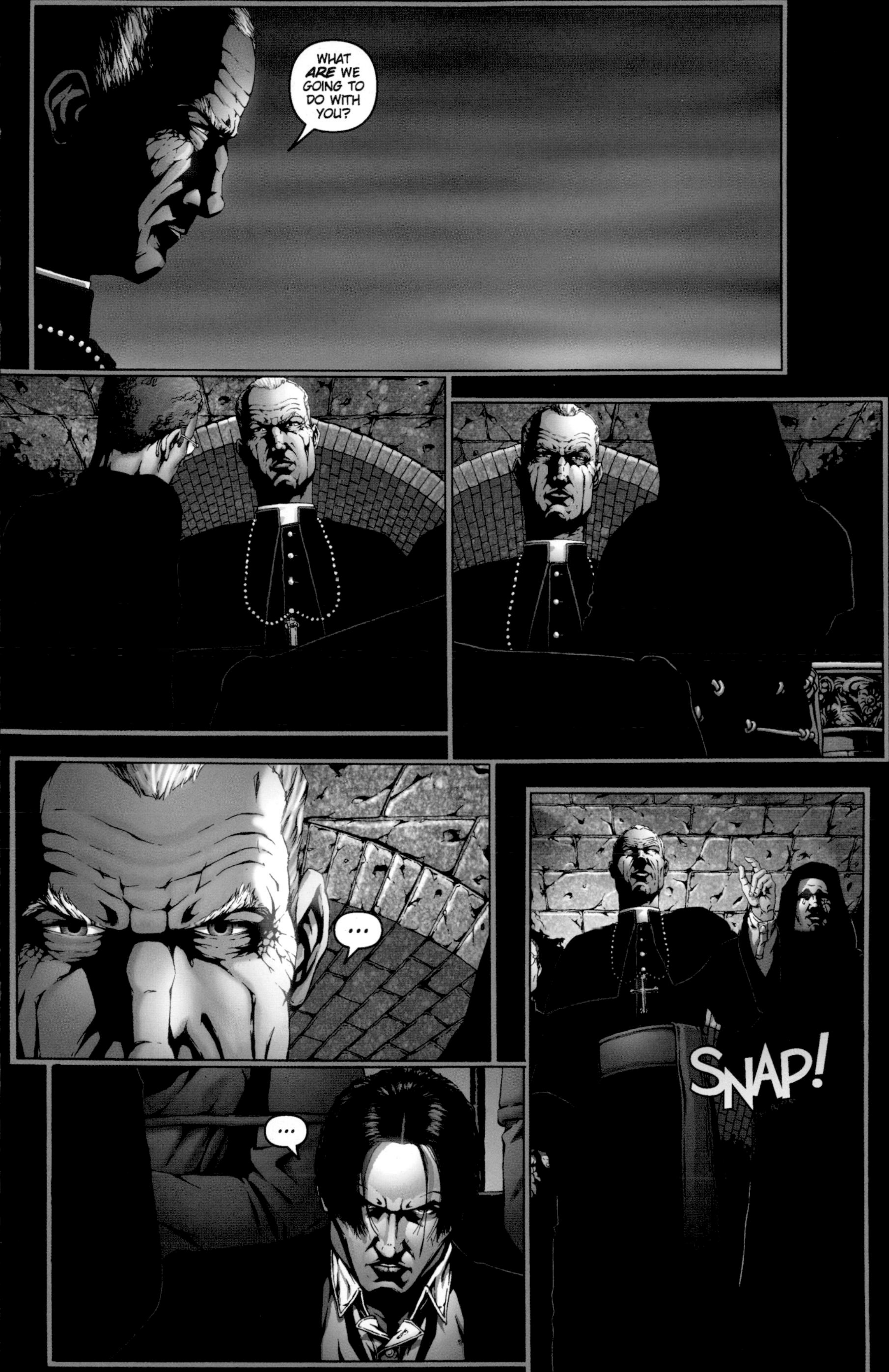
WHAT ARE WE GOING TO DO WITH YOU?
...
...
SNAP!

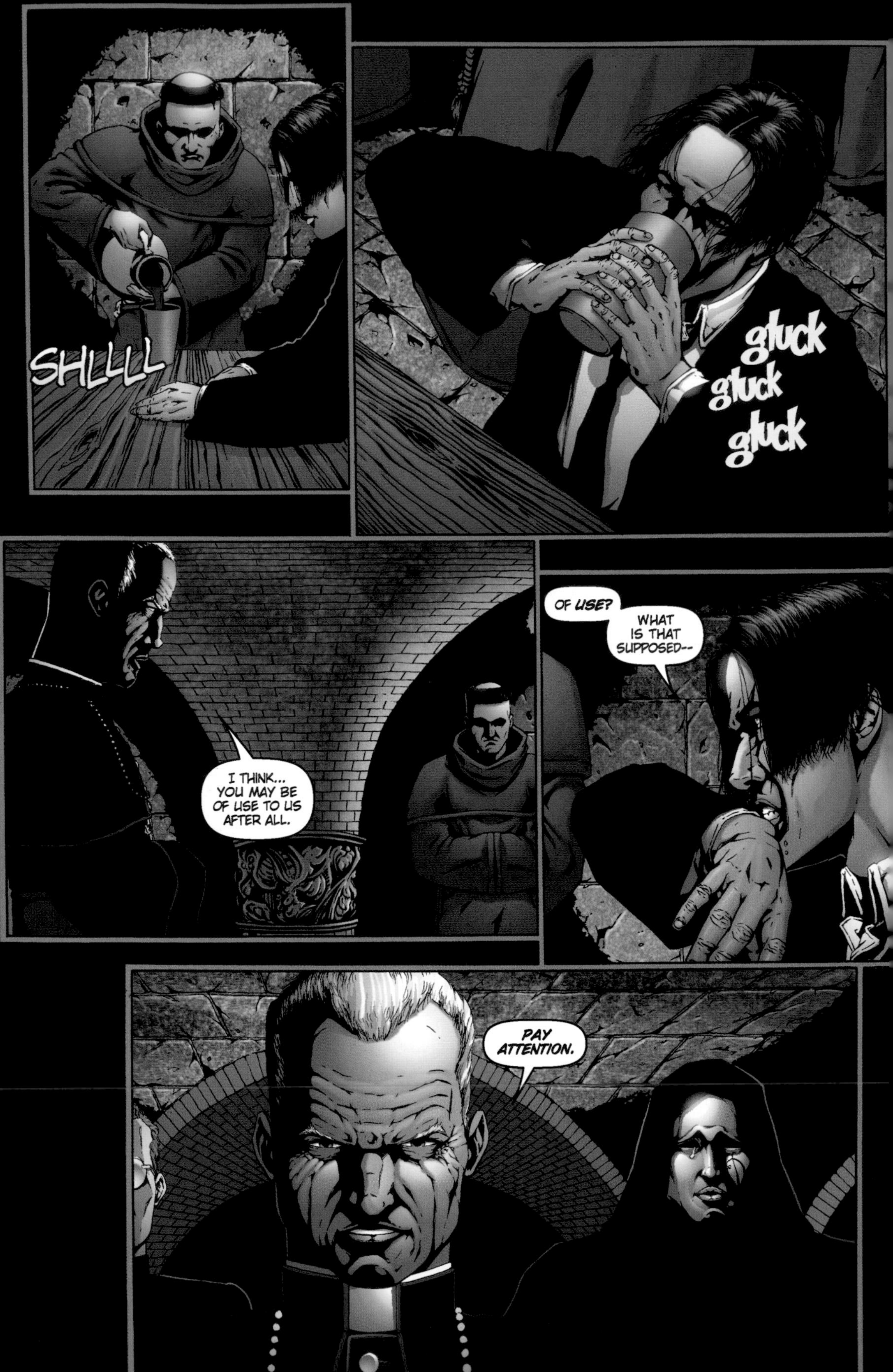
SHLLLL
gluck
gluck
gluck
I THINK... YOU MAY BE OF USE TO US AFTER ALL.
OF USE?
WHAT IS THAT SUPPOSED--
PAY ATTENTION.

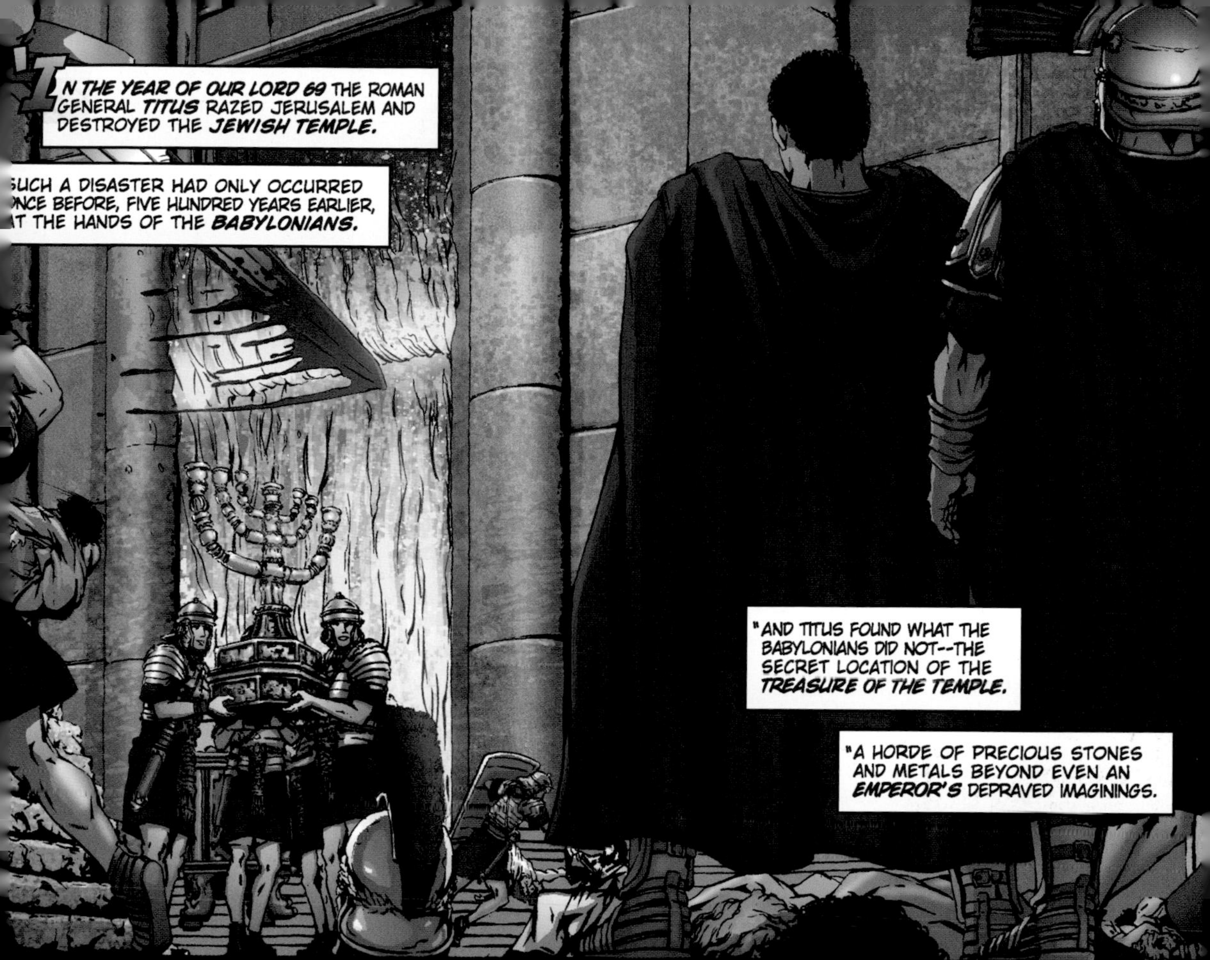
IN THE YEAR OF OUR LORD 69 THE ROMAN GENERAL TITUS RAZED JERUSALEM AND DESTROYED THE JEWISH TEMPLE.
SUCH A DISASTER HAD ONLY OCCURRED ONCE BEFORE, FIVE HUNDRED YEARS EARLIER, AT THE HANDS OF THE BABYLONIANS.
"AND TITUS FOUND WHAT THE BABYLONIANS DID NOT--THE SECRET LOCATION OF THE TREASURE OF THE TEMPLE.
"A HORDE OF PRECIOUS STONES AND METALS BEYOND EVEN AN EMPEROR'S DEPRAVED IMAGININGS.
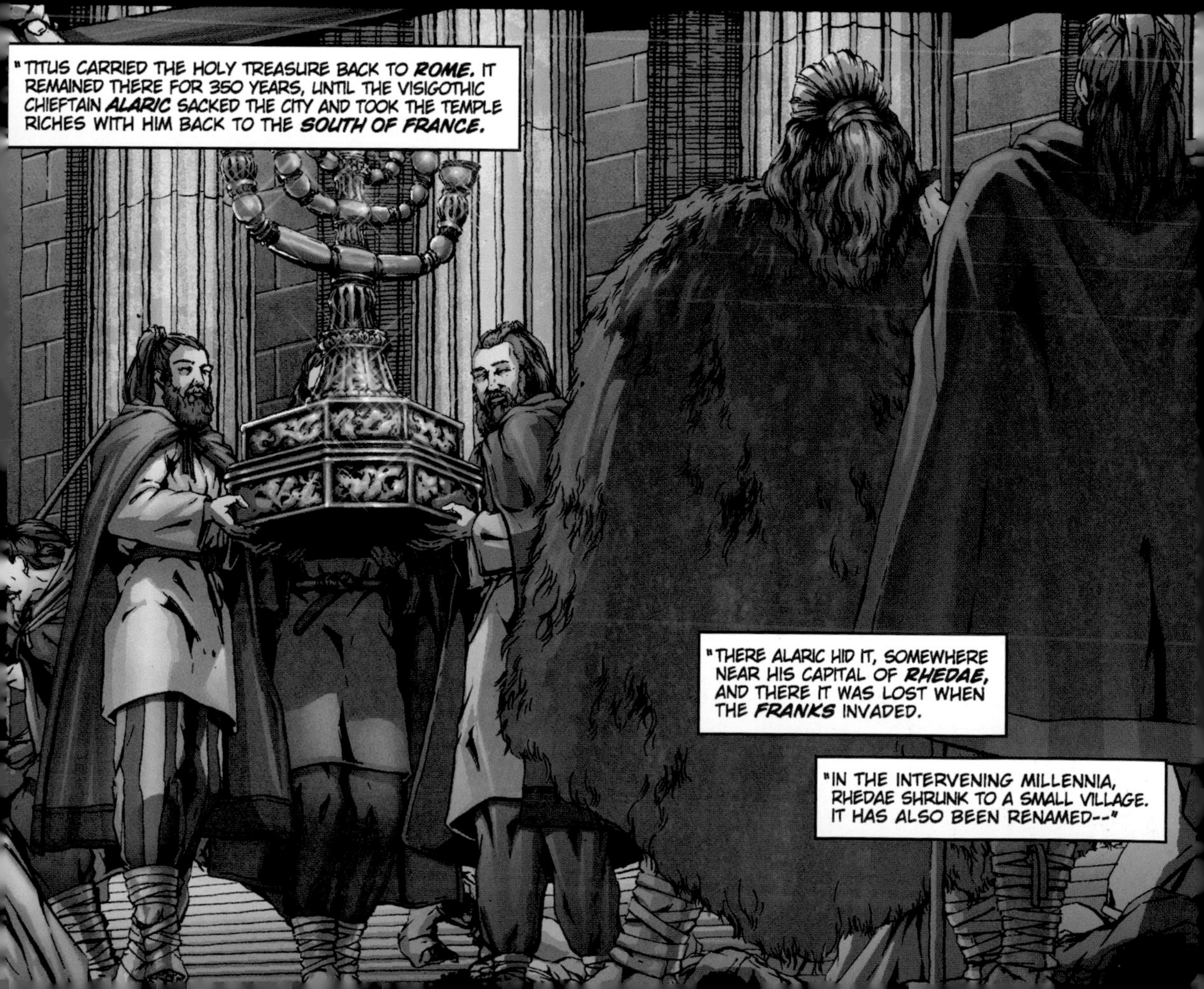
"TITUS CARRIED THE HOLY TREASURE BACK TO ROME. IT REMAINED THERE FOR 350 YEARS, UNTIL THE VISIGOTHIC CHIEFTAIN ALARIC SACKED THE CITY AND TOOK THE TEMPLE RICHES WITH HIM BACK TO THE SOUTH OF FRANCE.
"THERE ALARIC HID IT, SOMEWHERE NEAR HIS CAPITAL OF RHEDAE, AND THERE IT WAS LOST WHEN THE FRANKS INVADED.
"IN THE INTERVENING MILLENNIA, RHEDAE SHRUNK TO A SMALL VILLAGE. IT HAS ALSO BEEN RENAMED--"

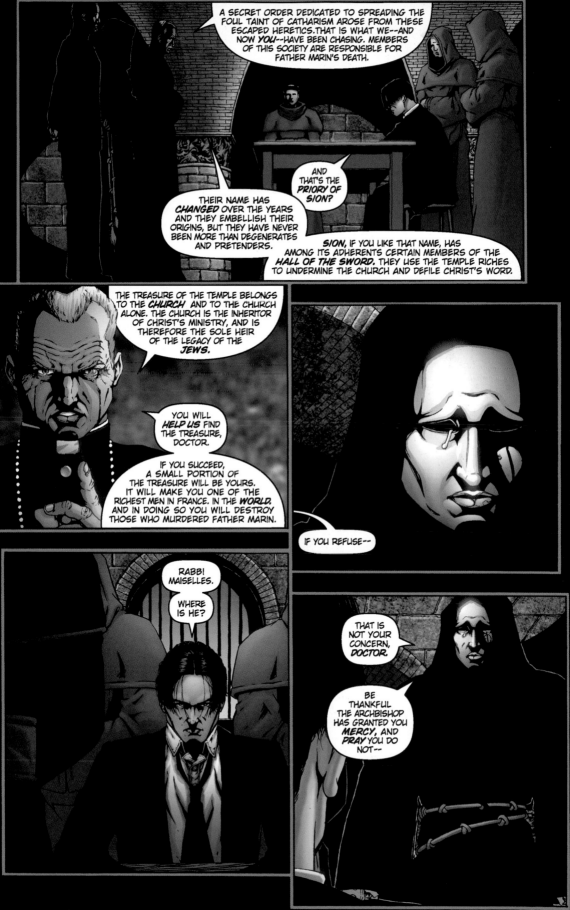

*FEDERAL REPUBLIC OF AMERICA

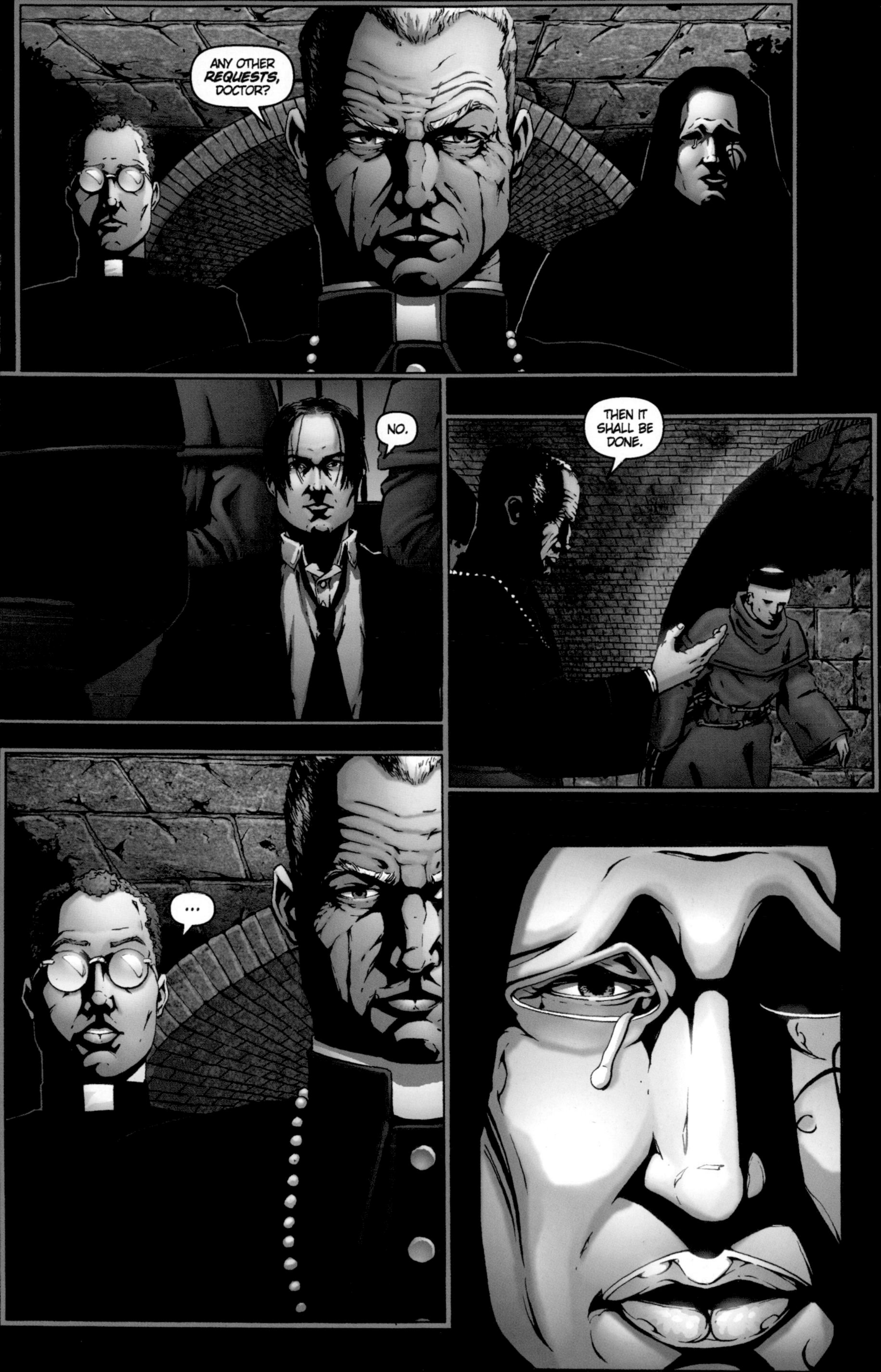
ANY OTHER REQUESTS, DOCTOR?
NO.
THEN IT SHALL BE DONE.
...

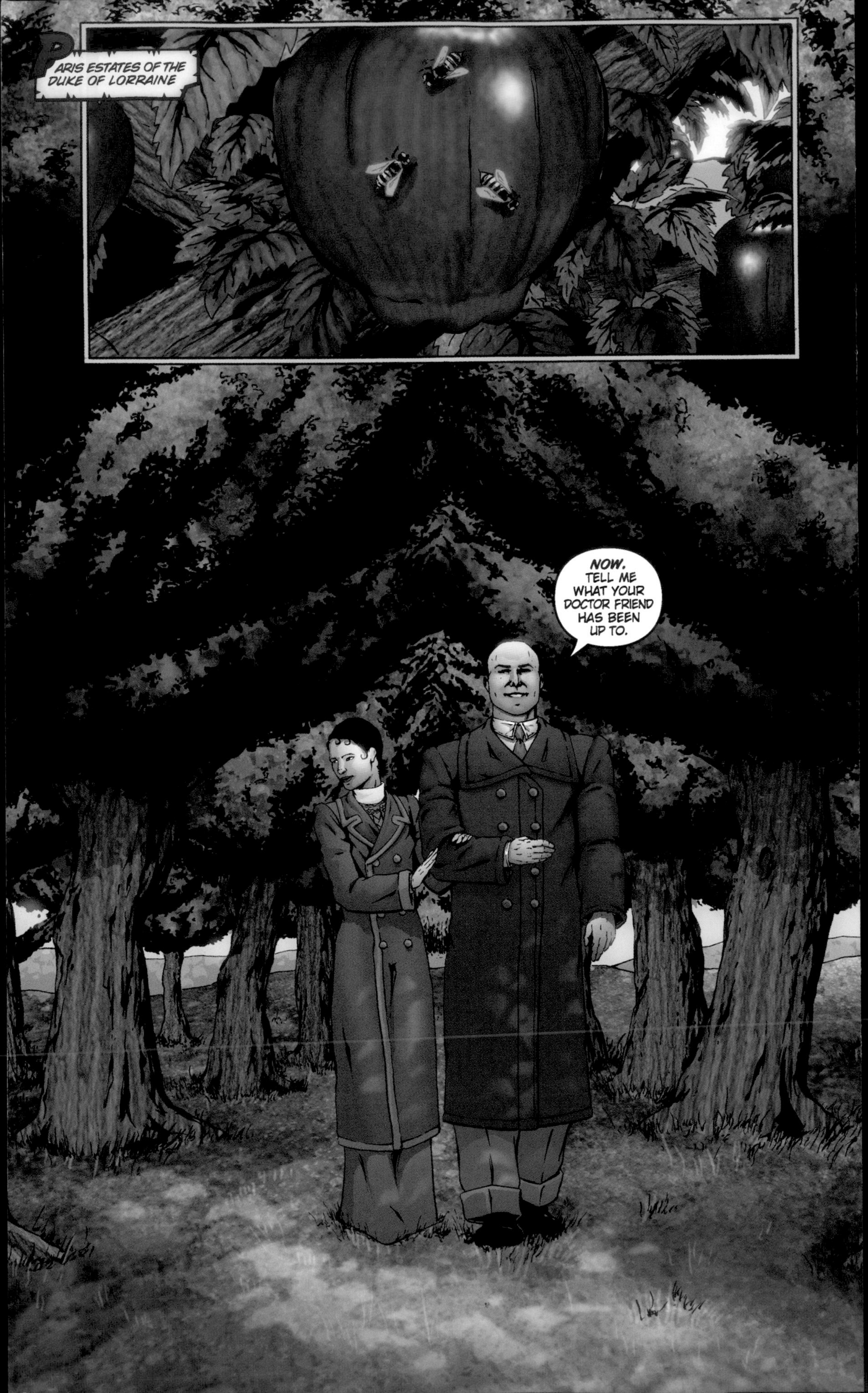
PARIS ESTATES OF THE DUKE OF LORRAINE
NOW. TELL ME WHAT YOUR DOCTOR FRIEND HAS BEEN UP TO.

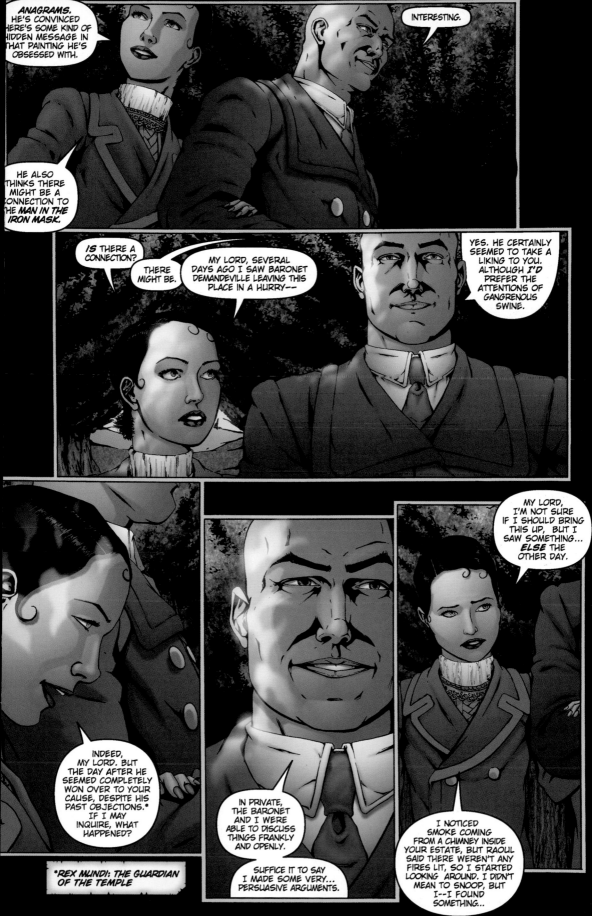

*REX MUNDI: THE GUARDIAN OF THE TEMPLE

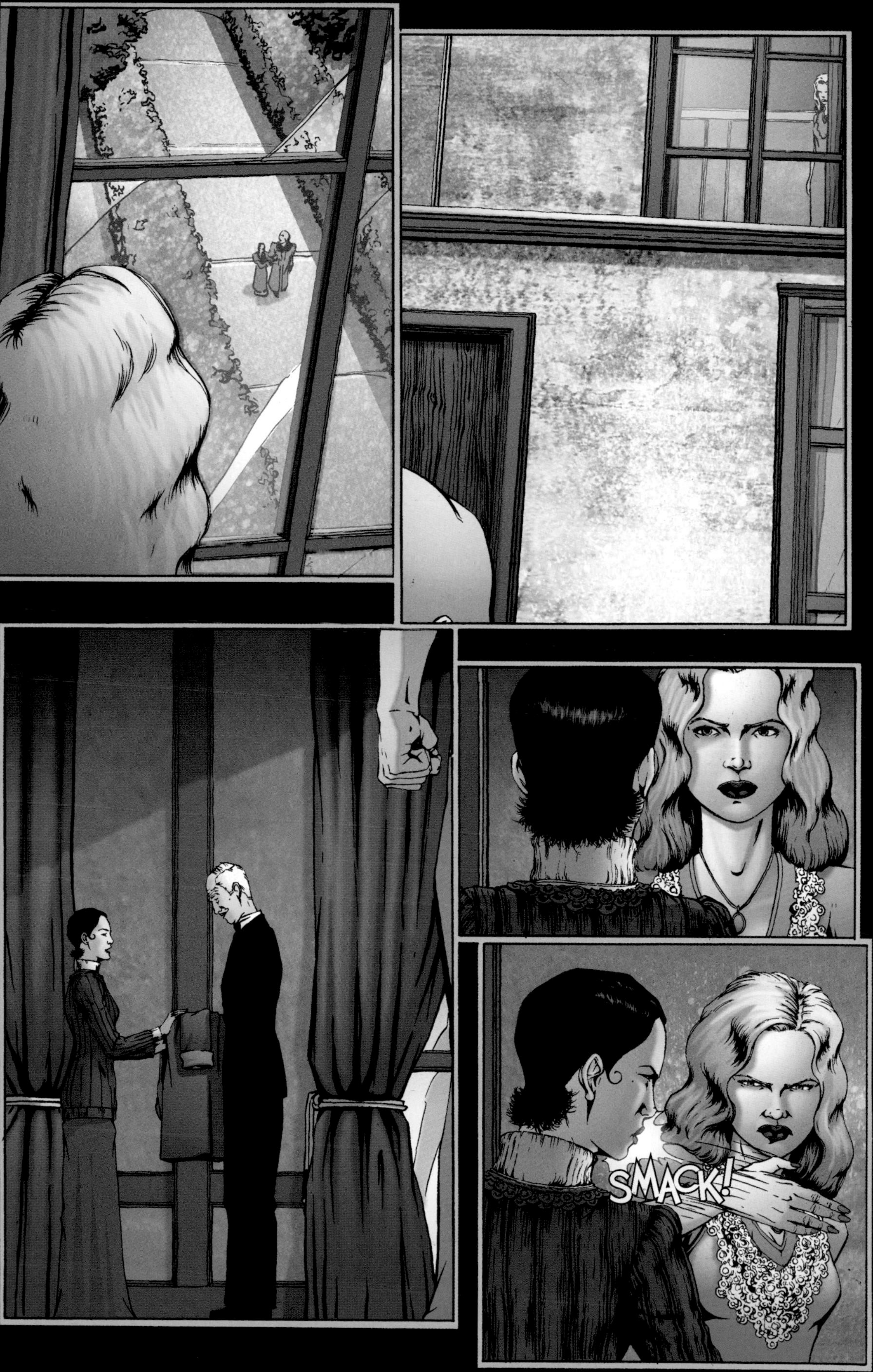
SMACK!

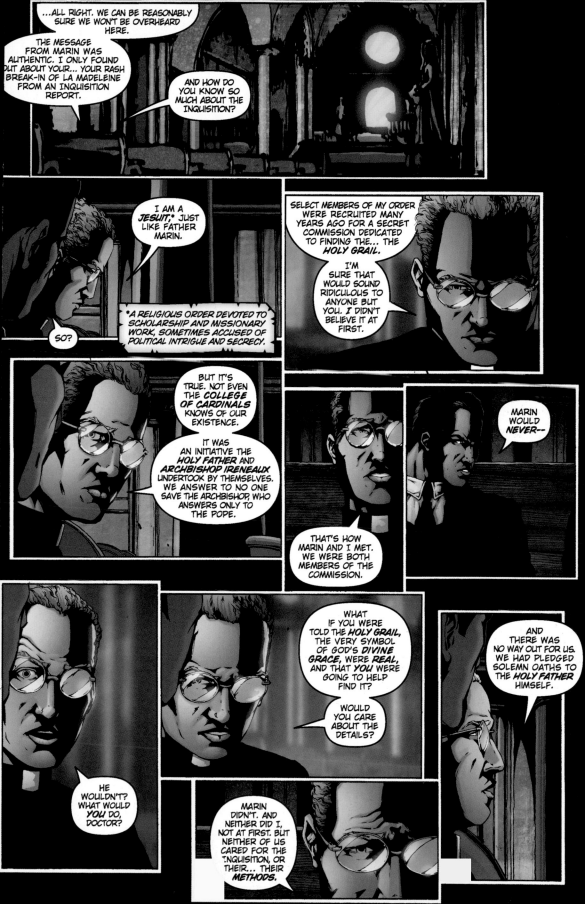

THE VENERABLE HOUSE OF DeMEDICI

This may be the last thing I ever write. I assumed the whore would die, but Dumont? The priest? If the Man in White can kill a priest, he can kill me just as easily. And there's nothing I can do about it, save hope someone finds the contents of this box.

I gave the scroll over to be destroyed, as ordered, but not before making this photostatic copy. I have no idea what to make of it, but it must be very important to have cost so many lives.

TO WHOMEVER FINDS THIS:
I hope you can make better use of it than I. And if I die, I hope you can bring down the bastards that do the dirty deed.

Hugo De Medici

REST IN **HELL,** DEMEDICI.

TTLKTHRAMYNNGENTTJNARATPFTSTICI
ARESTERVAETEXTEJRSTTCAYPTIRTSNSVISPEP
PLFTTAESTEEXVNGETNTTODAEREDIXALTER
TSETVTXTVDDXJSCARJORTISYVTYERATCVHMTRA
hENVTVMNONXVENŸTTGRECENPATSDENA
GENTES? dTXTNVFEMhOČCNONQVSTADEE
AdCVTMSEDQVhMFVRELRTETLOVCVIOShCAh
NMTVRPOTRAhETEdTXTTEJRGOTEShVSSTN
EPVLGTVRAEMSEAESERVNETILLQVDPAVPJER
hEMTTSNOhLTISCVMFMEAVTETMNONSES
VILTEROTZVRhAMVQLTAEXTMVdACTSTq
ARVNTNONNPROTEPRTESVMETANTVMMSE
EhTqVEMKSVSCTAOVTTAMORRTVTSCPOGT
RVTNCTPEJSSACEHCdOTVMVMTETLAZCAR
LVTAMYLVTTPROPYTERTLhXVMAhThGN
dEhANTTINTESVM

MARIN. AT LAST.

AT LAST, I HAD THE SCROLL YOU DIED FOR.

BUT WHAT SECRETS DID IT HIDE?

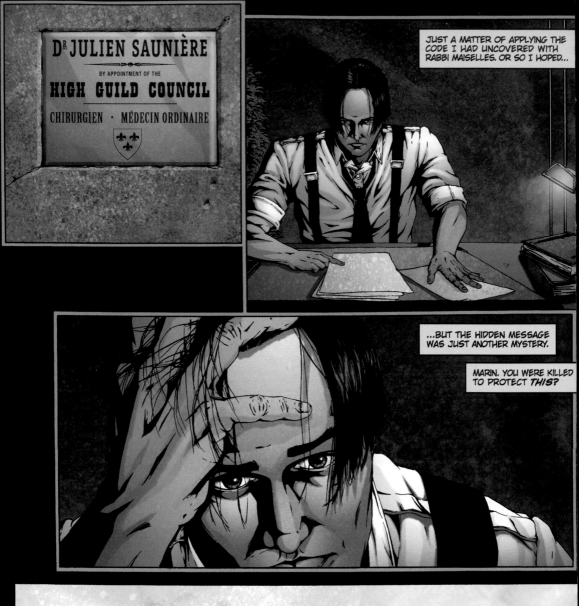

TO DAGOBERT II KING, AND TO SION BELONGS THIS TREASURE AND HE IS THERE DEAD

BEZU BLANCHEFORT RENNES LE CHATEAU LA SOULANE SERRE DE LAUZET

End of Book Two

Le Journal de la Liberté

Paris's leading anglophone newspaper • vol. 205, no. 97 • Oct. 28, MCMXXXIII

Editors in Chief: M. Tait Bergstrom, M. Matthew Pasteris. **Story Editor:** M. Arvid Nelson. **Art Editors:** M. EricJ, M. Jeromy Cox. **Photography Editor:** M. Alexander Waldman. **Layout Supervisor:** M. William Kartalopoulos. **Editors Emeritus:** M. Clark A. Smith, M. Howard P. Lovecraft, M. Robert E. Howard. Redacted by the Holy Parisian Inquisition under the direction of His Excellency Archbishop Emile-Jean Ireneaux. Le Journal de Liberté is printed under the benign auspices of his most puissant majesty KING LOUIS XXII of FRANCE.
GOD SAVE THE KING.

Papal Seal

of Approval

INQUISITORS UNCOVER CHILD SMUGGLING RING

Destitute street waifs abducted and sold into slavery in Cordova and Asia Minor; "despicable" says Inquisitor.

Paris, 13th Arrondissement – A six month-long Ecclesiastical investigation into a child smuggling ring culminated in success the other day when Inquisitors raided the offices of Mathieu Cancelier, a prominent Paris businessman.

Inquisitors discovered "around a dozen children, hog-tied and gagged," in a secret compartment in the basement of Cancelier's offices, according to Church authorities. The children were aged five to twelve, mostly urchins from the nearby Village d'Ivry shantytown.

"They were all in pitiful condition. It was apparent they had not eaten for days and had received very little water. Some showed signs of physical abuse," Brother Jean-Pierre, lead Inquisitor on the case, said.

Cancelier was taken into custody and has been charged with multiple counts of abduction of a minor and intent to engage in human trafficking.

Father Antonio Dolcino, the Inquisition lawyer assigned to prosecute the case, said the Church would seek Cancelier's execution.

"Cancelier is a monster without any regard for Christ's laws. We think we have a very strong case and likely he will be swinging from a rope within a few months."

Cancelier was not made available to comment on the charges. Cancelier's council, Pierre Modot, insists his client is not guilty.

"Mr. Cancelier has assured me he is completely innocent of these charges," Modot said.

He offered no explanation for the presence of the children or the secret dungeon in Cancelier's office. "A detailed and plausible vindication is forthcoming, pending our own private investigation," he said. "My client may be the victim of a conspiracy by business rivals. He is a wealthy man. Why would he risk everything he has by taking part in illegal activities?"

Le Journal investigators have discovered Cancelier is in arrears for several years of taxes, and his textile manufacturing businesses are deeply in debt.

Inquisitors received a tip from an anonymous informant which lead to the discovery beneath Cancelier's office.

"In cases like this, we rely heavily on informants. It is impossible to predict when and where the fiends will strike," Brother Jean-Pierre said.

He believes the children were destined for a "fate worse than death" in the lands of the Ottomans and Cordovans.

"Most of these children would have ended up as slaves," he said. "It is not uncommon for the Mohammedans to castrate their boy slaves, or for children to end up working in brothels. This is the most despicable crime I can think of."

Cancelier probably captured the children by enticing them with promises of food or money, Dolcino said. "In some cases he opportunistically abducted them off the street," he said.

More arrests many be pending.

"We have uncovered the names of a number of people we are anxious to talk to," Dolcino said. "Mr. Cancelier could not have run this operation by himself. This is by its very nature an international, multiparty operation. We have only uncovered the tail of the serpent." Dolcino decline to speculate further.

Carmelite nuns are working to reunite the shaken children with their families. Orphans will be placed in the care of the Church.

"All things considered, they are in good condition," Sister Mary-Line, assigned to care for the children, said. "One only wonders how many children before them have been carted off to oriental brothels and harems like so much human cattle."

Saved from a fate worse than death." Joyous children reunited with parents after their harrowing ordeal. Photo: Eugène Atget, Senior Photographer.

⁕ INSIDE ⁕

RUMORS SPARK ANTI-JEWISH RIOTS IN PRAGUE

Prague, Holy Roman Empire – At least one hundred people died and many more were injured last night in a riot in the Jewish quarters in the Czech city of Prague. The riots also left dozens of Jewish businesses and homes destroyed.

The strife broke out when a four-year-old boy was discovered missing. The child's father, Frantisek Uzelacová, suspected "certain Jews had kidnapped the child," according to city officials.

Uzelacová suspected the child's captors had killed the child and drank his blood, the so-called "blood libel."

Although the boy was found several hours later fishing on the Vltava River, widespread anger incited by the rumor had gained irresistible momentum.

"There was simply nothing we could do until the mob subsided," Vladimír Solnicka, mayor of Prague, said.

Inquisition officials said they were likewise incapacitated.

"Such things happen from time to time. It is regrettable, but we do not have the resources to confront mass disorder of this magnitude," a Church official said.

One priest, Father Vjaceslav Otcenásek, said he offered his church as a sanctuary.

"The mob respected the sanctity of Christ's house, but there were not many who made it through the doors, no more than a few dozen," he said.

Emperor Rudolph expressed his "outrage" in an official response to the violence.

Despite the statement, the Jews of Prague seemed despondent about reparations or trials for their attackers.

"Who would willingly confess to taking part in this?" Rabbi Slot-
continued on page A12

Russian and Japanese Naval Vessels Exchange Bowshots

Northern Sea of Japan – Russian and Japanese naval officials each accused the other of territorial violations yesterday in a tense stand-off in the northern Sea of Japan.

A Russian fishing vessel was spotted in waters claimed by both nations. A Japanese warship arrived, "forcing our navy to respond in kind," Russian cruiser captain Nikolai Kuznetsov said.

Although the warships exchanged fire, neither side claims to have aimed for the other vessel.

"This was a demonstration only, but the Tzar will only tolerate so much impudence from these devils
continued on page A8

❋ Inquisition Blotter ❋

Don't Eat the Pies!

Two young lads were caught "attempting to commit the sin of onanism" into a large batch of tarts in a Fifth Arrondissement pâtisserie, according to Inquisitors. The name of the pastry shop is being withheld "to protect the interests of the owner."

The two boys, Jean Duchamp and Guillaume Benet-Pantin, both aged 14, were remanded to the care of their parents.

"These miscreants did not complete their vile act, so we took no further action," said Brother Marcel, the Inquisitor on the scene. "But had they successfully cast their seed onto the pastries, we would have responded appropriately." Marcel said such a response could include "amputation of the offending member, as prescribed by scripture."

The owner of the pastry store was visibly shaken by the episode.

"Seems like every time I turn around someone is trying to use my baked goods for a purpose other than what G-d intended. Why can't these kids just go drill a hole in a watermelon?"

A Gladiatorial League of Sorcerers?

According to some Inquisition officials, it's possible. Early yesterday morning inquisitors and gendarmes responded to complaints of a disturbance deep within the Cimetière Montparnasse.

Gravedigger François St. Honoré reported the disturbance.

"There were explosions, flashing lights, all colors, and weird chanting it sounded like," St. Honoré said. "I didn't dare go near the place where it was going on."

Inquisitors on the scene found evidence of a "pitched battle involving the occult sciences." According to Brother Jean-Marc, the lead investigator, there were also signs the fight was part of a "coordinated spectacle."

"There's evidence a crowd numbering as many as one hundred individuals gathered to watch, almost like a tennis match," Brother Jean-Marc said.

But it doesn't mean the fight was a stage performance.

"There is physical evidence suggesting this was a serious melee, perhaps a fight to the death," a source within the Gendarmerie said. Brother Jean-Marc refused to comment further.

According to investigators, the scene is reminiscent of several others found over the past few weeks, in the Jardin des Tuilleries and the quays of the 12th Arrondissement,

amongst other places.

"We cannot rule out the possibility this is the work of morbid individuals who gather together by moonlight to observe and presumably gamble on violent sorcerous contests," Brother Jean-Marc said. "But it is impossible to say anything save they are exceedingly well-organized. They disperse very quickly and leave little behind in the way of physical evidence."

St. Honoré, the gravedigger, is convinced this theory is correct.

"I tell you, I saw shapes and shadows of people moving around the monuments and headstones a few minutes before the lights and noises started up," he said. "They were like ghosts. This job is creepy enough without crazies blasting up the grounds late at night."

Dope Fiends Using Catacombs to Smuggle Opiates

Inquisitors have uncovered a suspected network of "dope-runners" utilizing Paris's 18th century catacombs to transport and stash their merchandise.

Overcrowding in Paris graveyards became so acute in the late 1700s that corpses would overflow into people's wine cellars, and the noxious rainwater runoff from overcrowded burials poisoned drinking water.

City officials were forced to convert ancient Roman limestone quarries in catacombs, wherein were stacked hundreds of thousands of human bones, transported from gravesites above ground.

Transportation of a different sort is going on nowadays.

"We did not make any apprehensions, but we saw clear signs of traffic in certain catacombs in the Third Arrondissement," Brother Christof, the Inquisitor assigned to the case, said. "In addition, we located and destroyed a considerable quantity of laudanum, presumably stashed for sale or transportation at a later time."

The network of limestone tunnels beneath Paris is perfect for smugglers, Christof contends.

"It offers criminals and subversives the perfect medium through which to move from place to place quickly and undetected," he said.

Tracking down the elusive smugglers may be a gigantic undertaking.

"No one really knows exactly how big the network of catacombs is. Some people even think it continues all the way to Montmarte, but I doubt that," Anastasia Bourdain, chairwoman of the Paris Athenaeum, said. "Still, there are

certainly many unexplored passageways underground. It would be almost impossible to find someone who didn't want to be discovered."

Servant's Corpse Found Outside Hotel

Workers at the upscale Hôtel Duc de Berry discovered the mutilated corpse of a young woman, the servant of a visiting English dignitary, early yesterday morning.

Inquisitors who responded to the report confess they are puzzled by the crime.

"The body was discovered in an alley behind the hotel but seems to have been moved shortly after the commission of the crime," Brother Matthew, a novitiate Inquisitor on the scene, said. "But there's no indication of where the crime itself took place."

"There's something ritualistic about it. Three stab wounds to the neck, and any one would have been enough to kill. The last blow nearly decapitated her," Dr. Antoine Laborde, forensic attache from the Guild of Physicians, said.

Further details of the case are not forthcoming, as an investigation is underway. Hotel management declined to comment on the incident. The slain girl's master could not be reached.

Lower House Member Caught With His Pants Down (or Off)

Baron Georges Deleaval, standing member of the Hall of the Robe, was caught lying down yesterday—naked and handcuffed to a bed in an establishment known to Inquisitors as a "den of iniquity and habitation for women of ill repute."

Lord Deleaval's clothes and possessions, including money and jewelry, were "not present" according to Brother Eustache, who arrived in response to complaints from hotel occupants of shouting and thumping in Lord Deleaval's room.

"Looks like a shakedown," Eustache said.

Not so, according to Deleaval.

"It was simply awful," Deleaval said. "I happened on a young woman who told me her mother needed medical care beyond her means. I offered to help, as would any Christian gentleman. Imagine my surprise when, upon entering the building she claimed was her mother's residence, three young, muscular brutes jumped me and knocked me unconscious. The next thing I knew I was exposed and chained to a bed."

"There were no injuries anywhere on Lord Deleaval's body

that I could see," Eustache said.

Occupants of the building t... different story from the lord.

"I saw his lordship g... upstairs with a young boy, I'd about sixteen, with a few bottle... apricot oil, a pair of handcuffs, some hotsauce. Anyways, you... guess what they were up to," a building resident who spoke the condition of anonymity.

Lord Deleaval was release... the care of his wife and childre...

Watching the Detectives

Marchioness Philippa Amb... deBouron was briefly detaine... Inquisitors yesterday after physically assaulted a man... contends was a private investiga... whom her husband hired to "... low her every move."

Jacques Gittes, the man... flamboyant young marchio... assaulted, is in fact a charte... private investigator, although i... not clear he was actually stalk... Lady Philippa.

But the lady's opinion of ... was quite apparent to those w... overheard the scuffle.

"The lady called him a num... of names I shall not repeat... the sake of modesty," an umbr... salesman who witnessed the in... dent said.

Inquisitors on the scene... not charge Gittes, as they de... mined he was not responsible... the disturbance.

"This is not Lady Philip... first run-in with the Inquisiti... nor do we expect it to be her la... said Church officials on the sce... "She has a history of vituperat... and combative behavior."

Lady Philippa was released... the care of Lord deBouron, wh... twice his wife's age.

Prominent Rabbi Taken into Custod...

Inquisitors and Gendarme... officers stormed the home of Ra... Albert Maiselles yesterday evenin...

Eyewitnesses heard ... thumping and shouting in ... rabbi's apartment, whereafter ... and an unknown male compani... were directed into a black van.

Brother Moricant, the rank... Inquisitor on the scene, declin... to comment on the abductio... Archbishop Ireneaux mov... quickly to enjoin the matter, se... ing it from public scrutiny.

The whereabouts of Ra... Maiselles and his companion ... unknown. Maiselles was respec... amongst the Jews of Paris for ... extensive occult knowledge.

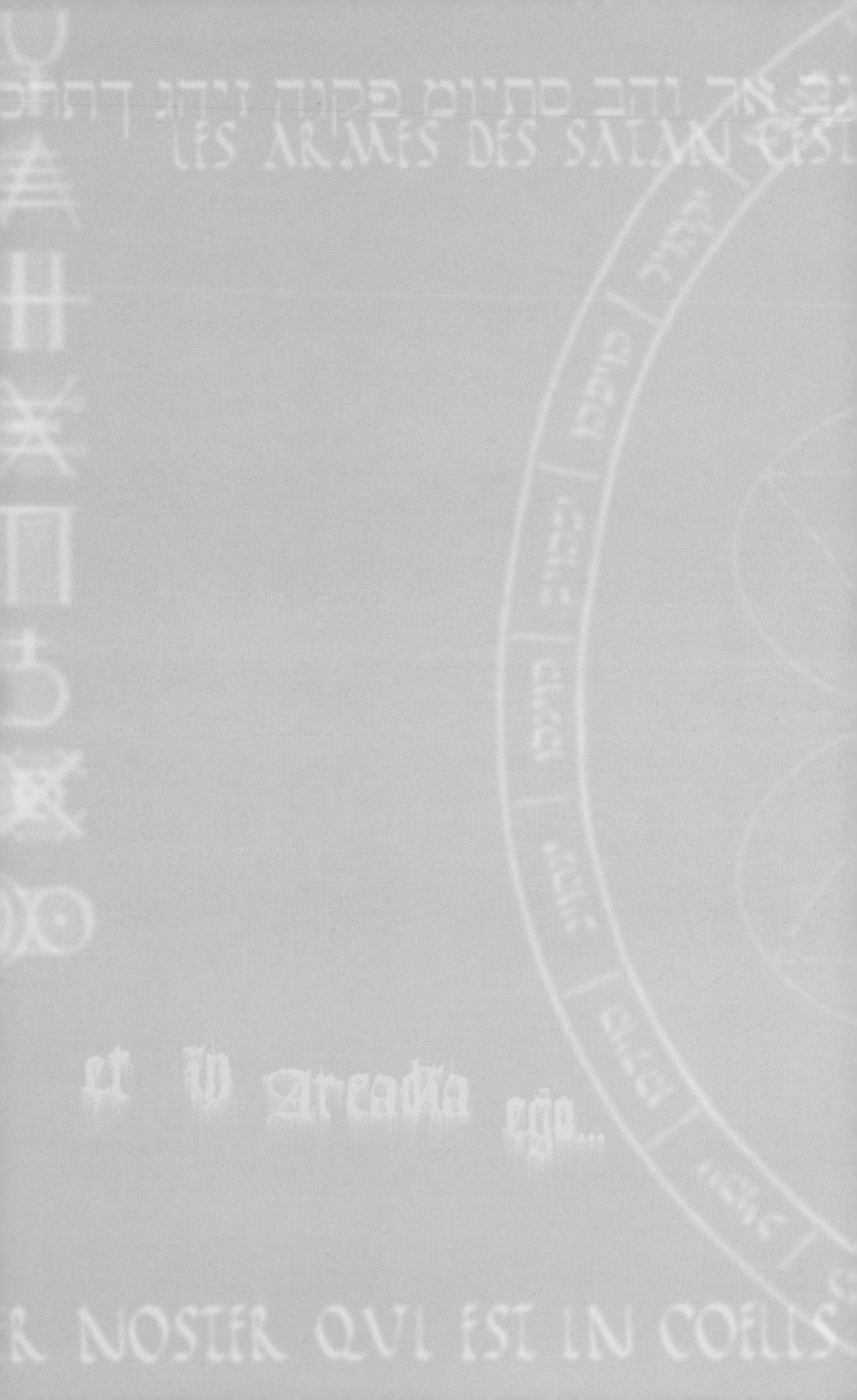
LES ARMES DES
et in Arcadia ego...
R NOSTER QVI EST IN COELIS

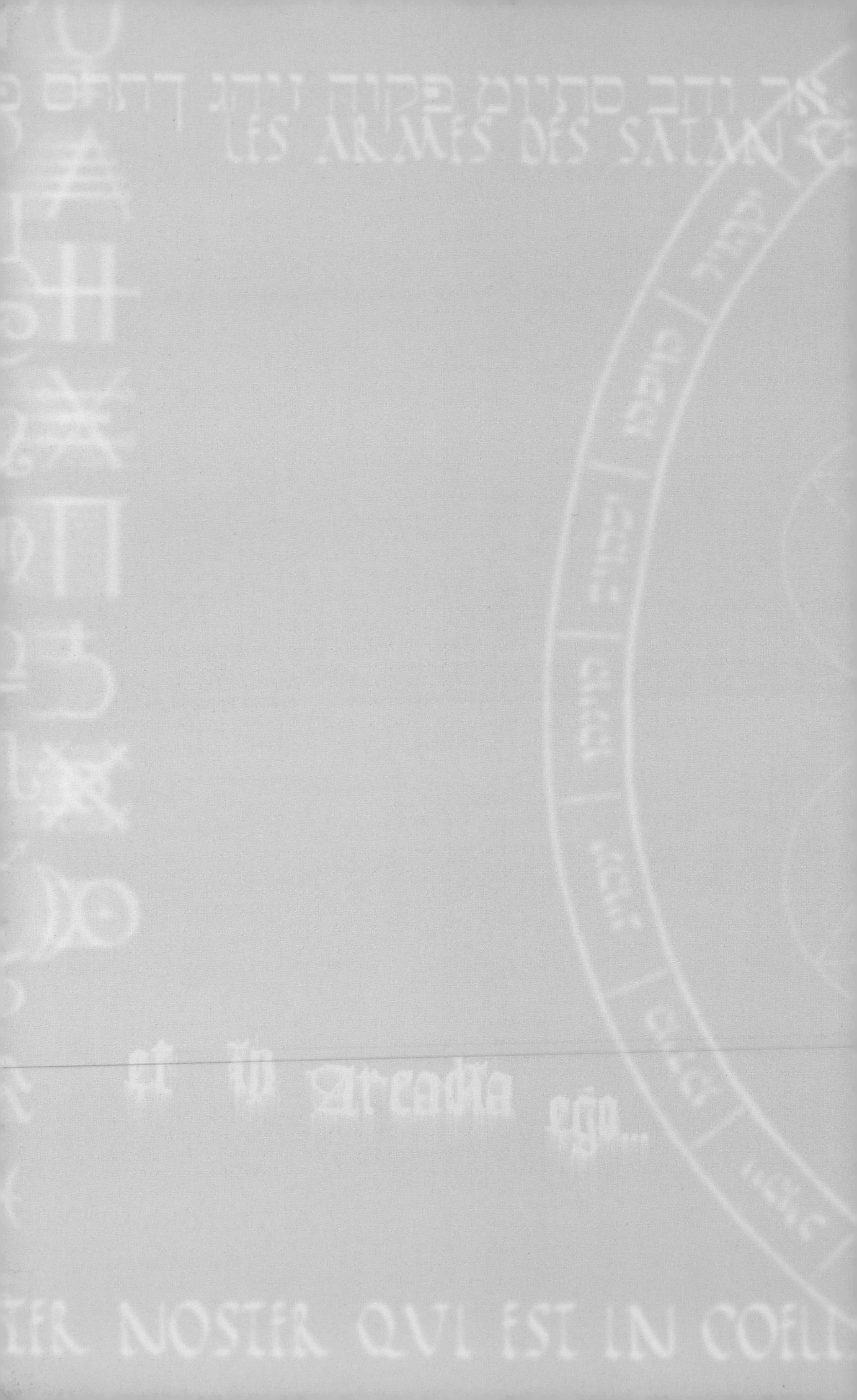
LES ARMES DES SALAM
et in Arcadia ego...
TER NOSTER QVI EST IN COELI

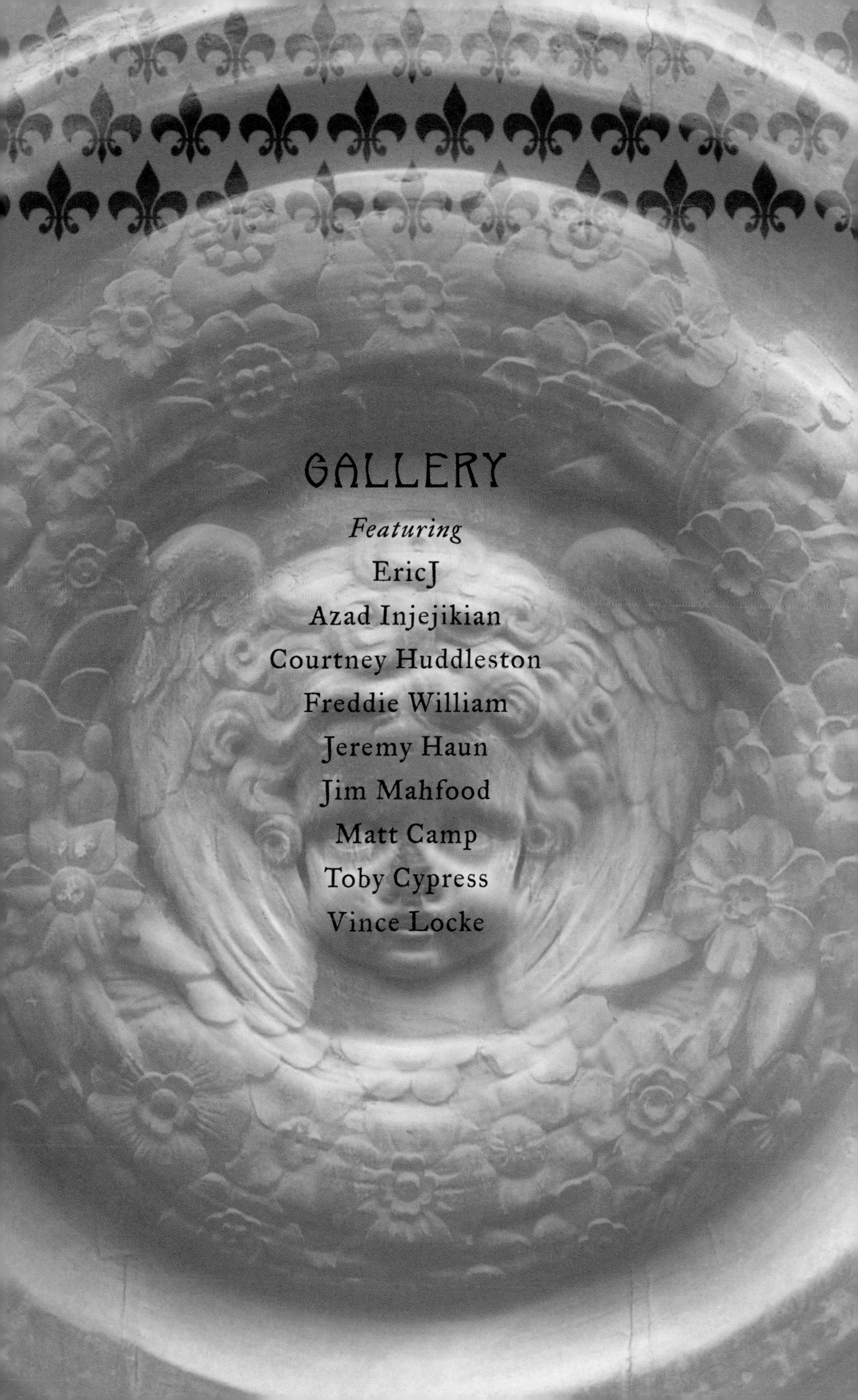

GALLERY

Featuring

EricJ

Azad Injejikian

Courtney Huddleston

Freddie William

Jeremy Haun

Jim Mahfood

Matt Camp

Toby Cypress

Vince Locke

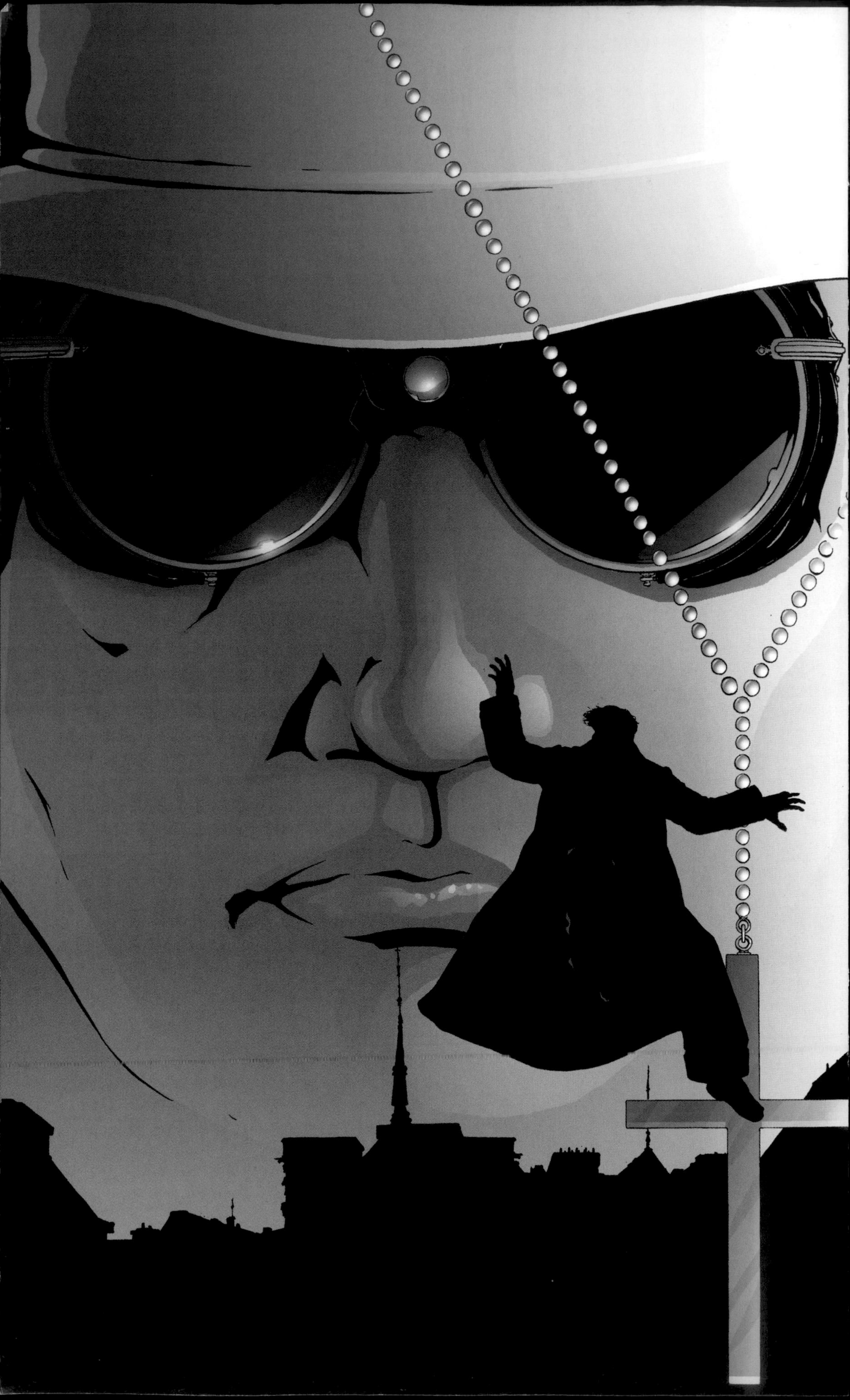

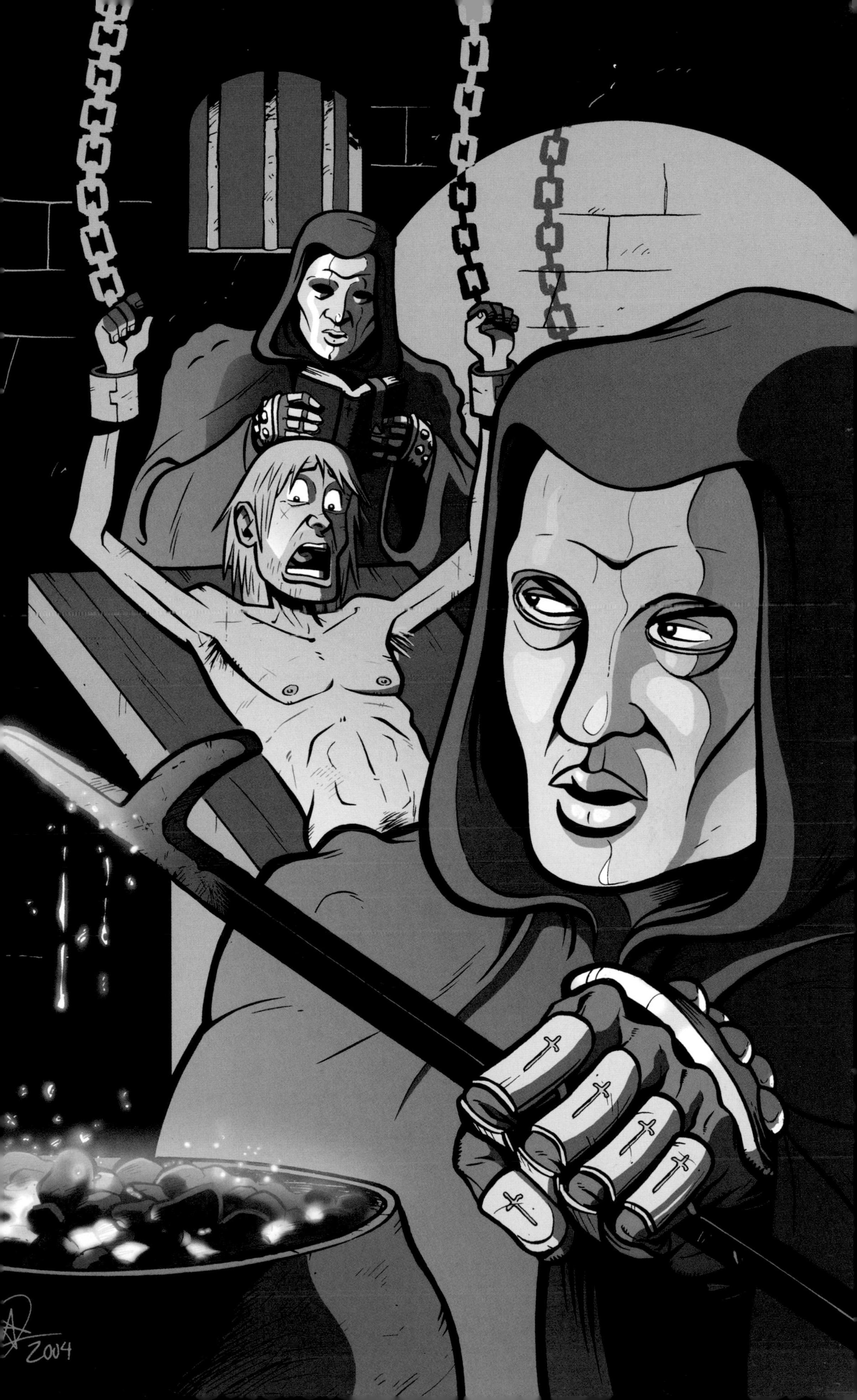
2004

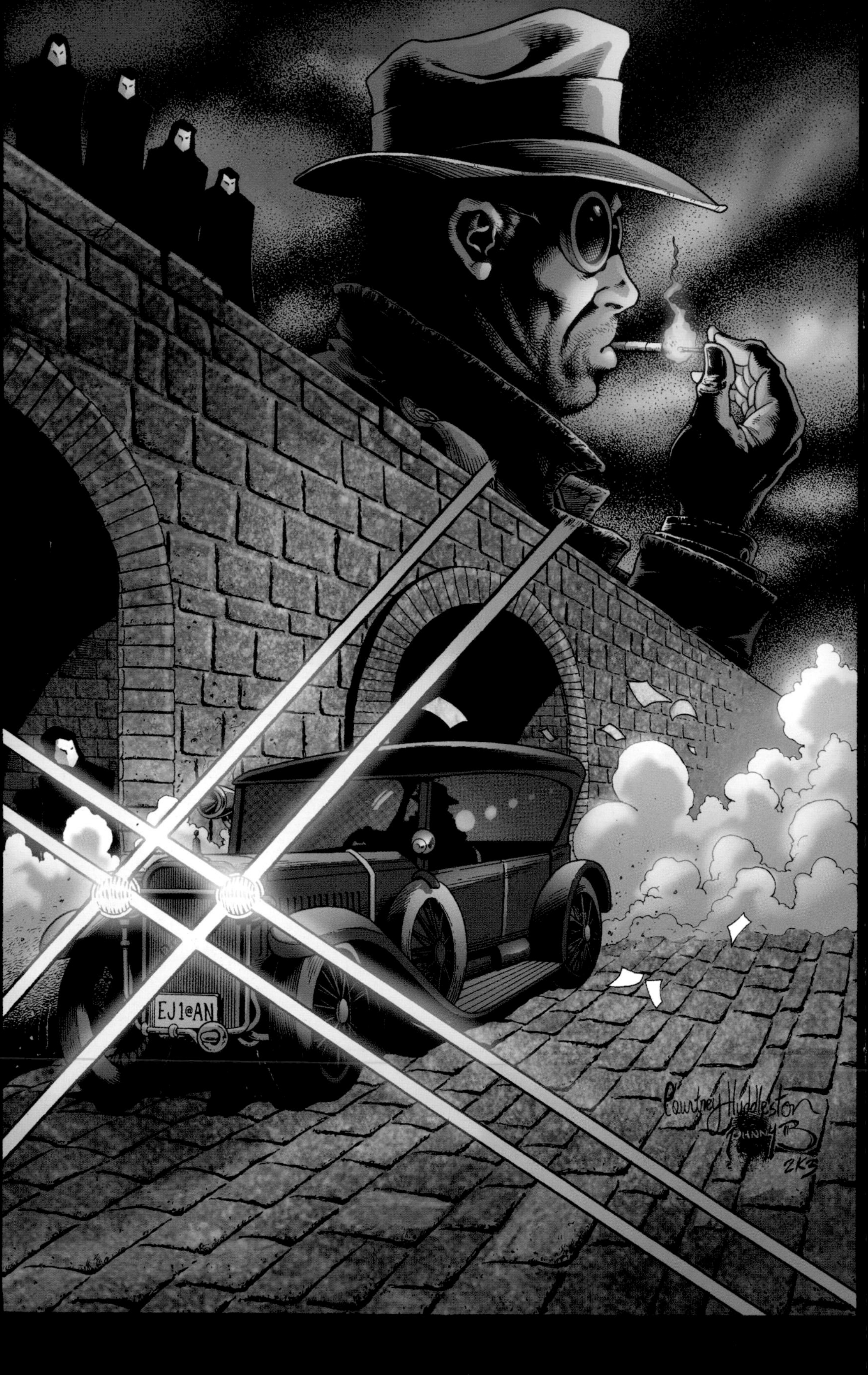
EJ1@AN
Courtney Huddleston
2K3

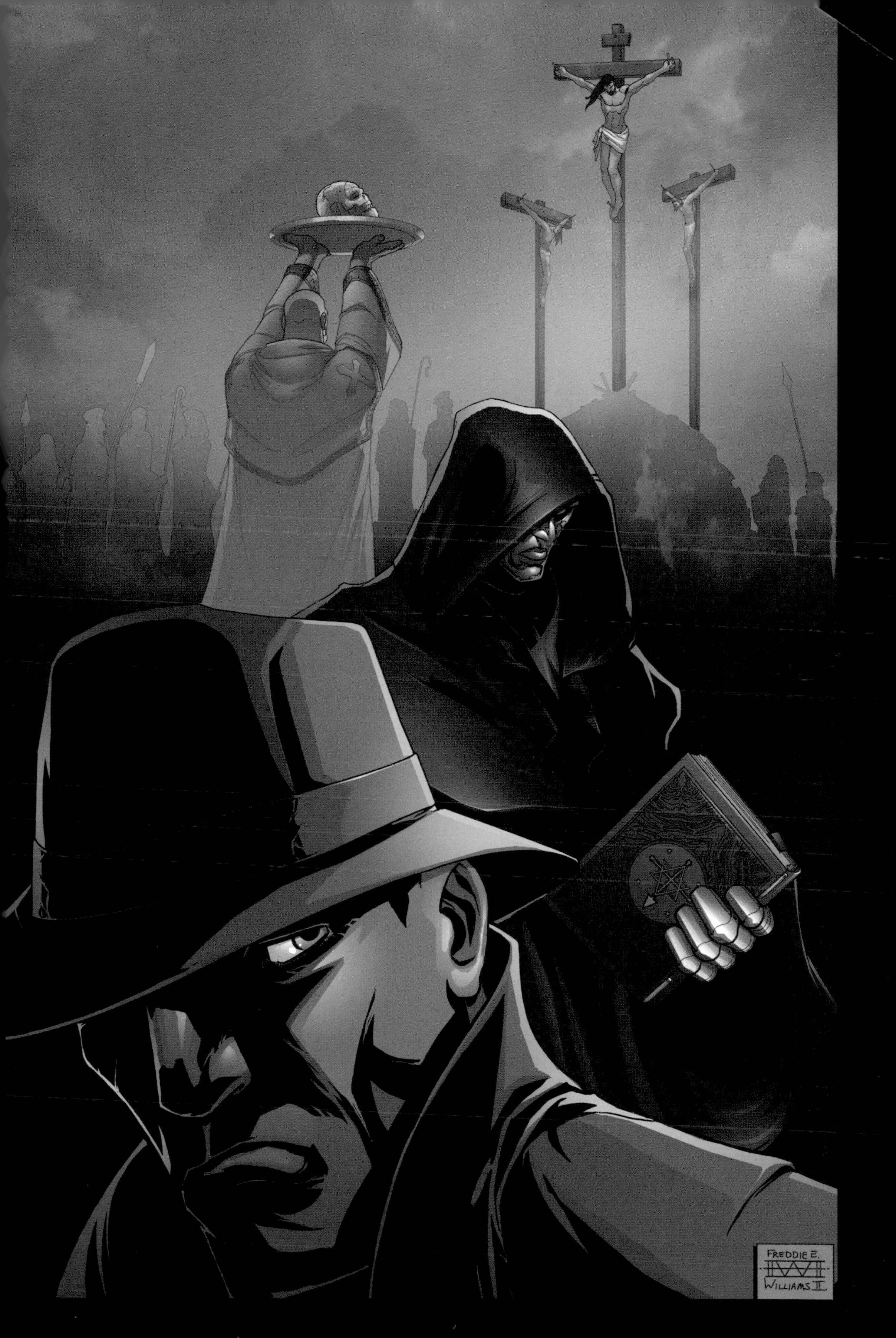
FREDDIE E.
WILLIAMS II

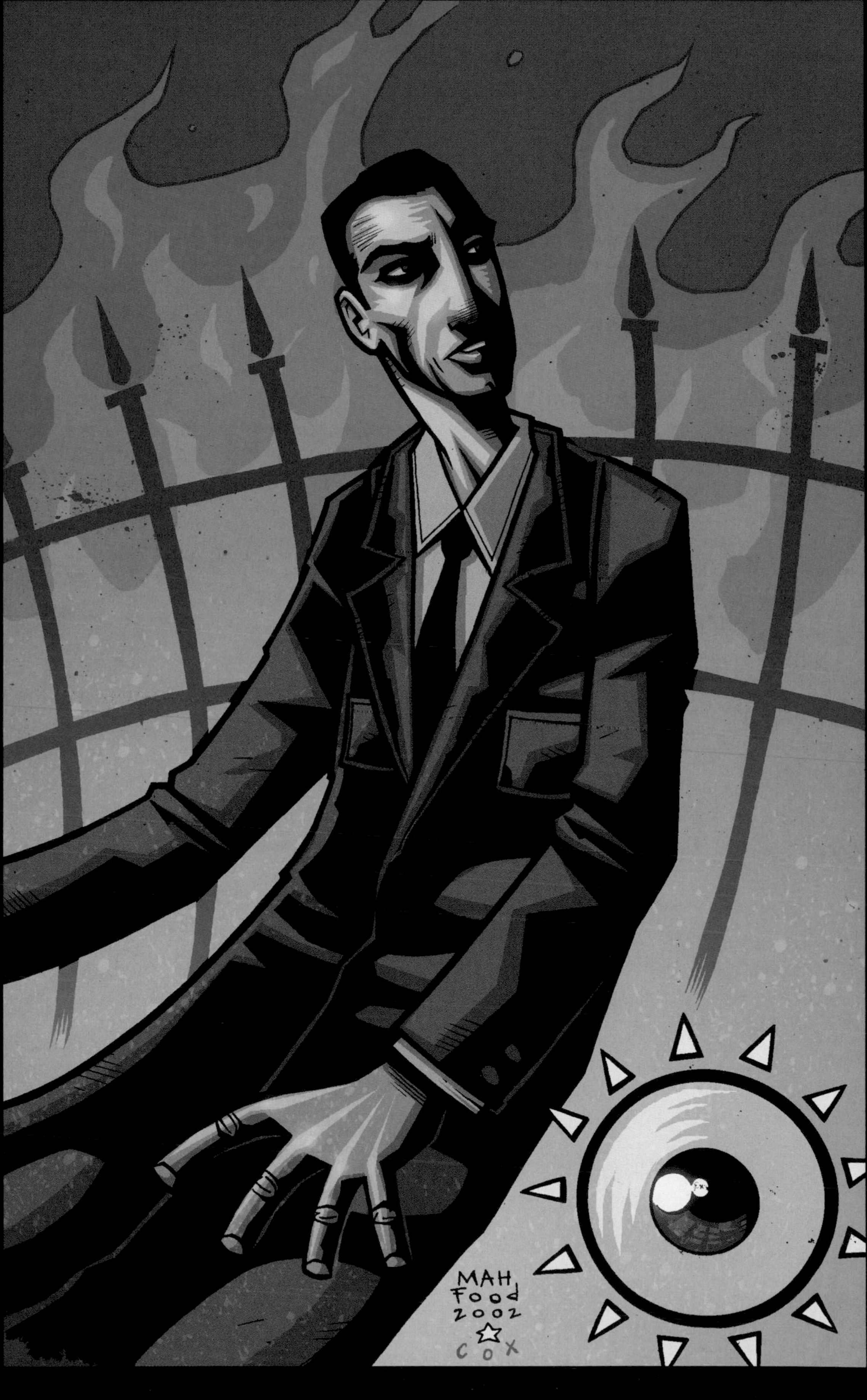
MAH Food 2002
COX

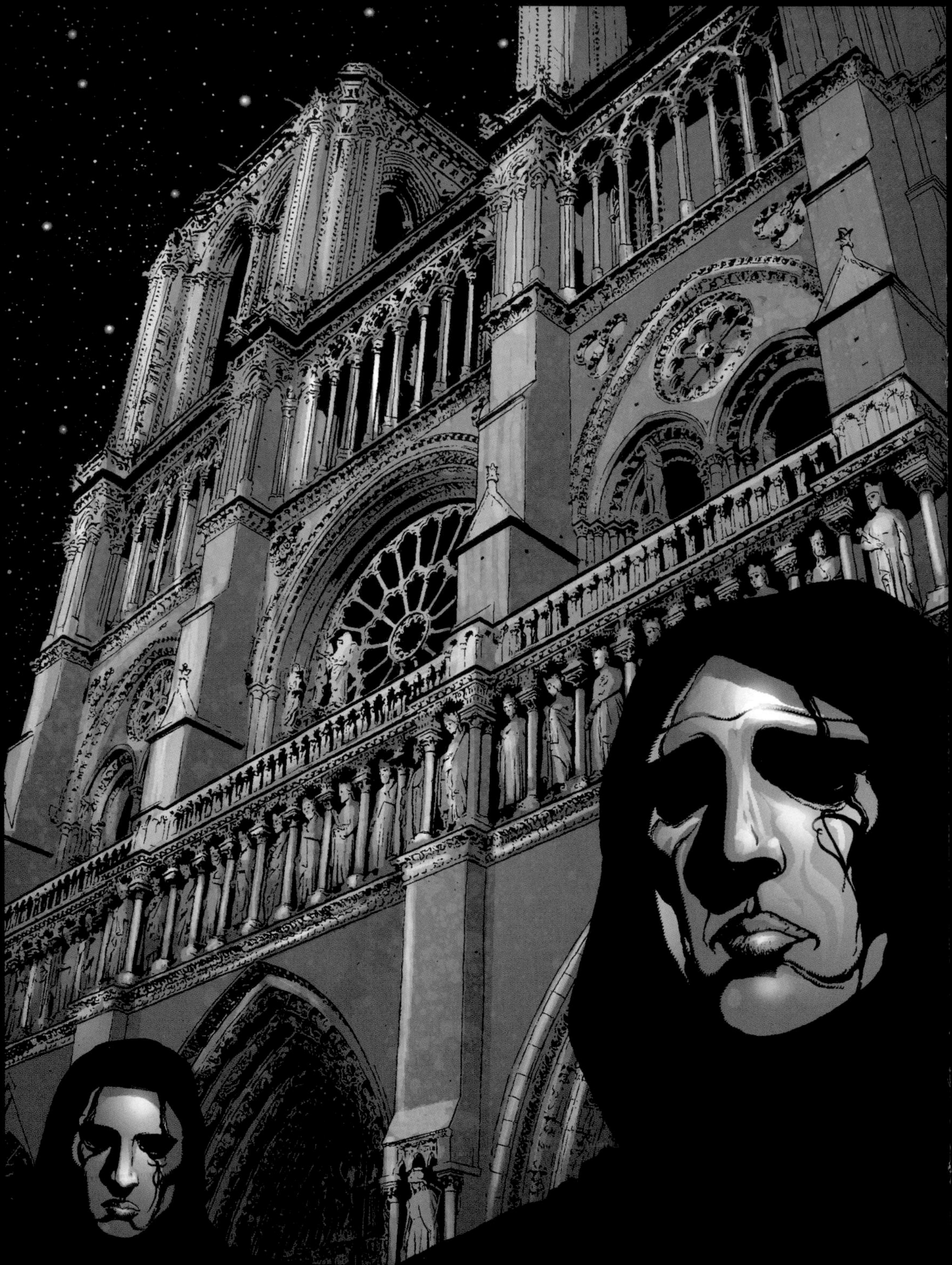

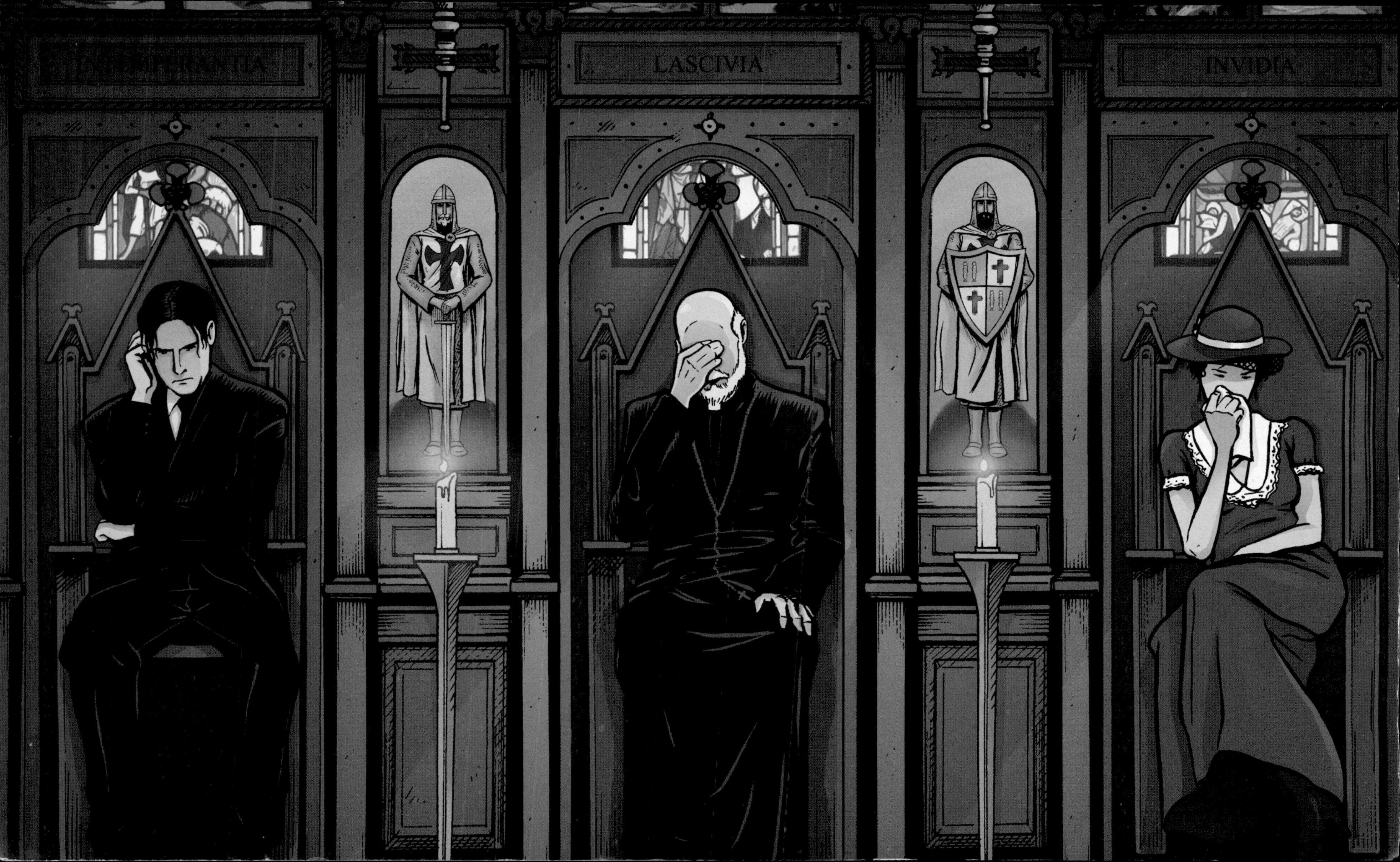
INTEMPERANTIA
LASCIVIA
INVIDIA

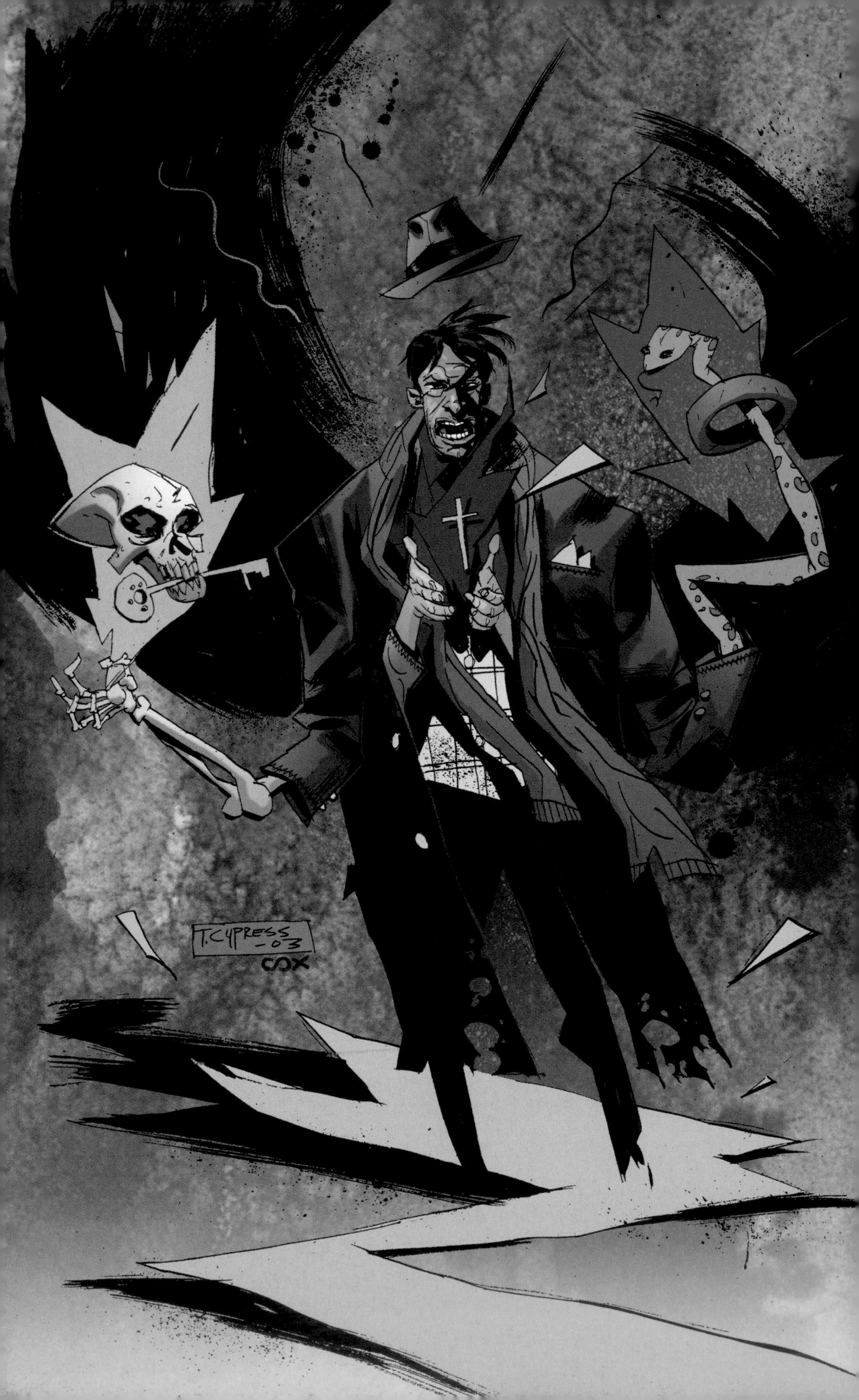
T. CYPRESS -03
COX

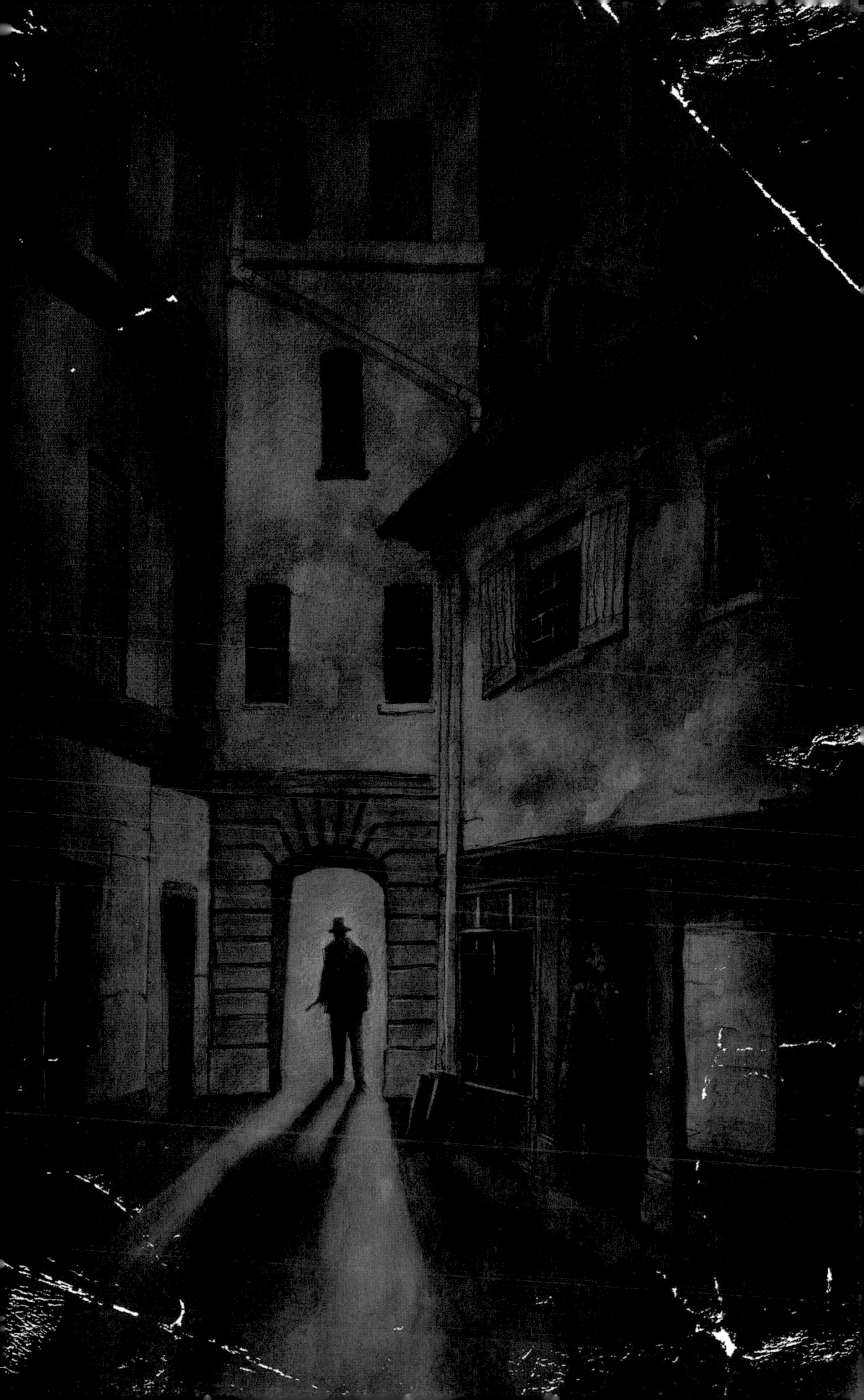

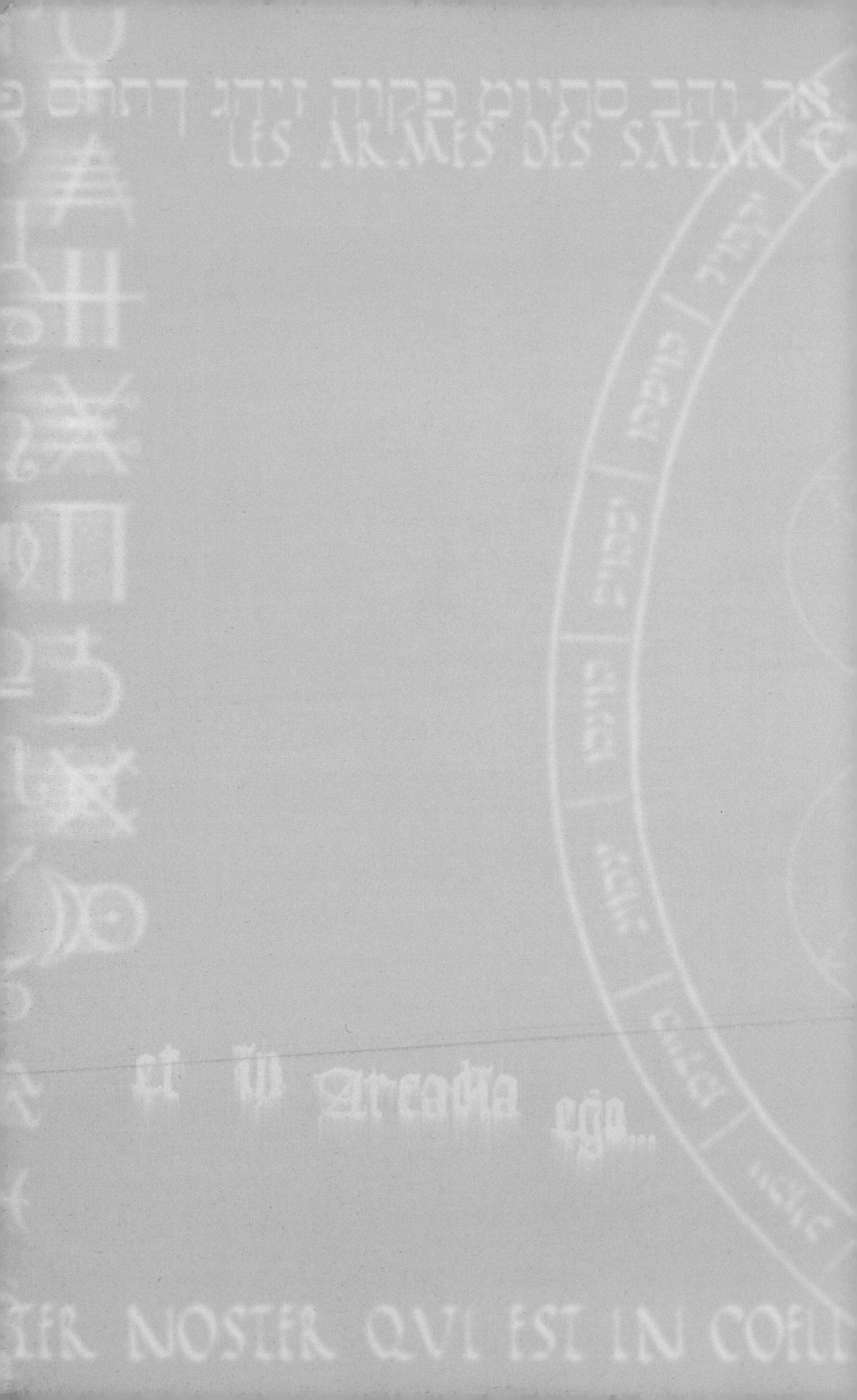
LES ARMES DES SATAN
et in Arcadia ego...
TER NOSTER QVI EST IN COELI

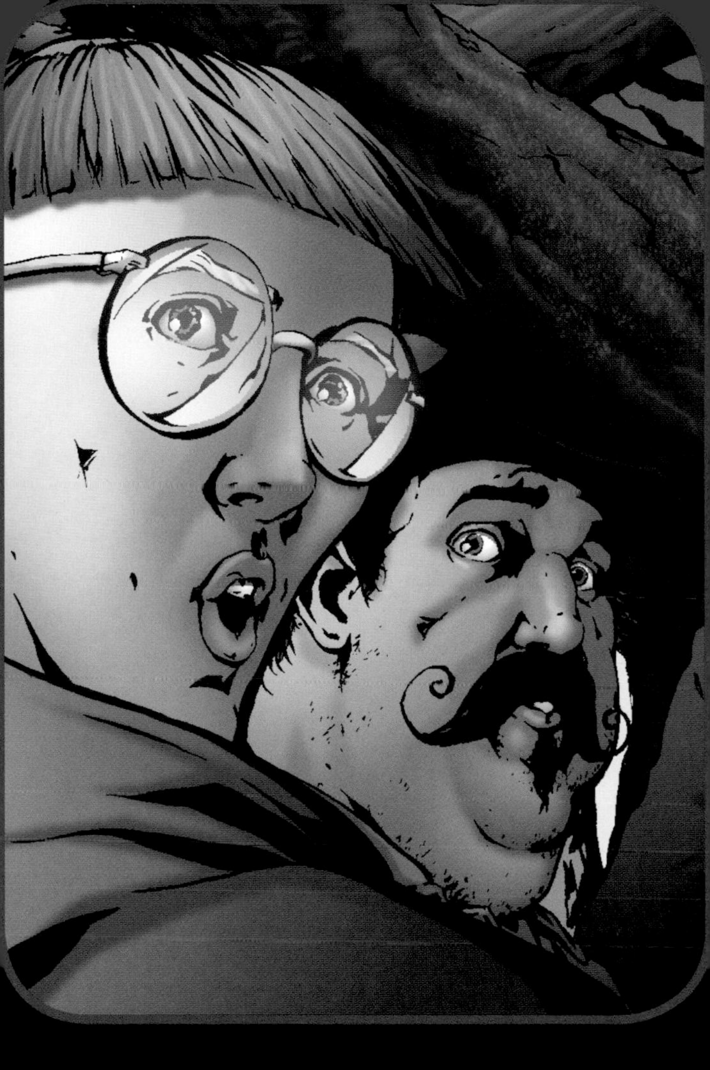

BROTHER MATTHEW

WELCOME TO PARIS

BROTHER MATTHEW:
Welcome to Paris

an introduction by Arvid Nelson

FOLLOWING IS A FIVE-PAGE colophon to "Blessed are the Meek," as of yet the one and only Brother Matthew mystery, my online comic strip that was printed for the first time in *Rex Mundi,* Book 1.

"Welcome to Paris" was also meant as a prelude to Brother Matthew's second investigation, titled "Hill of Martyrs." I wrote "Martyrs" four years ago, but I haven't had the resources to publish it. There's just not a lot of money to be made giving things away for free on the Internet. At least I haven't figured it out.

"Martyrs" is twice as long as "Blessed are the Meek," and I'm much happier with the writing. Hopefully I'll be able to get it done before too much longer. Thanks for picking up Book 2, and making the continuation of Brother Matthew's adventures all the more likely.

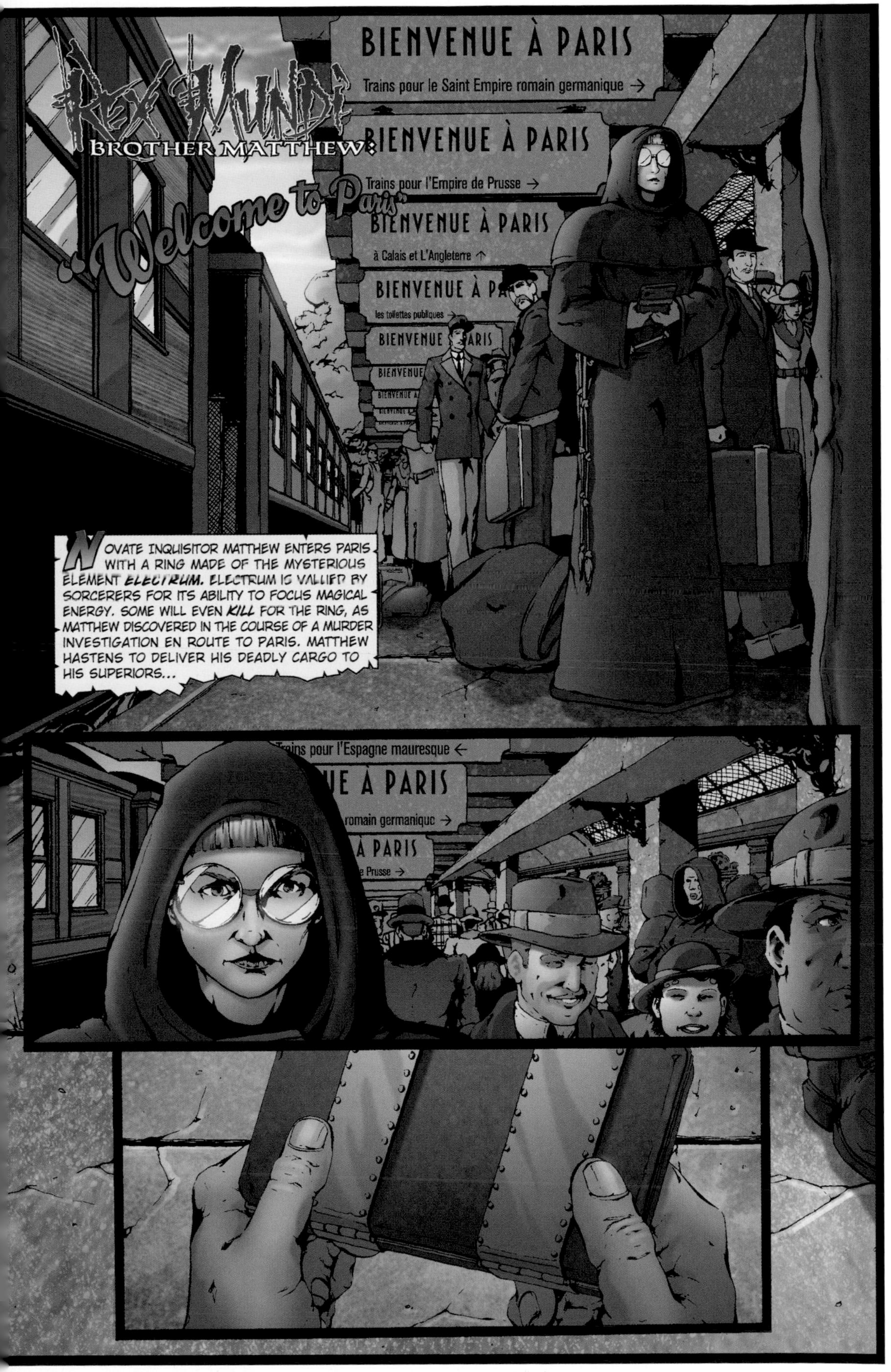
REX MUNDI
BROTHER MATTHEW:
"Welcome to Paris"
BIENVENUE À PARIS
Trains pour le Saint Empire romain germanique →
BIENVENUE À PARIS
Trains pour l'Empire de Prusse →
BIENVENUE À PARIS
à Calais et L'Angleterre ↑
BIENVENUE À PA
les toilettes publiques →
NOVATE INQUISITOR MATTHEW ENTERS PARIS WITH A RING MADE OF THE MYSTERIOUS ELEMENT ELECTRUM. ELECTRUM IS VALUED BY SORCERERS FOR ITS ABILITY TO FOCUS MAGICAL ENERGY. SOME WILL EVEN KILL FOR THE RING, AS MATTHEW DISCOVERED IN THE COURSE OF A MURDER INVESTIGATION EN ROUTE TO PARIS. MATTHEW HASTENS TO DELIVER HIS DEADLY CARGO TO HIS SUPERIORS...
Trains pour l'Espagne mauresque ←
UE À PARIS
romain germaniquc →
À PARIS
e Prusse →

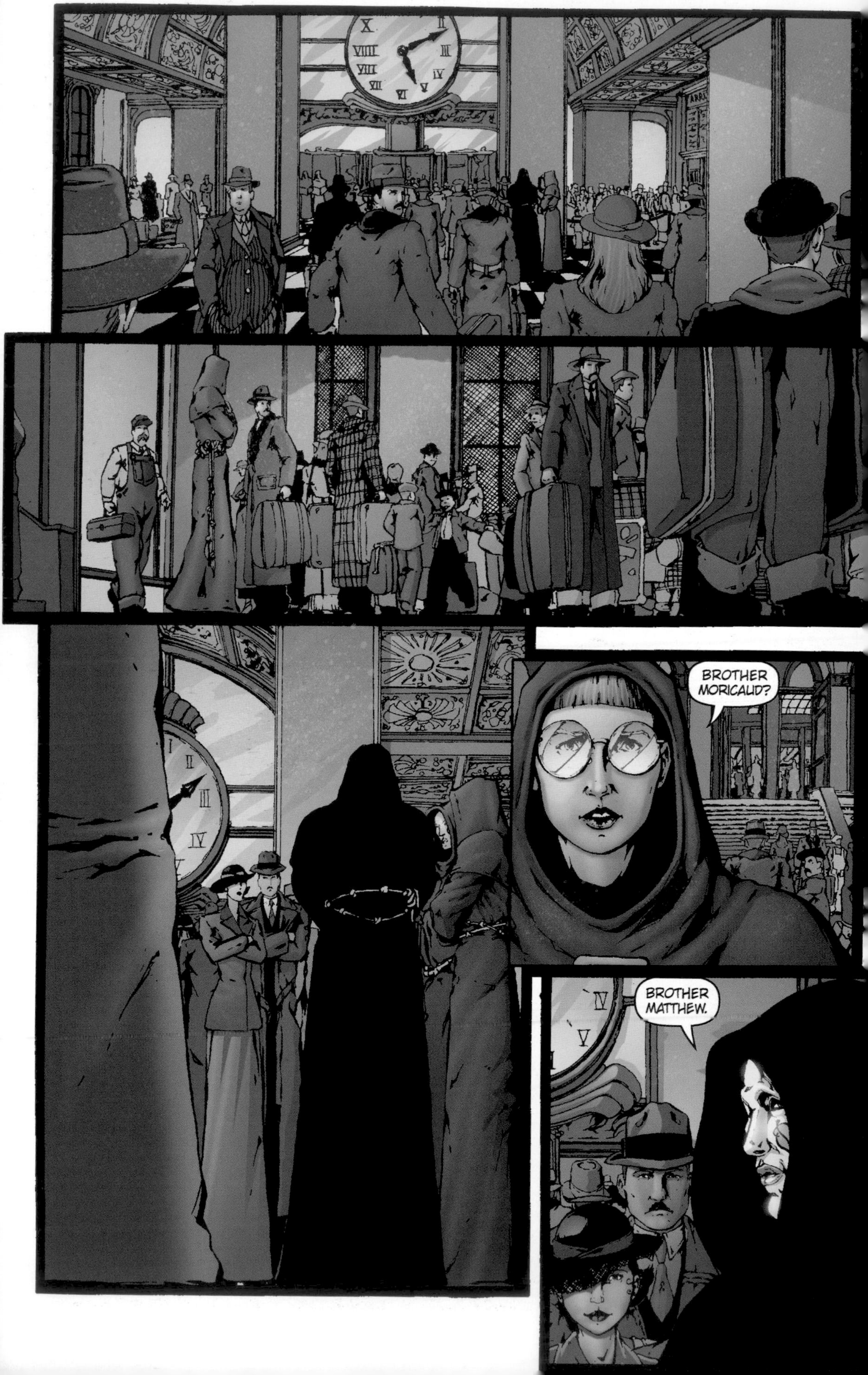
BROTHER MORICAUD?
BROTHER MATTHEW.

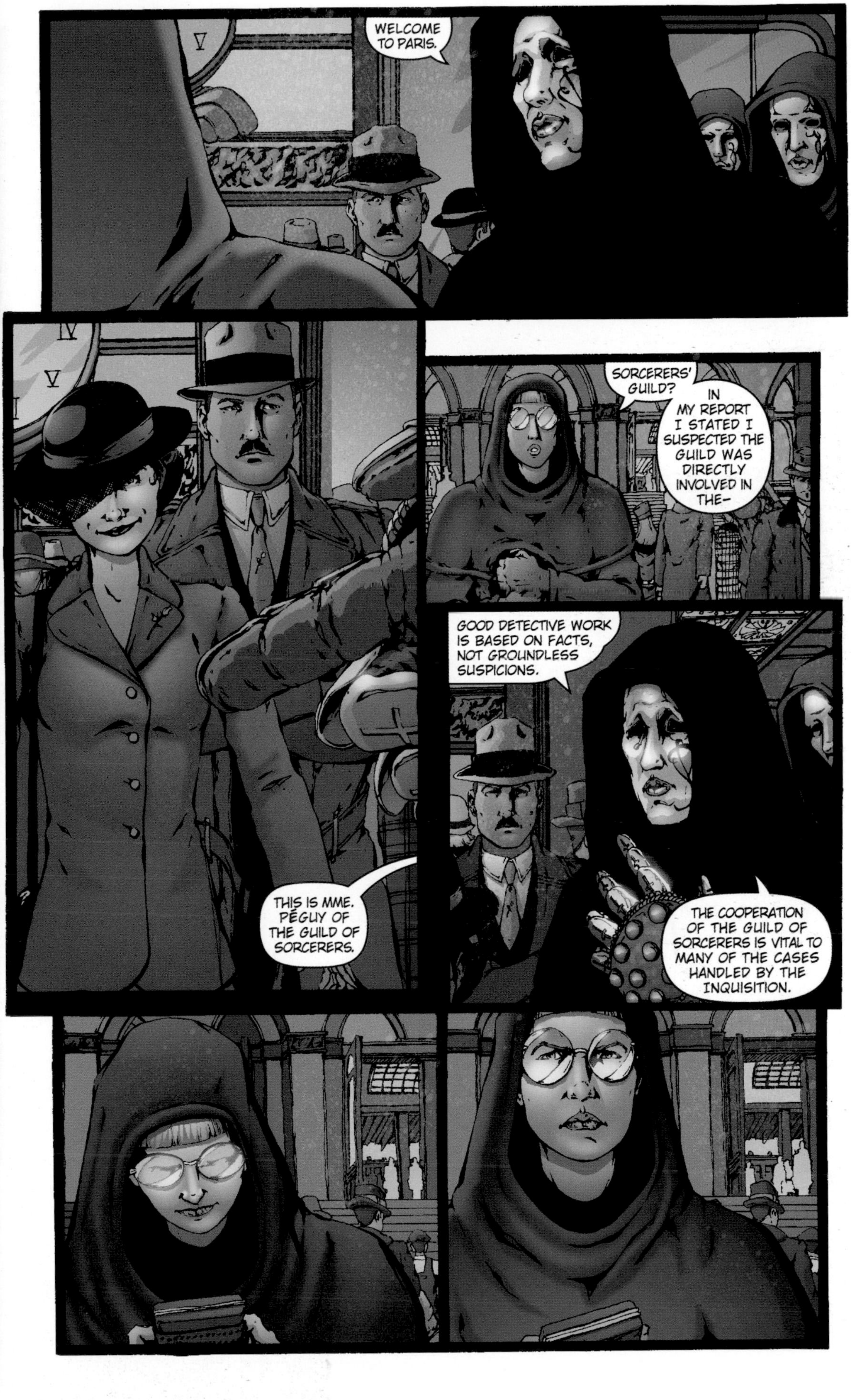

WELCOME TO PARIS.
THIS IS MME. PÉGUY OF THE GUILD OF SORCERERS.
SORCERERS' GUILD?
IN MY REPORT I STATED I SUSPECTED THE GUILD WAS DIRECTLY INVOLVED IN THE–
GOOD DETECTIVE WORK IS BASED ON FACTS, NOT GROUNDLESS SUSPICIONS.
THE COOPERATION OF THE GUILD OF SORCERERS IS VITAL TO MANY OF THE CASES HANDLED BY THE INQUISITION.

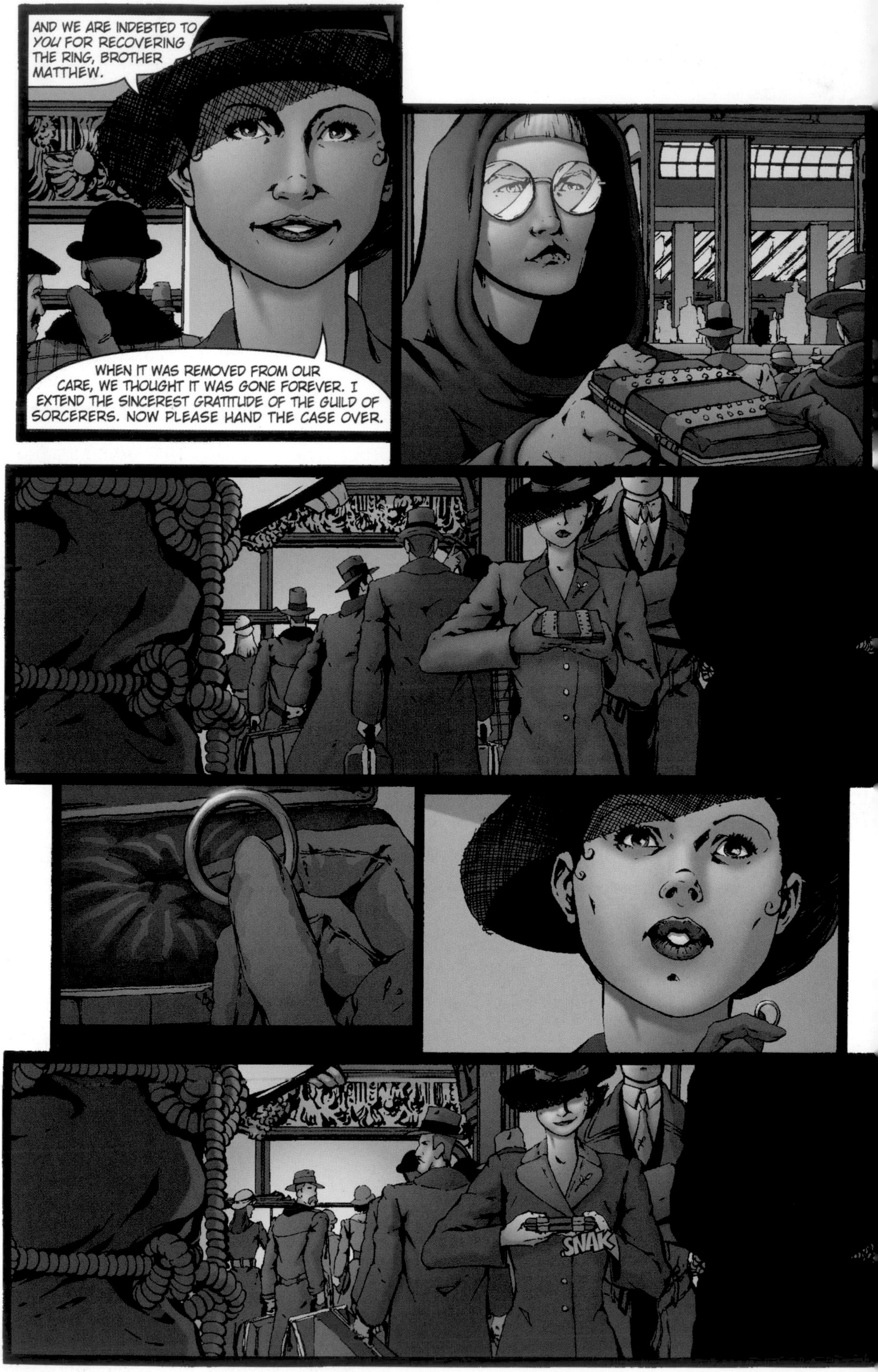
AND WE ARE INDEBTED TO *YOU* FOR RECOVERING THE RING, BROTHER MATTHEW.
WHEN IT WAS REMOVED FROM OUR CARE, WE THOUGHT IT WAS GONE FOREVER. I EXTEND THE SINCEREST GRATITUDE OF THE GUILD OF SORCERERS. NOW PLEASE HAND THE CASE OVER.
SNAK

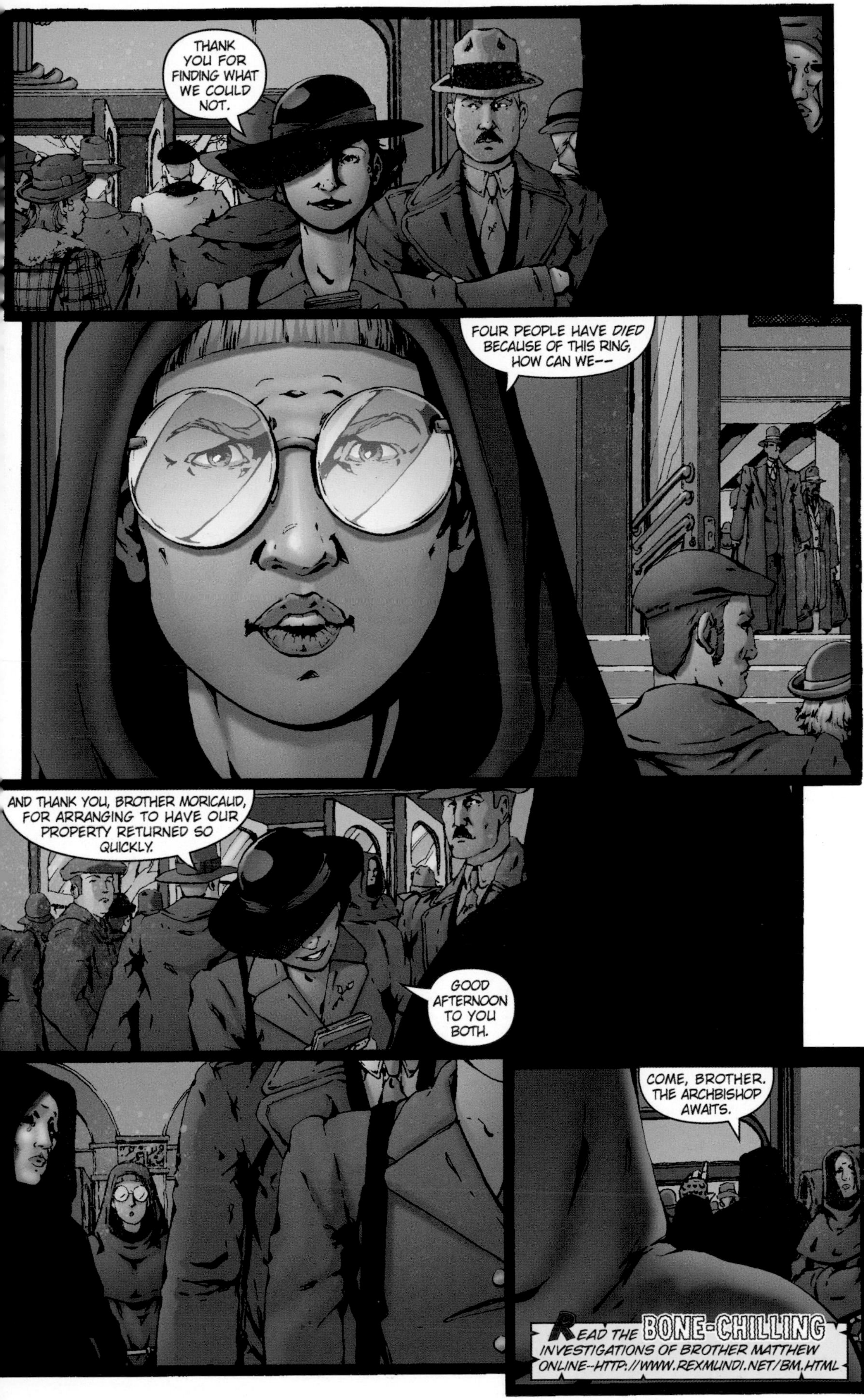
THANK YOU FOR FINDING WHAT WE COULD NOT.
FOUR PEOPLE HAVE *DIED* BECAUSE OF THIS RING, HOW CAN WE--
AND THANK YOU, BROTHER MORICAUD, FOR ARRANGING TO HAVE OUR PROPERTY RETURNED SO QUICKLY.
GOOD AFTERNOON TO YOU BOTH.
COME, BROTHER. THE ARCHBISHOP AWAITS.
READ THE BONE-CHILLING INVESTIGATIONS OF BROTHER MATTHEW ONLINE--HTTP://WWW.REXMUNDI.NET/BM.HTML

ALSO FROM DARK HORSE BOOKS

REX MUNDI
BOOK ONE
The Guardian of the Temple
ARVID NELSON • ERICJ
JEROMY COX

REX MUNDI VOLUME 1: THE GUARDIAN OF THE TEMPLE

Arvid Nelson, EricJ, Juan Ferreyra, and Jeromy Cox

A quest for the Holy Grail unlike any you've ever seen begins here—in a world where the American Civil War ended in a stalemate, the Catholic Church controls Europe, and sorcery determines political power!

ISBN-10: 1-59307-652-5 / ISBN-13: 978-1-59307-652-8

$16.95

ARVID NELSON
ERICJ
JEROMY COX
JIM DI BARTOLO
JUAN FERREYRA
REX MUNDI
The Lost Kings

REX MUNDI VOLUME 3: THE LOST KINGS

Arvid Nelson, EricJ, Jim Di Bartolo, and Juan Ferreyra

Julien furthers his investigation, only dimly aware of the forces tugging him down the trail of clues that lead to the doorstep, literally, of the Duke of Lorraine—a powerful man who seeks to provoke a massive, globe-spanning war that will soak the world in blood.

ISBN-10: 1-59307-651-7 / ISBN-13: 978-1-59307-651-1

$16.95

Mike Mignola Jill Thompson Evan Dorkin
Kurt Busiek Keith Giffen Gary Gianni and others
The Dark Horse Book of
MONSTERS

DARK HORSE BOOK OF MONSTERS

Mike Mignola, Gary Gianni, Evan Dorkin, Jill Thompson, Kurt Busiek, Keith Giffen, Arvid Nelson, Juan Ferreyra, and more.

Mike Mignola takes Hellboy on a monster-crunching mission, Arvid Nelson and Juan Ferreyra reveal deadly secrets in a Rex Mundi story, and many more of the most talented folks in comics tell terrifying tales in this fourth addition to Dark Horse's Eisner-nominated books of *Hauntings*, *Witchcraft*, and *The Dead*.

ISBN-10: 1-59307-656-8 / ISBN-13: 978-1-59307-651-6

$15.95

BOB FINGERMAN'S
RECESS PIECES

RECESS PIECES

Bob Fingerman

Bad things are brewing in the halls of The Ben Turpin School. When a science project goes wrong, only the prepubescent children are spared the fate of zombification . . . but can they escape being eaten alive? George Romero covered night, dawn, and day, but how about recess?

ISBN-10: 1-59307-450-6 / ISBN-13: 978-1-59307-450-0

$14.95

AVAILABLE AT YOUR LOCAL COMICS SHOP OR BOOKSTORE! • To find a comics shop in your area, call 1-888-266-4226.

For more information or to order direct visit darkhorse.com or call 1-800-862-0052 Mon.-Fri. 9 A.M. to 5 P.M. Pacific Time. Prices and availability subject to change without notice.

DARK HORSE COMICS *drawing on your nightmares*

darkhorse.com

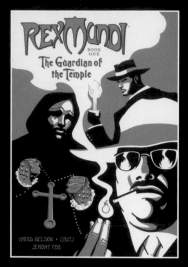

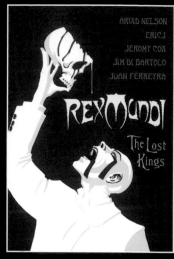

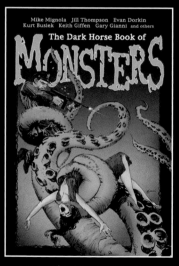

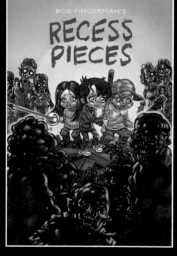

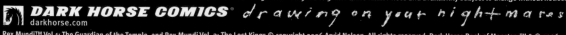

ALSO FROM DARK HORSE BOOKS

THE 13TH SON
THE BOOK SAYS HE'S REAL AND HE KILLS MONSTERS!
HOW MANY TIMES DO I NEED TO TELL YOU — THERE'S NO SUCH THING AS THE 13TH SON!
WORSE THING WAITING

13TH SON: WORSE THING WAITING
Kelley Jones

The 13th Son is a creature like nothing this world has seen before. Humans are not his target. It's the other monsters who walk this earth who live in fear of his enormous and terrifying powers.

ISBN-10: 1-59307-551-0 / ISBN-13: 978-1-59307-551-4

$12.95

a cal mcdonald mystery
LAST TRAIN TO DEADSVILLE
steve NILES
kelley JONES

LAST TRAIN TO DEADSVILLE: A CAL MCDONALD MYSTERY
Steve Niles and Kelley Jones

It's supernatural private eye Cal McDonald's most spine-chilling (and side-splitting) case yet, as some Beverly Hellbillies take him into the heart of a Southern California backwater brimming with monsters and mullets.

ISBN-10: 1-59307-107-8 / ISBN-13: 978-1-59307-107-3

$14.95

Mike Mignola
Jill Thompson
Evan Dorkin
Kelley Jones
Eric Powell
Gary Gianni
and others
The Dark Horse
BOOK OF THE DEAD

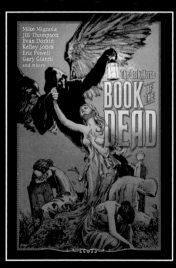

THE DARK HORSE BOOK OF THE DEAD
Kelley Jones, Mike Mignola, Jill Thompson, Evan Dorkin, Eric Powell, Gary Gianni, and others

The latest in Dark Horse's line of horror anthologies, *The Dark Horse Book of the Dead* features tales of the risen and hungry dead from comics notables including Mike Mignola, Gary Gianni, and Conan creator Robert E. Howard.

ISBN-10: 1-59307-281-3 / ISBN-13: 978-1-59307-281-0

$14.95

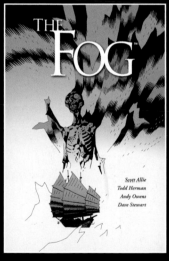

THE FOG
Scott Allie
Todd Herman
Andy Owens
Dave Stewart

THE FOG
Scott Allie and Todd Herman

Fourteen years ago, a group of Shanghai traders fled their native land and the curse that haunted it. But the curse has found them again, as a sinister fog wreaks terrible changes on their small, seaside town in this chilling prequel to the 2005 film.

ISBN-10: 1-59307-423-9 / ISBN-13: 978-1-59307-423-4

$6.95

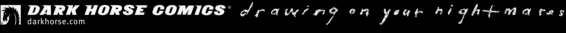

ALSO FROM DARK HORSE BOOKS

damn nation
ANDREW COSBY
J. ALEXANDER

DAMN NATION
Andrew Cosby and J. Alexander
Overrun by a vampire plague, the United States is quarantined from the world. Yet, not everyone on Earth wants to see America cured.
ISBN-10: 1-59307-389-5 / ISBN-13: 978-1-59307-389-3
$12.95

THE GOON
VIRTUE AND THE GRIM CONSEQUENCES THEREOF
by Eric Powell

THE GOON VOLUME 4: VIRTUE AND THE GRIM CONSEQUENCES THEREOF
Eric Powell
The Goon fights his way through a horde of killer robots and creatures from another dimension to help save his sometimes friend and ally Dr. Hieronymous Alloy.
ISBN-10: 1-59307-456-5 / ISBN-13: 978-1-59307-456-2
$16.95

HELLBOY
THE BOOK THAT INSPIRED THE MOTION PICTURE!
SEED of DESTRUCTION
MIKE MIGNOLA • JOHN BYRNE

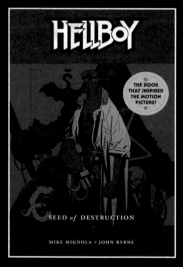

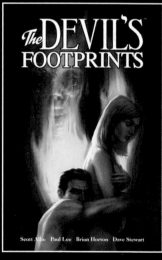

HELLBOY VOLUME 1: SEED OF DESTRUCTION
Mike Mignola and John Byrne
Sent to investigate a supernatural mystery, Hellboy discovers the secrets of his own origins, and his link to the Nazi occultists who promised Hitler a final solution in the form of a demonic avatar.
ISBN-10: 1-59307-094-2 / ISBN-13: 978-1-59307-094-6
$17.95

The DEVIL'S FOOTPRINTS
Scott Allie Paul Lee Brian Horton Dave Stewart

THE DEVIL'S FOOTPRINTS
Scott Allie, Paul Lee, Brian Horton, and Dave Stewart
Even after death, William Waite's foray into black magic continues to plague his heirs. Now it's up to his youngest son, Brandon, to protect his loved ones using the only means possible—witchcraft. But supernatural forces are unpredictable, and Brandon's good intentions just might destroy everything he's trying to save.
ISBN-10: 1-56971-933-0 / ISBN-13: 978-1-56971-933-6
$14.95

AVAILABLE AT YOUR LOCAL COMICS SHOP OR BOOKSTORE! • To find a comics shop in your area, call 1-888-266-4226.
For more information or to order direct visit darkhorse.com or call 1-800-862-0052 Mon.-Fri. 9 A.M. to 5 P.M. Pacific Time. Prices and availability subject to change without notice.

DARK HORSE COMICS® *drawing on your nightmares*
darkhorse.com